SMOKE AND MIRRORS

In memory of those who went down to the sea in ships

in the turbulent years of the First World War;

who fought because words like Duty, Honour, Sacrifice

had meaning.

SMOKE AND MIRRORS

Q-Ships against the U-Boats in the First World War

DEBORAH LAKE

First published 2006
This edition first published 2009

The History Press
The Mill, Brimscombe Port
Stroud, Gloucestershire, GL5 2QG
www.thehistorypress.co.uk

British Library Cataloguing in Publication Data.
A catalogue record for this book is available from the British Library.

ISBN 978 0 7524 5055 1

Typesetting and origination by The History Press
Printed in Great Britain

CONTENTS

ACKNOWLEDGEMENTS

Any writer who treads the paths and lanes of military non-fiction rapidly runs into debt: a debt of gratitude to curators, librarians, enthusiasts and others who all freely give their time and willing assistance. The list that follows is not in any way an order of merit. Every name is on a level par with every other.

Simply for convenience, I first thank the staffs of the Imperial War Museum in Documents Section, Printed Books, and the Photographic Department. Close on their heels come the staff of the National Maritime Museum and those of the National Archives (which I feel should still be called the Public Records Office) at Kew. Without exception, every member of staff provided willing help during my visits with even the most irritating and abstruse enquiries.

When it comes to enormous collections, I have to single out Kurt Erdmann of the Bundesarchiv-Militärarchiv at Freiburg. He dealt with my e-mail requests with charm and politeness, hunted down a particular U-boat war diary, and assisted my researches with considerable professional tolerance.

I also record an ongoing debt of gratitude to the Central Branch of the Northumberland County Library at Morpeth. Municipal libraries remain the jewel in the crown of Victorian civic endeavour; that some politicians seem to believe that they are irrelevant and expensive in the modern age is simply a sad reflection of misguided priorities.

If I mention other individuals, it is because they preside over smaller kingdoms with rather fewer staff. Despite this, they give a personal service with charm and efficiency. My thanks go to George Malcolmson of the RN Submarine Museum; to Allison Wareham of the RN Museum Library; and to Matt Little of the Royal Marines Archive at Eastney. All of them have suffered my e-mails and telephone requests for sometimes esoteric information; they all have displayed enviable patience and good humour. And, again, they willingly ransacked their collections for the answers.

I also owe thanks to Emile Ramakers of the Bibliotheek Maastricht in the Netherlands. He triumphantly produced documents that the world may have thought had vanished long ago. Among my Dutch contacts, Caspar Nijland spent several long hours on my behalf tracking down information in the deepest recesses of the Dutch shipping archives. I also thank Bernd Langensiepen whose knowledge of Goethe makes mine appear puny.

I must also thank Sue Satterthwaite for her courtesy in drawing my attention to her account of the life and career of Lieutenant Charles Bonner who served with Gordon Campbell on *Pargust* in 1917. This has enabled me to revise this text to ensure greater accuracy in respect of the officer's career. Details of her book are in the bibliography.

If no man is a hero to his valet, it is possibly also true that no author is a heroine to their agent. Malcolm Imrie deserves a special vote of thanks for his patience and efforts on my behalf. I also have to thank Jonathan Falconer of Sutton Publishing for his help and encouragement.

Michael Lowrey very generously, without hesitation, made available almost any U-boat diary for which I asked. He also read this book in its early manuscript version to steer me away from the more hideous mistakes that I made in U-boat actions.

Michael Forsyth also read the manuscript with a clinical gaze that saved me from various bear-traps. He also transcribed and translated some of the more illegible entries of watch officers in the German Imperial Navy as well as correcting my elementary errors.

That said, all and any inaccuracies in translation are entirely my responsibility.

I thank copyright holders for their permission to quote material; it was impossible to trace some owners. If anybody feels their copyright has been infringed, I will be happy to include the appropriate acknowledgement in further editions.

As always, I thank Vanessa Stead for her steadfast support. Not only has she proofed the manuscript several times in its various incarnations; she has also shielded me from domestic routine including telephone calls from people who wish to sell double glazing, demands for food from hungry cats, and a variety of other distractions.

PREFACE

This book is about valiant men. It deals with British decoy vessels in the First World War, the 'Q-ships' and their opponents, the German U-boats. Readers who seek a long list of vessels used as decoys must search elsewhere. For this book is about the men who fought. Enthusiasts who desire excruciating detail as to how many rivets held a conning tower to a U-boat hull will look in vain for such information here. These pages look at the human story of one aspect of the 1914–18 war at sea.

Most books about Q-ships that appeared between the two world wars were in English. Not surprisingly, they often seem to be written in red, white and blue ink, with a dust jacket of the Union flag. Even later books tend to be one-dimensional.

Without doubt, the men who served on decoys performed great deeds. Other heroes also sailed the seas. The men of the Imperial German Navy's underwater arm, too, fought with valour for their country. They, too, faced the prospect of an unpleasant death.

Any book that touches on the First Battle of the Atlantic needs to nod in the direction of the gorilla that squatted firmly outside the offices of the British and German Admiralties. That was the land war. For both sides, destruction of the enemy's supply lines meant, eventually, that his fighting soldiers would starve. In essence, it was siege warfare on an epic scale. The land war dominated. The land war decided priorities.

The men who went to sea helped decide the outcome on the Western Front, the Dardanelles and the Mediterranean, and the fate of Austria-Hungary. Politicians on both sides accepted that the civilian population might face hardships. That was regrettable. If men, munitions, supplies did not reach the trenches, the inevitable result was defeat.

One perennial problem in writing about the period is the simple one of measurement. The British employed the imperial system of feet and inches; Germany used the metric system. With naval affairs, further complications arise. Both sides used knots or nautical miles per hour.

Both sides used sea miles to express distance, although this is rarely stated in logbooks. It is taken for granted.

I have chosen the easy option and left all measurements as they were originally written, even when I have paraphrased sources. In practice, this makes little difference. A comparison of a U-boat's war diary and that of a Q-ship reveals that the Kapitänleutnant declares he opened fire from 6,000m. His opposite number informs his admiral that the range was 6,000yd. The U-boat commander commends his gunners for their accuracy at 3 nautical miles. The Q-ship captain agrees. The landlubber with an extremely long tape measure would accept $3\frac{1}{2}$ miles as accurate. To litter the text with conversions on every page is impractical. Better by far to retain the measurements with which those who fought, and sometimes died, were familiar.

For non-metric English-language readers, therefore, I suggest that it is useful to remember that 10cm equates to 4in; that 80 yd is very close to 74m; and that 8km is indistinguishable from 5 miles except by the arithmetically obsessed.

Minor liberties occur with both British and German ranks. In the Royal Navy, the rank known today as lieutenant commander did not appear until shortly before the war began. It was a grade, designed to distinguish between lieutenants. All received the advancement when they reached eight years' seniority. It was not a promotion. It was an automatic process to mark a senior lieutenant. The rank, originally, was written as 'lieutenant-commander'; other navies had a similar ranking. The German equivalent was Kapitän-Leutnant. In both instances, I have simply adopted current practice and ditched the hyphen.

The 24-hour clock has only become familiar in recent years. During 1914–18, logbooks, diaries, documents of all kinds stuck to a.m. and p.m. or their equivalents in other tongues. Where these times appear in original texts, I have retained them. Otherwise, I have used the present version of the clock, hence 1410hr, not 14.10 or 2.10 p.m.

For readers who may wonder about the relative importance of the letters RN, RNR and RNVR that follow a British naval officer's name, the rule is essentially simple. RN means a regular officer. RNR means an officer of the Reserve. This is not some superannuated mariner but a merchant navy officer who has agreed to serve in the Royal Navy in the event of war. RNVR applies to Volunteer Reserve officers who, unlike the RNR, usually had no formal qualifications but were enthusiastic amateur yachtsmen and the like.

As usual, the lower deck, the ratings, summed up the differences in simple language: 'A naval officer is an officer and a gentleman. An RNR officer is a seaman but no gentleman, and an RNVR officer is a gentleman but no seaman.'

I also ask the indulgence of Scottish, Irish and Welsh readers. It is a fact that the inhabitants of Continental Europe habitually refer to 'England' and the 'English' when they mean 'British'. When a Fregattenkapitän refers to the 'English Navy', he intends no insult to Gaels and Celts. In the interests of accuracy, I have not corrected quotations where this occurs; and I use it when paraphrasing recorded thoughts of mainland Europeans.

Place names familiar to the men of 1914–18 have remained. Queenstown has not changed to Cobh, nor has Danzig become Gdansk. Astute readers will find others. This is not because I wish to deny developments in world political history. Simply, it is more convenient for the reader and, I believe, more accurate, to keep the names that the men of the Q-ships and U-boats knew and used.

Readers may occasionally notice an apparent enormous discrepancy between a U-boat commander's estimate of a ship's size and its register size. This brings us into the thorny area of tonnage. This apparently simple measurement is, in fact, strewn with maritime caltraps. I have, in general, attempted to use 'displacement tonnage' which is the actual weight of the vessel and its contents. This is the figure normally quoted for naval vessels. Merchant ships follow a more esoteric course.

Reference sources, from varied authorities, use different measurements. Ships are described by 'gross registered tonnage', which is the internal volume of a vessel plus cargo space available on deck; the same ship may also be defined by 'net registered tonnage'. This is the 'gross registered tonnage' less the volume of space that does not hold cargo, such as the engine rooms, bunkers and so forth. To confuse matters even more, these tonnages, based on volume, are expressed in gross tons, measurement tons or cubic metres. As these sizes often influenced port and pilotage fees, owners preferred low tonnage assessments. Governments opted for higher ones.

When gross, net or displacement tonnage do not serve, a ship can be specified by its 'deadweight tonnage'. This is the maximum weight the ship can safely carry when fully loaded. This includes the crew, fuel, water and other stores.

As a final complication a ton may be long, short or metric; a measurement ton or a freight ton.

Luckily, U-boat commanders had a simple way to calculate size. All they had to do was to estimate how many litres of water the hull beneath the surface displaced. As 1 litre weighs almost precisely 1 kilogram, the answer in metric tons was immediate.

It was all exceedingly simple. As long the captain got the first bit right.

For submarines, tonnage varies simply as to whether the boat is above or below the surface. In general, I have used surface tonnage. It is for this reason that figures of tonnage sunk is, at best, an uneasy compromise between several sets of conflicting figures. Any readers who wish to quarrel with my statistics, therefore, are asked to refrain from sending rude letters via the publisher.

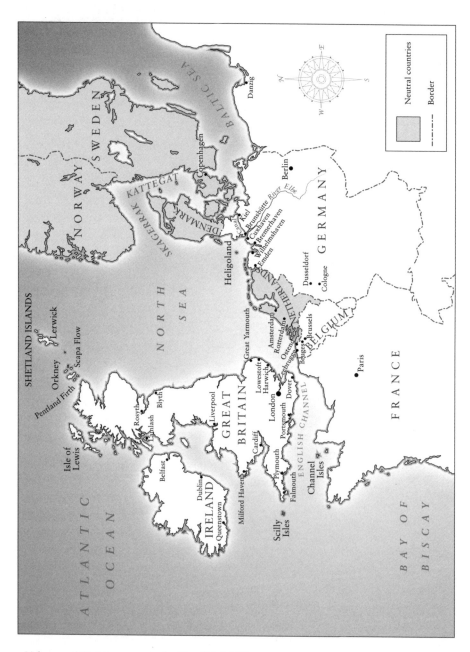

U-boat and Q-ship waters in the First World War.

PROLOGUE

On 15 October 1918, HMS *Cymric*, based at Granton on the Forth, sank the final victim to fall to the Admiralty's Special Service Ships, the mystery vessels known as 'Q-ships'. *Cymric*, a barquentine of 226 gross tonnage, carried one 4in gun, two 12-pounder guns and a single $7\frac{1}{2}$in howitzer, each one concealed from sight.

At 1520, approximately 50 miles out to sea from the Northumberland port of Blyth, in visibility of 6,000yd, her captain and lookouts spotted a large submarine, dead ahead on an opposite course. The alarm sounded. The crew went to action stations.

When the suspect was off the starboard bow, the *Cymric*'s captain decided she was friendly. He told his gun crews to stand by, nonetheless, in case the stranger proved hostile.

U 6. A German U-boat. The letter and number showed clearly on her conning tower. More, crewmen manned it, close to a large gun on a platform in front of the tower. An ensign flew from a short mast, indistinguishable against the sky. The submarine came up on the beam, at an angle of 90 degrees. The captain stared hard. So did the other men on the bridge. *U 6*. Nobody doubted it. Clearly unable to dive, she showed a bold front, making off to Germany as fast as she could on the surface.

Cymric hoisted the White Ensign. Rumours of peace suggested that the war would soon end. No reason, all the same, to let a Hun escape. The stranger did not react to the Royal Navy's battle flag. Seconds ticked away. *U 6* continued on her escape course.

The Q-ship opened fire a near half-minute later. The starboard 12-pounder fired twice, both shells falling short. The 4in gun made a direct hit with its first round. Its shot flew into the hull on the waterline in front of the conning tower. The 12-pounder found the range. Its third effort also smacked into the pressure hull on the waterline, this time some 10ft behind the conning tower.

Both guns continued to fire. After about ten rounds, a man on the after deck waved a white object. At the same time, a thread of black smoke curled into the air above the conning tower. *Cymric* ceased fire.

The submarine maintained its speed and course. It was close to vanishing in the smoke and haze when the decoy opened fire again. Escape was not an option.

ONE

THE DJINN ESCAPES THE BOTTLE

Their Victorian Lordships at the Admiralty detested underwater craft by whatever fancy name their inventors called them. The world's most powerful navy had no interest in crackpot contraptions. The Admiralty saw no point in devices whose purpose was to destroy proper warships by stealth. Only inferior fleets had any interest in such infernal machines. The Russians, perhaps, who envied Britain's hold on India. The French, almost certainly. Despite their status as allies in the Crimea, they were not totally to be trusted.

The designers of such imbecilities were cranks, eccentrics, wild-eyed visionaries, even lunatics, according to taste. Certainly not serious inventors. So said the Lords Commissioners to anyone who cared to listen.

A Dutchman produced the first practical submarine. Employed at the Court of James I, Cornelis Jacobszoon Drebbel invented a whole series of useful products. He formulated a scarlet dye, devised a thermostat for a self-regulating oven, easily adapted to control a successful incubator for duck and chicken eggs, produced a perpetual motion machine, developed the double convex lens microscope and designed a chimney.

One day in 1621, before the king and thousands of onlookers, he and some intrepid oarsmen demonstrated a wooden rowing boat, encased in greased leather, on the Thames. They submerged and moved underwater 12ft below the surface. Hollow tubes poking above the water solved the vital problem of air supply. Although these failed to keep the air fresh, Cornelis had a trick of his own. He uncorked a large jar in which was the result of another experiment. 'Salt-petre,' Cornelis explained vaguely, 'broken up by the power of fire, was thus changed into something of the nature of the air.' In simple terms, he had discovered how to make oxygen a mere 150 years before anybody else.

Drebbel produced three submersibles. Rumour later claimed that James I actually took a journey in one. This was probably an inspired piece of royalist propaganda. The shambling, uncouth, tobacco-loathing, honours-hawking, penny-pinching, buttocks-fondling James I and VI was no by-word for heroism. Reviled by many Scots because he left his own country to enjoy the luxury of the English throne, he inspired precisely the same emotion in many of his new subjects.

The Jacobean Navy took no interest in the Dutchman's invention. No lucrative orders for wooden submarines came his way. Despite his achievements, Drebbel ended his days a poor man, the keeper of a tavern. His wife, Sophia, may have been responsible. She allegedly spent their money 'entertaining sundry lovers'.

Drebbel spawned imitators. A number of craft, usually converted rowing boats that sank on command, entranced the public. On rare occasions, the boats returned to the surface, an even more fascinating achievement. In the century after Drebbel showed the way, inventors filed some fourteen or more patents in England for submersibles.

In 1747, one Nathaniel Symons developed a ballast tank. Water flowed into leather bags. The vessel sank. Strong hands wrung out the bags. The boat rose. It was a technological triumph, a small step on the road of progress.

War produces inventions. The severe unpleasantness between the American Colonies and the British government from 1775 to 1786 inspired an Irish emigrant, David Bushnell, a graduate of Yale. He decided to destroy the British fleet in Boston Harbour by underwater attack. George Washington declared that he was 'of great mechanical powers, fertile in invention and a master of execution'. He undoubtedly made an impression. The parsimonious Washington personally financed Bushnell's experiments.

The inventor named his underwater machine *American Turtle*. With no massive industrial base to support him, he nonetheless produced a watertight hull; propulsion that drove the submersible forwards, backwards, upwards and downwards; a steering system; variable ballast; a primitive breathing device; what modern military men call a weapons delivery system; and a two-bladed screw to drive it along.

Bushnell weighted *Turtle* with a lead-filled base to both stop it rolling wildly in rough water and to achieve neutral buoyancy. As an engineer, he could recite, without thinking hard, Archimedes' great discovery. If the weight of a body submerged in water equals the weight of the water it displaces, it will tend neither to sink nor to rise. Neutral buoyancy – the principle that enables all submarines to work. By taking on water

to make it heavier, developing negative buoyancy, the submarine goes
down. Pumping out the same water produces positive buoyancy. The
submarine rises.

Made of oak, *American Turtle*, a mere 7ft long and 4ft wide, looked
like two vertical tortoiseshells joined together. Others considered that it
resembled an enormous upright walnut. To make it watertight, Bushnell
bound the machine with iron bands, then covered it with pitch.

The single operator perched upright on a seat akin to a bicycle saddle.
With the hatch closed, he saw nothing. A judicious coating of phosphorescent fox-fire, more properly known to botanists as bioluminescent
rhizomorphs, remedied the problem.

On top of *Turtle*, vents provided air when the hatch was clear of the
surface. Two flaps closed as the vessel submerged. Once it was under
water, the air supply lasted for about thirty minutes.

The crewman sat behind an oar that turned the screw to move the
vessel. A similar oar above him gave extra control for descending or
surfacing, as well as the ability to stay at a particular depth. Bushnell had
thoughtfully provided a depth gauge of his own design. A foot-operated
rudder took care of the steering. A compass told the operator in which
direction he pedalled.

In early 1776, Bushnell decided that *American Turtle* was ready to
annihilate the Royal Navy. Most of the British fleet had already sailed
from rebellious Boston to a more welcoming Halifax in Nova Scotia.
A few vessels, though, remained in New York Harbour.

Turtle moved to The Battery in Manhattan, where General Israel
Putnam and 9,000 Continental soldiers stood guard. Ezra Bushnell,
the inventor's brother, could operate *Turtle* with nonchalant skill but he
needed several weeks to adjust to the intricate tidal conditions between
The Battery and Governor's Island. Finally, David and Ezra were satisfied.
Turtle was ready to destroy the British fleet.

The brothers chose HMS *Eagle*, the flagship of Lord Howe, the British
commander, as their target. Putnam authorised the venture. Ezra fell sick
with fever, but another Ezra stepped forward. Sergeant Ezra Lee of the
Connecticut Militia volunteered to be the new operator.

Two months slipped by as Lee learned to master *Turtle*. Close to midnight on 6 September 1776, a rowing boat towed the submarine halfway
to Staten Island. Lee lowered himself into the wooden submarine, fastened
the hatch, and so became the first and only non-commissioned officer ever
to command a United States submarine.

Lee pedalled. He kept going until he reached the 64-gun *Eagle* unobserved. In the dark, the one-third of the egg-shaped contraption above the water scarcely showed. Lee took in ballast and *Turtle* submerged. The sergeant inched forward until certain he was under *Eagle*. Ezra gently pumped out water until *Turtle* bumped against the flagship's keel.

Bushnell's ingenious weapons system came into play. In theory, an iron auger bit, worked from inside the vessel, fixed a screw to the enemy hull. A rope ran from the screw to a mine of Bushnell's own design. When the submarine retired, the mine detached itself from *Turtle*. This started the clockwork of the tethered mine.

Lee drilled without success. Bushnell either forgot, or never knew, that England's wooden walls were sheathed in copper. Where marine weeds did not penetrate, neither did a primitive corkscrew.

The sergeant surfaced, gulped air, tried again. More failure. At last, exhausted, sweating, aware that the tide was on the turn, he gave in. Lee dumped all his ballast water to pedal furiously for safety in the growing dawn. *Turtle* showed up starkly in the early light. An inquisitive British patrol set out from Governor's Island to investigate the unusual shape in the water. Lee abandoned the 250lb burden of the mine. His aching thigh muscles, with less weight to move, pushed the *Turtle* towards safety.

The mine exploded.

Howe prudently moved his ships to lower New York Bay. The Royal Navy apparently took little notice of the new threat. No ships' logs or reports to London mention the incident. But, whether myth, truth or simple exaggeration, naval warfare had changed. The submarine menace had arrived.

Turtle made two more attempts to sink a British ship. On one, tide and currents overcame willing muscles. On the other, in the calmer waters of the Connecticut river, the frigate HMS *Cerberus* escaped unscathed although a schooner close by blew up with the loss of several lives.

George Washington, as a mark of esteem, personally authorised Bushnell's commission into the Continental Army's Corps of Engineers. When the war ended, Bushnell went to France to sell his design. He returned, disillusioned, in 1795. Before he left, though, Bushnell published details of his invention. Another American, Robert Fulton, who lived in Paris, seized on the idea.

Fulton, an accomplished miniature painter, a builder of canals, designer of a rope-making machine and practical engineer, tackled the problems with skill and determination. As the infant Republic grappled with its new calendar, Fulton wrote to the French Directory on 22 Frimaire in Year 6 of the Republic, more easily recognised as 13 December 1797:

> Considering the great importance of diminishing the power of the British Fleets, I have Contemplated the Construction of a Mechanical Nautulus: A Machine which flatters me with much hope of being Able to Annihilate their Navy; hence feeling confident that Practice will bring the Apparatus to perfection; The Magnitude of the object has excited in me an Ardent desire to Prove the experiment: For this Purpose, and to Avoid troubling you with the Investigation of a new Project, or the Expense of Carrying it into effect; I have Arranged a Company who are willing to bear the Expense, and undertake the Expedition on the following Conditions:

After which, the American got down to business. He wanted 400 livres, or £1,400, per gun for every destroyed ship that carried more than forty guns. For ships less than 40 tons, which carried less armament, he required 2,000 livres, or £6,000, per gun. No paper money accepted. Cargoes and property from every ship would pass to Fulton and his company. In a final flourish, he asked for letters of marque for all his men so that, if they were captured, an enemy would treat them as prisoners of war and not pirates.

The French haggled. As Fulton had not built a 'Nautulus', this was hardly surprising. In a further letter, the inventor shrewdly emphasised that the 'destruction of the English Navy will ensure the independence of the seas and France, the nation which has the most natural resources and population, will alone and without a rival, hold the balance of power in Europe'.

Compelling words. If the 'diving boat' achieved this, it was worth consideration, especially as payment was strictly by results. The Minister of Marine, Vice-Admiral Eustache Bruix, appointed a committee to consider the pestering inventor's idea. They duly produced a long and detailed report.

Fulton's idea, they decided, was feasible and highly desirable. It was, they agreed, 'a terrible means of destruction', but one particularly suitable for France as the British had a much stronger navy. Even the entire destruction of both fleets would favour the French. The committee approved construction.

Fulton's machine would hardly have looked totally out of place a century later. Roughly cigar-shaped with pointed bow and tapering stern, it showed off a conning tower that served as both hatch and periscope. It had a snorkel tube. The space between the double hull contained the water ballast. The submarine also had a forward diving plane and a vertical rudder. In a leap of technology, compressed air spat out the water ballast. *Nautilus* also pioneered the use of two propulsion systems, one for surface use and one for under water. Submerged, the boat relied on muscle power from her crew of three. A hand crank turned a four-bladed propeller. Above the waves, a sail provided the push.

In 1801, the craft sailed 70 miles in five days. The crew attempted to close on two English brigs. They made off as soon as the strange vessel appeared. Royal Navy captains knew about the 'Mechanical Nautulus'. British spies kept the Lords of the Admiralty fully informed of developments in the enemy camp.

Fulton's original design had an iron drill, like *Turtle*. By 1802, he had abandoned this idea. He also replaced the candles that lit the interior with a glass porthole which, he claimed, let in sufficient light to read a watch 25ft down.

General Napoleon Bonaparte, now modestly enjoying the title of First Consul of the Republic, showed keen interest in Fulton's efforts. The American had, indeed, solved most of the problems associated with underwater craft.

Unfortunately for Fulton, Napoleon appointed a new Minister of Marine. The choleric Admiral Decrès wasted little time on Bonaparte's fad. He flatly rejected the idea. France had not yielded the seas to England. The invention had no future in naval warfare, although it might be useful against pirates or Algerian corsairs.

A depressed Fulton decided to try his luck in England. He now had not only a working submarine to sell. He had his own brand of mines as well. Once more, he wrote to the highest in the country with his proposals and, helpfully, his scale of payment.

Again, a committee considered the ideas. His underwater craft met with rather less enthusiasm than it had in France. The politicians, though, liked his mines. These were a long way from black spheres with horns. Fulton's largest creation was 18ft long, square-sectioned with wedge-shaped ends. It weighed 2 tons. All of his mines used clockwork detonators. Fastened to an enemy hull by a grapnel, they seemed an excellent way to attack the French invasion fleet at Boulogne.

A first attempt, in October 1804, failed. Only one of five bombs destroyed a target. A small pinnace and crew were blown to pieces. Despite the secrecy that surrounded the expedition, the news rapidly reached the popular press. Much indignation ensued. Not for the failure but for the underhand method. Public and Navy alike considered it unfair. It broke the rules of warfare.

A second attempt at Calais in December also achieved nothing.

Fulton, undismayed, badgered Pitt for action. The American, with some reason, believed that the Royal Navy deliberately hampered his efforts. Two public demonstrations that satisfactorily destroyed the targets persuaded the government to finance a third expedition.

Fulton met Admiral Lord St Vincent. He wanted to tell the admiral how mines would wipe out the French fleet. The acerbic naval officer gave him short shrift. 'Pitt', he told the inventor, 'was the greatest fool that ever existed, to encourage a mode of war which they who commanded the seas did not want, and which, if successful, would deprive them of it.' With those words, he set the official policy of the Royal Navy for decades to come.

Pitt, ever the pragmatic politician, considered it better to have Fulton on the British side than on the French. St Vincent, like practical military men throughout the ages, wasted no time on those who mouthed theory but were woefully short of experience.

The third expedition on 27 October 1805, once more against Boulogne, achieved nothing. Days later, news of Nelson's victory at Trafalgar convulsed the whole of Britain. The invasion threat vanished. Fulton's schemes withered.

He returned to America. Seven years later, rumours of his 'submarine bombs' during the War of 1812 ensured that British naval officers remained extremely wary of attack when anchored in harbour.

Four decades later, another inventor decided that the way to destroy enemy ships was from beneath the surface. In 1840, 18-year-old Wilhelm Sebastian Valentin Bauer, the son of a corporal in the Bavarian army, joined the military himself. A serious youth, he studied mathematics, chemistry and physics in his spare time.

In 1848, he volunteered to serve in the German Federation Corps in the First Schleswig-Holstein War against Denmark. Bauer ended up on the island of Alsen, where the Danes defended a vital bridge. The Germans wished to destroy it. The Danes, equally determined, preferred it intact. With a fine field of fire, Danish guns menaced anything that approached. The Bavarian, having watched cavorting seals around Alsen, decided that a submersible vessel would serve the purpose very well indeed. That could arrive undetected, plant explosives, and leave unchallenged. The problem was solved. All he had to do was to design a mechanical seal.

In 1849, the Germans and Denmark agreed peace terms, and the Bavarian volunteers returned home. Schleswig-Holstein continued to fight alone for independence. Bauer left the Bavarian army to sign for the Schleswig-Holstein service.

The Danes blockaded Kiel. Bauer produced plans for a submersible to attach mines to the besieging ships. He called his invention *Der Brandtaucher*, which satisfactorily translates as 'Firediver'.

In return for thirty gold marks from the War Ministry, Bauer produced a working model, shaped roughly like the inspirational seals, in which an oversized clockwork motor drove a three-bladed screw to produce an impressive performance. A large lead weight on a threaded bar that ran almost the full length of the model boat controlled horizontal trim. Ballast tanks, operated by hand pumps, allowed *Brandtaucher* to submerge or surface. In the bow, a pair of leather gloves, operated from inside the submarine, allowed a man to fix mines to enemy hulls.

All Bauer needed for a full-size boat was money. The Schleswig-Holstein treasury had none to spare. An undaunted Bauer did what visionary inventors have always done: he appealed to the public. The citizens chipped in, as did the army who rather wanted to win the war. Despite everyone's efforts, they failed to raise enough to build *Brandtaucher* as originally conceived.

The Schweffel und Howalt iron foundry, given the task of building *Brandtaucher* on a limited budget, cut corners. Thinner sheets than specified made up the metal hull. Loose weights replaced adjustable ones. Water ballast, once carefully contained in compartments, sloshed around the keel instead.

The finished vessel, 8m long, flat-sided, weighed 30 tons. On the bright, moonlit night of 18 December 1850, Bauer, with Ingenieur Hest, Steurmann Wiedemann and Matrosen Witt and Thomsen, displayed *Brandtaucher* to a large and admiring crowd. The craft did not submerge, as there was no on-board ballast. Instead of clockwork, a large treadmill that would not have disgraced the local jail drove *Brandtaucher* across the bitterly cold water of Kiel Harbour.

The submarine ambled at a majestic 3 knots through drift ice. The crew panted to turn the treadmill at twenty revolutions per minute. The crowd cheered. The Danish spies among them made mental notes. News of Bauer's invention swiftly reached the Danish fleet. Equally smartly, the Danish ships withdrew further out to sea.

During the next weeks, Bauer and his two seamen pedalled around Kiel Harbour to test the machine. The authorities became impatient. They wanted *Brandtaucher* to dive, destroy Danish ships and return in triumph. Wars are, after all, for winning.

On 1 February 1851, *Brandtaucher* eased her way into the harbour. With the hatch firmly closed, Bauer prepared to dive. He opened the ballast valves. Water gurgled in. The loose weights slid towards the tail. Everything not nailed down slid towards the stern. The flat iron plates buckled under the strain. Rivets popped. The North Sea sieved in through the seams.

After fifty-four seconds of terror, *Brandtaucher* hit the seabed, stern-down, at an angle of 34 degrees. The treadmill had broken free. The pumps could not cope. In the darkness, the three men heard only the ominous trickling of water as it flowed into the hull.

Bauer was a remarkable man. He did not panic. Self-taught in physics, he knew they could escape. He needed only to persuade his companions to encourage the water to come in. The external and internal pressures would equalise as the hull filled. When they matched, the crew could open the hatch to escape. Whether sweet reason or the brutally large spanner that Bauer meaningfully waved convinced Witt and Thomsen, the inventor got his way. They opened the valves. Water rushed in. The air compressed. The hatch opened. The three intrepid adventurers hurtled to the surface in a bubble of air.

Unshakeable in his ideas, Bauer hawked them around the courts and palaces of Europe. He demonstrated a model to Prince Albert, an irrepressible enthusiast for technical devices, at Osborne. With royal backing, the Thames-side yard of John Scott Russell, a leading naval architect, began work on Bauer's new boat. Increasing suspicion on both sides caused the Bavarian to leave England before completion of his design. Scott Russell's men finished the submarine. They took it to the river for tests. It sank.

Bauer found more encouragement in Russia. The Tsar and his advisers, locked in the Crimean conflict with Britain and France, needed something, anything, to threaten the Allied fleets that blockaded their coast. Bauer designed a new submarine, *Der Seeteufel* although the Russians preferred the French rendering of *Diable-Marin*. Twice the size of *Brandtaucher*, her most warlike excursion honoured Tsar Alexander II's coronation. A quartet, dignified by the title of orchestra, played patriotic melodies from the bottom of the harbour.

Allegedly, Bauer conducted 134 diving trials of his boat. They appear to have achieved little. The vessel spent her days either on the surface or motionless on the ocean floor. Movement under water was a major problem.

Bauer designed a 24-gun submersible, powered by steam. The Russians decided that it would not work. In any event, the Crimean War had ended. A disappointed designer left Russia in 1858, but he continued to preach the values of underwater vessels. When Prussia went to war against the old enemy, Denmark, Bauer volunteered for the Navy. His flow of new ideas, some extremely perceptive, failed to reach fruition. He never built another submarine.

In the American Civil War, only the North had an effective navy. The Confederates faced the familiar challenge of breaking a blockade. Less industrialised than the Union, the South nonetheless countered the Federal Navy's supremacy with commerce raiders, armoured ships, rifled naval guns and mines.

The war was the first conflict in which mass production and tech-nology played a significant part. The production of muskets, previously largely made by hand, became almost fully automated. Machines shaped the elaborate wooden stocks and butts, metal parts flowed from specially designed equipment.

In the South, private inventors flourished. A government with little formal routine supported their efforts. In the North, an entrenched bureaucracy that also supplied funds hampered rapid development. War was no excuse for bending established rules.

A New Orleans consortium that included Horace Lawson Hunley, a Customs officer, and two practical engineers, James McLintock and Baxter Watson, designed a submarine. When New Orleans fell to the Union in 1862, the three men hastily moved to Mobile, Alabama, to continue their work. They launched their third prototype, known variously as 'the fish boat' or 'the porpoise' in July 1863.

After successful trials, she moved to Charleston in South Carolina. Good financial reasons pushed them there. The South Atlantic Blockading Squadron of the Federal Navy patrolled the coast with iron resolution. The destruction of a Union ship brought a high cash bounty. Smashing the blockade was essential for Southern victory.

In August 1863, Lieutenant George Gift of the Confederate Navy helped prepare the 'very curious machine for destroying vessels' for despatch by train. With cheerful disregard for secrecy, he described the 40ft 'torpedo fish-boat' in a letter to his fiancée:

In the first place imagine a high pressure steam boiler, not quite round, say 4 feet in diameter in one way and $3\frac{1}{2}$ feet the other – draw each end of the boiler down to a sharp wedge shaped point. The 4 feet is the depth of the hold and the $3\frac{1}{2}$ feet the breadth of beam. On the bottom of the boat is riveted an iron keel weighing 4000 lbs which throws the center of gravity on one side and makes her swim steadily that side down. On top and opposite the keel is placed two man hole plates or hatches with heavy glass tops.

These plates are water tight when covered over. They are just large enough for a man to go in and out. At one end is fitted a very neat little propeller $3\frac{1}{2}$ feet in diameter worked by men sitting in the boat and turning the shaft by hand cranks being fitted on it for that purpose. She also has a rudder and steering apparatus.

Embarked and under ordinary circumstances with men, ballast etc. she floats about half way out of the water & resembles a whale. But when it is necessary to go under the water there are apartments into which the water is allowed to flow, which causes the boat to sink to any required depth, the same being accurately indicated by a column of mercury. Air is supplied by means of pipes that turn up until they get below a depth of 10 feet, when they must depend upon the supply carried down which is sufficient for 3 hours! During which time she could have been propelled 15 miles!

The secret weapon was, indeed, made from a steam boiler. Lengthened and deepened, she took a crew of nine. The craft had two hatches, one forward and one aft, diving planes, removable iron ballast in addition to her water tanks, and a compass. General Pierre Gustave Toutant Beauregard, the Confederate commander at Charleston, found one innovation particularly fascinating. 'Light', he noted, 'was afforded through the means of bull's-eyes placed in the manholes.'

The general liked unusual weapons. Under his aegis, the Confederates developed a steam-driven vessel, with a crew of four, known as the *David* design. About 18ft long, it had a 134lb spar torpedo, the standard mine on a pole. As it merely rode low in the water, rather than submerge, it was hardly a submarine.

Nonetheless, a *David* attacked a Union ironclad, *New Ironsides*, on 5 October 1863. The Confederates killed an ensign on watch with a shotgun blast before they detonated the mine. In the explosion, a cascade of seawater extinguished the *David*'s boiler. Outraged Federal sailors captured two of the crew. Sent to the North in chains to face a threatened court martial for using a devilish weapon, they never faced trial. Both sides soon agreed to an exchange of prisoners.

New Ironsides escaped relatively unscathed. The threat kept Union lookouts on edge. Anything in the water could be a floating bomb.

Like her predecessors, the Mobile blockade buster carried a spar torpedo. Once this was placed close to an enemy hull, the submarine would leave and detonate the mine from a safe distance. James McLintock had gone to Charleston with the boat. His cautious handling, allied with technical difficulties, exasperated the military. The Army seized her and replaced the civilian crew with Confederate Navy volunteers. On an early trial, unfamiliarity with the boat sent her to the bottom of the harbour when she dived with her hatch covers open. Five sailors died. An embarrassed military raised the wreck. Repaired, she underwent more trials, this time with a civilian crew from Mobile. Horace Hunley himself captained them.

Everything went well until 15 October 1863. On that day, submerged, Hunley made a simple error with the forward ballast tank. The boat buried its nose in the harbour silt and mud. She stuck fast. Water flooded in. This time, nobody had time to equalise the pressure. All eight crew drowned.

Fresh volunteers continued training and trials with the salvaged submarine, renamed CSS *H.L. Hunley*. Finally, on the chill, cold night of 17 February 1864, the submarine reached the sloop USS *Housatonic*, at anchor off Charleston. A vigilant lookout spotted *Hunley* in the moonlight as she approached. Despite a smattering of rifle and shotgun fire she reached the ship. The submersible planted her 135lb mine and backed away. Minutes slithered by as *Hunley* cleared the ironclad. The night split apart with a roar of flame.

The explosion shattered the *Housatonic*. She sank in less than three minutes with the loss of five sailors. For the first time in history, an enemy submarine had sunk a warship.

Hunley did not return home for 136 years. She went down on the return journey. Found in 1995 in almost perfect condition, raised in 2000, she is now preserved. Her crew of eight received honoured burial in Charleston's Magnolia cemetery. The first two crews of the *Hunley* lie close by.

While men in grey and men in blue fought and died at Shiloh, Antietam, Gettysburg, Chickamauga and the Wilderness, Europe watched the creation of a truly monstrous machine: the French *Le Plongeur*.

She had the right credentials. Designed in 1858 by a naval officer, Captain Simon Bourgois, the design gained the approval of the Corps of Naval Constructors. One member of the Corps, a naval commander, Charles Brun, who later became Director of Naval Construction, gave the project his full support to the extent of designing an amazing engine.

Work began on *Plongeur* in 1860. The boat was 45m long and displaced 420 tons, far more than any previous design. Iron plates fastened to a stunningly heavy keel formed her hull. The important development was an alternative to strong men with monstrous thighs to work pedals. She had an engine, driven by compressed air. One remarkable feature was a boat, bolted in position inside the hull, to carry twelve men. Internal pressure was kept slightly higher than that of the water outside to prevent seepage at the bolt fastenings.

On the surface, the French submarine behaved with decorum. Submerged, she became a recalcitrant beast. *Plongeur* employed a network of pipes, valves and pistons to move water ballast from one end of the hull to the other. This worked only slowly. The unfortunate creature, long, flat, unwieldy, had little grace as she porpoised through the water, apparently changing her depth as Gallic fancy took her.

The engine developed 80hp. The need to carry enormous bottles of 'fuel' dictated *Plongeur*'s size. Her bulk overwhelmed the engine while her traditional spar torpedo was hardly worth the weight of vessel behind it. It took no heart-searching for the French navy to abandon the project, despite the many advances incorporated in the design.

In 1872, the implacable Confederate James McLintock tried to sell an improved *Hunley* to the Royal Navy. The Admiralty, updating its plans for a war with the United States, intended to enforce the time-honoured blockade, should hostilities occur. Anything that challenged their plans interested them.

In the event, nothing came from McLintock's approach. It seems certain, though, that the papers reached the Royal Navy's Torpedo

School, HMS *Vernon*. Arthur Knyvet Wilson, whose lower-deck nickname of 'Old 'Ard 'Art' succinctly describes his disciplinarian reputation, took command of the school in 1876. More technically minded than many of his contemporaries, Wilson later wrote, in 1901, that during his time at the Torpedo School

> . . . a very well thought out design for a submarine boat was brought to my notice . . . which only required one small addition . . . to make it efficient. Experiments were carried out which proved the practicability of the one point in this invention which was novel, and the inventor was given no further encouragement. . . . A very similar course has been adopted with all the various submarine boats which have been brought forward since. Each design has been carefully examined and sufficient experiment has been made in each case to ascertain its probable value. It has then been quietly dropped with the result of delaying the development of the submarine boat for about 20 years.

Wilson let a modest cat out of a dark bag. Their Lordships did indeed keep wary eyes on submersible development. They discouraged any progress for good reasons as Wilson made clear: 'Now, we cannot delay its introduction any longer, but we should still avoid doing anything to assist in its improvement in order that our means of trapping and destroying it may develop at a greater rate than the submarine boats themselves.'

Not only the submersible started to assume practicality. The spar torpedo, the mine on the end of a long stick, had limited use as a weapon. To place it involved difficulty as well as danger. Neither could it successfully cope with a moving target. As the American Civil War ended, Captain Giovanni Luppis of the Austro-Hungarian navy produced the answer. He designed a small boat that carried an explosive charge. Steam or clockwork powered his invention, which, vitally, could be steered by cords from its parent vessel.

A small propeller and pistol detonator on the nose provided a brilliant firing mechanism. While the boat approached its target, the propeller spun. As the propeller spun, it unscrewed a safety lock on the detonator. When the lock opened fully, the charge exploded.

Luppis found it hard to convince his admirals that his invention had a use. An Englishman, Robert Whitehead, boss of a marine engineering firm in the Adriatic port of Fiume, believed it had. In 1868, the pair unveiled their self-propelled or 'auto-motive torpedo'. Driven by a compressed-air motor, retaining the original firing device, the 135kg weapon had an 8.2kg warhead. A range of 180m, allied to a speed of 6 knots, scrawled a warning to surface ships. An improved prototype with a 270m range soon appeared.

The Royal Navy took notice. The new invention might be slow. It might not go very far. Improvements, however, were no more than a matter of time, of money. The essential fact was that the Luppis– Whitehead torpedo carried explosives to a distant target.

By 1870, the production version had a length of 4.9m, carried a 35kg guncotton warhead at 8 knots over 360m. Whitehead travelled to England. One hundred test firings amply convinced the Admiralty. They promptly bought rights to manufacture the design themselves. The ideal weapon for the submarine had arrived.

In the United States, an Irish immigrant, John Philip Holland, a New Jersey schoolteacher, peered at his students through wire-rimmed spectacles and dreamed dreams. Always interested in the potential of submarines, he sent his plans for a one-man submersible to the Secretary of the Navy. A blunt reply told him that it was not something to which anyone would trust himself.

Undeterred, the walrus-moustached Holland looked for financial support. An Irish nationalist, he did not need to look too far. The Fenians, revolutionaries for Irish freedom, came to his aid. Anything that could strike the detested Queen Victoria and her military a telling blow interested them. *Holland I* duly appeared. A mere 15½ft long, the boat took after a pencil, sharpened at both ends. The single operator necessarily wore 'diving dress'. The control room flooded each time the craft submerged.

There was one great advance. Holland's boat used a petrol engine. It did not work brilliantly but engineering had finally made the pedal genuinely obsolete. The prototype performed well enough to encourage the building of a larger version.

The Reverend George Garrett, an Anglican clergyman in Manchester, forked out £1,500 in 1879, to build a submarine to his own design. At 45ft long and 10ft in diameter, she similarly resembled a short stub of pencil, pointed at each end. With a deft touch of divine inspiration, Garrett named his creation *Resurgam*: 'I shall rise again'. A patent closed-system steam engine gave enough power to drive the boat underwater for four hours.

After successful trials of the vessel at Wallasey, the Royal Navy took an interest. *Resurgam* set out for Portsmouth in February 1880. Technical problems forced her into Rhyl. Repaired, but towed by a steam yacht, she left harbour on a gale-swept night. The steam yacht broke down. *Resurgam*'s crew left their boat to transfer to the yacht to lend a hand.

Since the conning tower hatch closed only from the inside, the submarine shipped water. The towrope parted. Down went *Resurgam*.

Garrett, low on funds like inventors before and after him, turned his eyes, not to heaven, but to Sweden. Thorsten Nordenfelt, an arms manufacturer, had an interest in submarines. They were the weapon of the future, and weapons turned a profit.

In 1881, Holland produced his second boat, 31ft long, armed with an air-powered cannon. Tests dragged on. The Fenians, anxious to send the Royal Navy to perdition, became impatient. Eventually, they stole their own boat, hiding it in a shed in Connecticut, where it stayed for thirty-five years.

Holland formed his own company, the Nautilus Submarine Boat Company. It took two years to produce its first boat, the *Zalinski*. Holland named it after Captain Edmund Zalinski, his major investor as well as inventor of the terrifying air-powered gun of the earlier boat.

In Europe, in the United States, designers of submersibles tried out their ideas. Claude Goubet of France built two generally ineffective boats that incorporated another innovation: power came from electric batteries. Technology spurred its way into creative minds.

Less useful than an electric boat was Josiah Tuck's *Peacemaker*. The American used caustic soda to propel his creature through the water. His anxious relatives, probably more concerned that he squandered the family's substantial wealth on his inventions, committed him to an asylum for the insane. Years later, hard-headed German designers investigated the same technique.

Thorsten Nordenfelt launched his submarine in 1885 in Stockholm. She used the same pattern steam engine as Garrett's *Resurgam*. *Nordenfelt I* weighed 60 tons, measured 64ft in length and carried a single torpedo tube. Speed and manoeuvrability were not her main assets. It needed twelve hours to build up sufficient steam for underwater travel. She took thirty minutes to submerge. Once under the surface, the Nordenfelt design behaved like an eccentric aunt with a mind of her own.

The Swede did not become wealthy by allowing such minor details as poor design to impede his progress. Specially trained, carefully chosen men demonstrated the invention before royalty, presidents and prime ministers. It always impressed.

The Greek navy bought one. Nothing more was heard of her.

Nordenfelt moved to England, establishing his works at Barrow.

The Turkish navy acquired two of his later design, *Nordenfelt II*, to counteract the threat from the Greek boat. Bigger and better, at 100ft long with twin torpedo tubes, Barrow built them in sections. They were shipped to Constantinople for final assembly. When the first boat tested her torpedo, she unhesitatingly tipped backwards to slide, stern first, to the bottom of the Bosporus. The second boat then languished in pieces for years at the Constantinople navy yard, before reappearing in August 1916. Originally named *Abdul Hamid*, she became the *Yunusbaligi* or 'Porpoise'. She entered the water. She sank.

Russia stumped up for *Nordenfelt III*. This was bigger still, at 123ft long, with a surface speed claimed to be 14 knots. On the delivery trip, she ran aground. The Tsar's navy took the opportunity to cancel their order.

Nordenfelt lost interest in submarines when they failed to make money. Rather than build them at a loss, he sold plans to interested governments. Germany was one.

The French designer Gustave Zede produced *Gymnote*, named for a species of electric eel, in 1888. She, like Goubet's boats, used batteries, an attribute that inspired her name. She managed 8 knots on the surface but the inventor had not allowed for recharging batteries at sea. This rather limited her usefulness.

The following year, Isaac Peral, a Spanish navy lieutenant, designed and built a fully functional submarine that successfully fired three of Whitehead's improved torpedoes during her trials. Officialdom failed to pursue his innovation.

The hunt for a practical submarine, a genuine weapon of war, quickened. The minuet of tranquil evolution gave way to the waltz, the quickstep, the polka of furious development as science expanded the horizons. The accumulator battery. The internal combustion engine. Mass production. Powered machinery. All made their mark.

In 1893, the United States government announced a competition for a new submarine. Holland entered his latest proposed design. The two other competitors were Simon Lake and George Baker. Lake's design was only on paper but Baker had a real, functioning submarine. Its steam engine for surface use also powered an electric motor that acted as a dynamo to charge batteries for underwater running. Lake's design incorporated wheels to allow the boat to run on the seabed. His knowledge of the ocean floor was, observers felt, limited.

Holland won the competition but no official orders followed. The Irishman copied Nordenfelt's approach. He inspired the rumour that foreign navies wanted his submarine. On 3 March 1895, the John P. Holland Torpedo Boat Company received a $200,000 contract for a steam-powered submarine. Holland fell out with the authorities over putting a steam engine into his design but there was no turning back. The US navy wanted submarines with steam engines, not dangerous petrol gadgets.

Holland was proved right. The 'official' boat, *Plunger*, never made it to the open water. She was launched in 1897, but the temperature in the fire room reached 137 degrees Fahrenheit at only two-thirds power. Not even American stokers could work in that temperature. Holland had already started work on a new boat, powered by a petrol engine.

In 1898, Simon Lake demonstrated his *Argonaut I* with a voyage across the open sea from Norfolk, Virginia, to Sandy Hook, New Jersey. At no point did his boat trundle along the bottom. The feat attracted a telegram from Jules Verne. The exploit, he enthused, would spur submersible development across the world. The famous author added that 'the next war may be largely a contest between submarine boats'.

Europe was not far behind the USA. In France, the *Gustav Zede*, 148ft long with a weight of 266 tons, took part in the French navy's annual manoeuvres. To the dismay and consternation of traditional admirals and their acolytes, the umpires ruled that she had successfully torpedoed a moored battleship.

The French announced a submersibles competition. Contestants needed to demonstrate a surface range of 100 miles and travel 10 miles under the water. The contest attracted twenty-nine entries. The winner, *Narval*, was 188ft long and weighed in at 136 tons. Its designer, Maxime Laubeuf, originally proposed a steam engine to power the boat, but a diesel engine soon replaced it.

By the end of the nineteenth century, the submarine had arrived as a weapon of war.

The djinn had escaped the bottle.

TWO

FRIENDS IN PEACE. FRIENDS FOR EVER

By 1914, the major European powers all had submarines. Sixteen world navies possessed 400 boats. The Royal Navy had seventy-five, a misleading number, for most were small and unable to patrol out to sea. Germany had fewer. When war came in fateful August, the Kaiserliche Marine had twenty-eight boats in service or close to commissioning, with more being built. Although the Imperial Navy had fewer submarines than either the British or French navies, their quality, their design and construction, were superior.

In Britain, Sir John Fisher, the First Sea Lord in 1904, seized upon the potential of the submarine with his usual enthusiasm. His enemies, of whom there were a good number, scoffed at 'Chinese Jack's' interest in the new weapons. 'Toys' and 'playthings' were the least offensive descriptions. Fisher controlled a service that devoutly believed in battleships with massive armament. Other navies agreed. The Japanese navy subsequently proved its truth when they destroyed the Russian Pacific Fleet by adroit use of heavy guns.

Sir George Goschen, the First Lord of the Admiralty from 1897 until late 1900, considered that the Royal Navy should have submarines, if only to see what they could do. His professional advisers thought likewise. The United States and the French navies took submarines seriously. If those two nations did, Britain had better know what she was up against. Goschen made the point, in typical language, to the House of Commons: 'The Hon. Member pointed out the enormous importance of submarine boats . . . I do not propose publicly to declare whether the Admiralty believes in submarine boats or not. . . . We do not wish to encourage or discourage other nations by stating . . . how great would be the danger of these submarine boats to ourselves.' Goschen chose not to mention that, two months earlier, he received a terse minute from the Senior Naval Lord – Fisher changed the title to First Sea Lord when he took office – that said plainly that the 'matter of submarine boats cannot be ignored and will have to be taken up by us – our first want is a design'.

Short days after Goschen's speech, Lord Rothschild provided an introduction for Isaac Rice, the new owner of the Holland Company and an extraordinary salesman, to the Admiralty.

By October the deal was done. Britain would build five boats under licence. The design included space for four torpedoes and three white mice. The mice formed an early warning system. They squeaked if poisonous fumes escaped from the primitive petrol engine. In practice, the rodent alarms broke down. Sailors stuffed them full of food. The mice spent much of their service careers in happy lethargy.

Viscount Selborne, Goschen's successor, announced the purchase in April 1901. Vickers Son & Maxim of Barrow-in-Furness won the contract. The vessels were 'to assist the Admiralty in assessing their true value'. Despite errors in the technical drawings from the Holland Company, darkly believed to be deliberate by conspiracy theorists, HM Submarine Torpedo Boat Number 1 entered the water on 2 October 1901.

The Holland design suffered from wide-ranging faults. A cupola instead of a proper conning tower marred stability. On the surface, petrol exhaust fumes persuaded crews to leave open the entrance hatch to keep the air fresh. With the boat low in the water, this practice invited flooding from any passing vessel. As the engine also produced a lively range of sparks with the ability to ignite the fumes, most Holland submariners preferred swamping to exploding.

The Admiralty appointed an outstanding officer as its first Inspecting Captain of Submarine Boats. Reginald Bacon, a protégé of Fisher's and described by him as 'the cleverest officer in the Navy', possessed a determined inventiveness that tackled any problem. He would, if required, have devised a scheme to move a battleship across the Gobi Desert. The limitations of the Holland submarine were a ten-course banquet for his quicksilver brain. In collaboration with Vickers, he redesigned it.

The result was half as large again. By 1904, the A Class entered service. They employed proper conning towers. Their batteries had twice the capacity of the Holland Class. The more powerful Wolseley 500hp petrol engine, however, tended to burn out its plugs, as well as turn piping white-hot. As the pipes ran throughout the submarine, their heated proximity to petrol tanks created heart-stopping alarm at regular intervals.

Bacon proposed, possibly in a moment of fine distraction, that the new vessels should bear names like proper ships. He produced suggestions. After a piercing scrutiny, their Lordships disagreed. Given the lower deck penchant for nicknames, HMS *Ichthyosaurus*, *Simosaurus*, *Plesiosaurus*, *Discosaurus*, *Pistosaurus* and *Nothosaurus* fortunately remained on file.

Playthings. Toys. No craft for gentlemen. The early volunteers endured countless insults from the surface fleet. The vagaries of primitive petrol engines, squalid crew conditions, the surroundings that dirtied even the most fastidious fingernails, led to gibes that submarine officers were mechanics, 'unwashed chauffeurs', nothing better than tradesmen. In socially stratified Edwardian England, this potent insult became absorbed and turned into a name of honour. 'The Trade' remains a title proudly acknowledged by submariners.

In the Navy manoeuvres of 1904, the umpires decided that Bacon's 1st Submarine Flotilla 'sank' two battleships. The submariners believed they accounted for more, but prejudice still ruled. The decision did not please the Commander-in-Chief of the Home Fleet, Sir Arthur Knyvet Wilson, that same officer who so firmly thwarted earlier developments. An Old Etonian, hereditary baronet, holder of the Victoria Cross, Wilson considered submarine warfare underhand and not worthy of a gentleman.

His dislike boiled over when an A Class 'torpedoed' his flagship. The submarine's commander surfaced to signal: 'Respectfully submit have torpedoed you. Respectfully submit you are sunk. Respectfully submit you are out of the exercise.' Wilson seized the semaphore flags from his yeoman of signals to reply personally: 'You be damned.'

Bacon left his post in 1904. He went to the Admiralty as Fisher's naval assistant. There he worked on the secret designs for the new revolutionary capital ship. Every navy in the world had copied previous British battleships with their mixed armament of 12in and 9.2in guns. The new class, driven by steam turbines, mounted only big guns. After time at sea to gain enough experience, Bacon took command of the first new ship. HMS *Dreadnought* carried ten 12in guns in five turrets. She roared along at 21 knots. Built and commissioned in the record time of fourteen months, she made every other fighting ship obsolete. Other nations immediately began to build dreadnoughts and super-dreadnoughts of their own.

A chorus of critics immediately condemned Fisher. They alleged that he threw away the Royal Navy's superiority at sea. In fact, he preserved it. Admirals in Japan, Italy, Germany and the United States all read, along with Fisher, an article in *Jane's Fighting Ships* by the Italian naval designer Cuniberti. This proposed the new type of ship that ignited Fisher's passion. While others pondered, Fisher acted. The secrecy and speed of *Dreadnought*'s building left every other navy behind.

Captain Edgar Lees succeeded Bacon. He, in his turn, handed over to Captain Sydney Hall. Both were capable officers, torpedo specialists, whose periods in command saw substantial development in underwater craft. Submarines became less like seals or sharpened pencils. They looked more like ships as designers realised that submarines spent more time on the surface than under the water.

A break with accepted practice came in 1910. Captain Roger John Brownlow Keyes became Inspecting Captain of Submarines at the behest of Sir Arthur Knyvet Wilson, now First Sea Lord. Keyes was no torpedo specialist. Neither had he served in submarines. He was a destroyer man. He described himself as a salt-horse with minimal technical knowledge. He was not an officer who stayed behind a desk to push around paper. A hero during the Boxer Rebellion, he had no lack of courage. No great administrator, he countered this with leadership in abundance.

Wilson required someone who agreed with him on the role of submarines. He wanted them to work in closer touch with the main fleet rather than operate independently. The suggestion that Wilson wanted an officer with good prospects of making admiral persuaded Keyes to take the post. Fisher was safely in retirement. This was one problem out of the new inspecting captain's way. Admiral Jack had little time for Captain Roger.

Keyes inherited sixty-one boats. Twelve venerable A Class, eleven outdated B Class, thirty-seven coastal C Class and *D1*, the first of her class. The shipyards had orders for eight more.

The new inspecting captain turned the submarine branch into an élite. Bold, intelligent, and occasionally eccentric officers joined the underwater flotilla. They proved their worth in the years ahead. Keyes also introduced much-needed improvements. He badgered authority for decent-sized depot ships to allow crews to sleep away from their cramped craft when in harbour. Despite his efforts, though, British submariners generally endured squalid conditions appropriate to the Navy of George the First rather than George the Fifth.

By 1914, the E Class were the latest submarines in Royal Naval service. Like their predecessors in the D Class, they were genuine blue-water boats, able to operate away from harbours and depot ships. With a speed of 15½ knots above water and 9½ knots below it, 178ft long with a displacement of 660 tons, they represented the new breed. Their torpedoes, equipped with a gyroscope to maintain a set course, could theoretically hit a target 11,000yd distant. They could safely submerge to 200ft. They had the same task as every other ship in the Royal Navy. Deny the seas to the enemy.

The Admiralty, often accused of technological myopia allied with wanton stupidity, evolved a policy that regarded the submarine as a decisive weapon of battle. The weapon was not yet perfect, but time would make it infinitely better.

The Kaiser's navy, at least officially, came late to the idea of submarines. Wilhelm, enamoured of big ships, wanted the biggest and best toys for his bath. The German General Staff, traditionalists to a man, saw no need for a navy. The Army was the conquering machine. If the All-Highest wished to play with ships, so be it, as long as he realised that their only use was for coastal defence.

Germany dominated Continental Europe. Wilhelm, though, wanted an empire, a proper empire with overseas colonies. To expand Germany's global influence, he needed ships. Ships that entered foreign harbours. Ships that hammered home the message of German might. Ships that emphasised Germany's power.

A fork-bearded genius created Wilhelm's navy. Grossadmiral Alfred von Tirpitz, an Anglophile of no mean order, admired and envied the Royal Navy. He believed that sea power brought prosperity. A country that controlled the oceans controlled its own fate. Britain itself was proof. She had an empire. She became the leading world power because she owned the world's largest fleet. Germany, too, needed a large navy, one with battleships, battleships, battleships at its heart. In 1897, an enthralled Wilhelm appointed him as Secretary of State for the German navy.

By 1901, Tirpitz had steered two Navy Bills through the Reichstag. They projected a Kaiserliche Marine of thirty-eight battleships and twenty cruisers. No submarines were contemplated. As the chairman of the Schiffbautechnische Gesellschaft, or Technical Shipbuilding Society, claimed in a speech in 1899: 'The present technical unreliability of the underwater vessels, especially the factor of lack of longitudinal stability, was such that one can see very little future for them. . . . The German naval authorities are right when they refuse to indulge in expensive and lengthy experiments with under water craft, but confine themselves to battleships, cruisers and sea-going torpedo boats.' The new German navy did not totally dismiss the Unterseeboot. The Torpedo Inspectorate, in particular, thought they had much to offer. As battleships and cruisers rattled down the slipways, the torpedo specialists investigated U-boats.

Nordenfelt's original 1885 design sparked serious interest. The Germans bought plans. The Danzigerwerft and the Kiel Germaniawerft both began to build a submarine. Steam-powered, 114ft long with a surface speed of 11 knots and a maximum of $4\frac{1}{2}$ knots under water, the 215-ton boats eventually joined the torpedo flotillas at Kiel and Wilhelmshaven for trials. Neither impressed.

German shipbuilders did not stop with the Nordenfelt boats. They built others from French designs as well as their own. In the autumn of 1903, the Kaiser and Prince Heinrich of Prussia visited the Germaniawerft shipyard to inspect one of the experimental boats. Named *Forelle* or 'Trout', she had a range of 25 nautical miles at a speed of 4 knots. Prince Heinrich not only took part in a diving trial. The royal hands steered the boat under water.

Despite this Imperial interest, Tirpitz refused to spend money on machines that only sailed close to the coast. He disliked any deviation from the task of building a powerful fleet. Rapid developments modified his opinions. U-boats, armed with torpedoes, could be respectable fighting vessels. When Russia ordered three submarines from the Germaniawerft, Tirpitz changed his mind.

The first official 'experimental' Unterseeboot received authorisation in 1905. On 4 August 1906, a salvage vessel lowered the finished craft into the water. In September, she went to sea under her own power. In November, she became *U 1*. The Kaiserliche Marine took delivery of her on 14 December 1906.

She was not greatly unlike her British A Class contemporary at 42m long and a displacement of 238 tons, but for one major exception. No hazardous petrol engine turned pipes white-hot. The German boat had a Körting paraffin motor that developed 400hp for surface running.

Her successors, laid down even before *U 1* began her trials, outstripped the British submarines. *U 2*, *U 3* and *U 4* each carried four torpedo tubes, two in the bow, two at the stern. The latter two boats also boasted a retractable 37mm deck gun.

Paraffin engines stayed as standard fittings until 1913. Among their major drawbacks was the large exhaust funnel that poured out white smoke by day and sparks and flames at night. Not until *U 19* appeared, equipped with Rudolf Diesel's twenty-year-old invention, did the U-boat finally come of age. So equipped, *U 19* travelled more than 4,000 miles at her top speed of 15½ knots. At half that speed, she went twice as far. Under water, she managed 80 miles at 5 knots without draining her batteries. Later boats had a greater range. German designers had taken the words of Tirpitz to heart. U-boats were no longer coastal huggers. They became ocean-going killers.

Developments in underwater craft, battleships, artillery or other forms of nastiness meant little to the ordinary citizen of 1914. War was unimaginable. Austrians, Germans, French, British all felt secure behind the shield provided by the great armies and navies. Even if a European war did break out, it would swiftly finish. Economically, war was impossible. Only a few politicians and retired generals believed otherwise. It was all talk anyway. The statesmen and diplomats resolved problems that might lead to war. They had in the past. They would in the future.

In June 1914, the Royal Navy sent some light cruisers to show the flag at Kiel Regatta. The Kaiser was in his element. Commodore William Edmund Goodenough, commanding the British 1st Light Cruiser squadron, recalled:

The Kaiser, when visiting the British flagship, wore the uniform of a British Admiral of the Fleet and said in that somewhat exaggerated phrase of speech to which he was addicted, that he was proud to wear the uniform worn by Lord Nelson.

His brother, Prince Henry, an honorary admiral in our own fleet said, 'This is what I have long hoped for – to see a portion of the British and German Fleets laying side by side in friendship in Kiel Harbour.'

The feeling between the more senior officers was friendly if rather dispassionate. With the more junior officers, the fraternisation was perfectly complete.

The glittering occasion ended abruptly. News of the assassination of Archduke Franz Ferdinand at Sarajevo on 28 June 1914 finished the festivities. The grey shapes of the British warships left Kiel. The ceremonial bunting vanished but HMS *Southampton* flew an unambiguous signal. 'Friends in peace, friends for ever.' Inexorably, the seconds ticked away to the outbreak of war.

By chance, later presented as shrewd forethought, the Royal Navy and reserves mobilised on 15 July 1914, the result of a decision made a year earlier. Economy, rather than keen anticipation of international tensions, determined the move. Practice mobilisation came cheaper than exercising the fleet at sea. Two days later, the Spithead Review saw, in the words of the First Lord of the Admiralty, Winston Spencer Churchill, 'the greatest assemblage of naval power ever witnessed in the history of the world'.

Most Britons believed that the Royal Navy was infinitely better than Kaiser Bill's. In terms of pure design, little separated British and German ships. More practical matters caused problems. British capital ships suffered in comparison because of their lack of beam. A series of Liberal governments, anxious to fulfil their promises of social benefits for all, kept beady eyes on military costs. They spent nothing on new docks. All new British ships had to fit existing facilities. This ensured that none of Fisher's dreadnoughts exceeded 90ft in width. In Germany, as the Kaiser airily explained to Admiral Sir John Rushworth Jellicoe in 1910, they built the docks to take the ships, not the other way around. In practice, German big ships were 10ft wider than British. This allowed thicker side-armour, a feature that made them less vulnerable to mines and torpedoes.

Technologically, King George's fleet lagged behind Wilhelm's navy. British ships still practised individual gun-laying in action. Their opponents used a director system in which all of the guns were trained, laid and fired by a master stereoscopic sight and rangefinder. The individual turrets merely followed the elevation and bearing of the master sight, every gun firing at the same target.

With shells, mines and torpedoes, the same story applied. Jellicoe, as Third Sea Lord in 1910, asked for an armour-piercing shell to penetrate an enemy at an oblique angle and burst inside. When Jellicoe returned to sea, Admiral Sir John Briggs succeeded him. No live wire, Sir John failed to sprinkle salt on the tail of the Ordnance Board. Wartime British shells broke up directly they hit armour plate.

Similar inertia dogged the development of British mines and torpedoes. To the Royal Navy, especially most of its gunnery specialists, such devices were the resort of weaker fleets. The gun, the queen of sea battles, sank enemy ships, not mechanical contrivances. Although the British pioneered the torpedo, development lagged behind that elsewhere. British torpedoes possessed a distressing ability to run deep or sink to the bottom when fired.

The story with mines was worse. They often broke from their moorings. They usually failed to explode. No thoughtful tactics existed for their employment. From 1914 to much of 1917, British minefields were essentially a waste of time and money. A reliable mine finally appeared after three years of war, copied from the German version. Mines and torpedoes became the stock-in-trade of the U-boat.

Admirals in neither Germany nor Britain really knew how to use the underwater arm. On both sides, initial thoughts suggested a defensive role. Both naval staffs agreed on one thing. The enemy would charge across the North Sea to attack battleships at anchor in ports and harbours.

This theory obsessed the German Naval Staff. They agreed that the Army would finish any European war in short order. The only thing the British could do, therefore, was to mount a surprise raid into the Heligoland Bight in an effort to destroy the High Seas Fleet. This led the U-boats to sway at mooring buoys, 20 miles out to sea. Ten miles beyond them, German destroyers patrolled. When the British hove in view, the destroyers retreated, chased by their enemy. The U-boats submerged and prepared to devastate the pursuing Royal Navy with mass torpedo attacks.

A study of previous wars convinced the Kaiserliche Marine that the Royal Navy would closely blockade the German coast. This would give the U-boats and destroyers generous chances to pick off enemy capital ships and detached vessels. This steady erosion of British numerical superiority would finally allow the High Seas Fleet to chance a full-scale engagement.

The British Admiralty, soon after the end of the Boer War in 1902, decided that Germany was the next enemy, not France. British sea policy in time of war had always been one of close blockade. To apply this to Germany needed Royal Navy control of the German North Sea coast, best described as a right angle. A close blockade needed to command the 150-mile hypotenuse between the Danish and Dutch borders. This, in turn, required the capture of one or more of the offshore islands – Sylt and Heligoland being particular favourites – for use as a forward base by British light forces. Behind them the First, or Grand, Fleet would steam ready to engage the High Seas Fleet when, in desperation, it tried to break out. The result, nobody doubted, would be another Trafalgar.

This rosy scenario created several problems. The Royal Navy's three major dockyards were Chatham, Portsmouth and Devonport. Ideally positioned for wars against the French, the Dutch and the Spanish, they had little use unless the Western Approaches, the southern half of the North Sea and the English Channel became battle arenas.

The arrival of Germany as the foe posed a difficulty. Attention had to be focused on the north. If the High Seas Fleet sallied out from Kiel, Cuxhaven and Wilhelmshaven, a clutch of British battleships cruising around the Isle of Wight could do nothing to stop them.

In 1903, the Admiralty decided to develop Rosyth on the Firth of Forth as a first-class naval base. 'First-class' in 'navalspeak' meant a port with a dockyard able to construct, equip and repair warships of any tonnage in every way. It would have a permanent stores depot that could supply every item a navy needed. In addition, its defences could see off any intruder.

As First Sea Lord, Jackie Fisher turned up his nose at Rosyth. He wanted to go further north, to the Cromarty Firth, to command the passage from the North Sea into the Atlantic. Still further north lay Scapa Flow in the Orkney Islands, 15 miles by 8, an enormous haven that could shelter the entire Royal Navy with room to spare.

Fisher failed to win that particular struggle. Rosyth was chosen. To sweeten the pill, either Cromarty or Scapa would become a second-class base, one that could do smaller repairs and held only essential stores. After some heated moments, the admirals chose the Cromarty Firth. They adopted Scapa Flow as a fleet anchorage in war, a consolation prize of little value as the Treasury decreed that it was too expensive to erect any defences there.

It took some while for dreams of a second Trafalgar to vanish. In 1911, the Commander-in-Chief Home Fleet issued a memorandum that set out British strategy if Germany and Britain went to war:

The present War Plans provide for a blockade of the Heligoland Bight by the 1st and 2nd Destroyer Flotillas, supported by the 1st, 2nd and 3rd Cruiser Squadrons, with the principal objects of:

preventing raiding expeditions leaving German ports in the earlier stages of hostilities:

preventing the German Fleet putting to sea without the British Commander-in-Chief knowing it and, when it is known to be at sea, conveying him such information as to its movements as will enable it to be brought to action by the British Main Fleet.

It was a plan worthy of Horatio Nelson. Sadly, mines, torpedoes, U-boats, destroyers and long-range coastal artillery made it an absurdity. Heligoland and Sylt dripped fortifications and defences. Even the crustier seadogs in Whitehall admitted defeat.

The new War Plan of 1912 tossed out the close blockade in favour of an 'observational blockade'. A line of destroyers and light cruisers would patrol from the south-western tip of Norway to the Dutch coast. Behind them, to the west, the First Fleet would wait. Dreams of Trafalgar still lived, for the Plan emphasised that 'the general idea . . . is to exercise pressure . . . by shutting off German shipping . . . through the action of patrolling cruisers . . . and supporting these cruisers and covering the British coasts by two battle fleets stationed so as to . . . bring the enemy's fleet to action should it proceed to sea with the object of driving the cruisers off or undertaking other offensive action'.

The new blockade line was 300 miles in length. It left unanswered the question of German hit-and-run attacks. Not even the British could manage an unbroken line of ships from Norway to Holland. U-boats and destroyers could pick off the blockaders, one by one, with little danger to themselves.

Only in July 1914 did the Admiralty's new War Plan embrace reality. Coincidentally, it also propounded the policy that helped win the war. The 'distant blockade' became the new policy. It proposed to close the two exits from the North Sea. The Channel Fleet would seal the Straits of Dover. The First Fleet, based in the Orkney Islands, would guard the line from the Norwegian coast to the Orkneys. It was sensible, practicable and the Law of Unintended Consequences duly clicked in. It handed the U-boats a prime part to play.

German naval policy never intended to send the High Seas Fleet on a desperate venture to destroy the Royal Navy in one mighty battle. The Kaiser's admirals based their hopes on piecemeal, isolated actions, to destroy a battleship here, to sink a cruiser there. The Kaiser personally decided on a strategic defensive policy, a policy supported by his Chancellor. An intact High Seas Fleet was a powerful counter when it came to imposing peace conditions on France and her allies after the Army won the land war.

As for the Unterseeboote, they were part of the fleet's defences. In Britain, however, despite the prevailing view that submarines did little more than get in the way of proper ships while simultaneously ruining exercises, some admirals and politicians feared their potential.

Churchill, the civilian First Lord of the Admiralty, had no doubt that the Germans intended to use U-boats against the Royal Navy. In a survey to the Committee of Imperial Defence on 11 July 1912, he observed:

> If ever there was a vessel in the world whose services to the defensive will be great, and which is a characteristic weapon for the defence, it is the submarine. But the German development of that vessel, from all the information we can obtain, shows that it is intended to turn even this weapon of defence into one of offence, that is to say, they are building not the smaller classes which will be useful for the defence of their somewhat limited coast-line, but the larger classes which would be capable of sudden operation at a great distance from their base across the sea.

One advocate of the submarine was Arthur Balfour, Prime Minister in 1902–5, a staunch supporter and partisan of Jackie Fisher. Balfour, convinced that it was a weapon for the weaker fleet, in letters to the former First Sea Lord pointed out that the real question was not whether Royal Navy submarines would make the enemy's position intolerable but whether his submarines would make the British position impossible. There was, Balfour believed, nothing to prevent German U-boats sealing every port whatever the British superiority in service vessels. An infestation of enemy submarines rendered a surface fleet impotent. Almost as an afterthought, he mentioned that a submarine could not capture a vessel at sea.

Fisher, on half-pay, remained as forthright and emphatic as ever. Among other ideas, he proposed a pre-emptive strike against Germany, a suggestion that filled even the bellicose Churchill, the political First Lord of the Admiralty, with dismay. International opinion, if not law, condemned such an idea.

In June 1913, Fisher turned his attention to the use of submarines and blockades with a long, written appraisal. He expanded on Balfour's gentle hint. An individual submarine, Fisher argued, could not 'capture the merchant ship; she has no spare hands to put a prize crew on board . . . she cannot convey her into harbour. . . . There is nothing else the submarine can do except sink her capture.'

This statement of the seemingly obvious shocked Prince Louis of Battenberg, the First Sea Lord. He was hardly mollified when Fisher admitted that such behaviour was 'freely acknowledged to be an altogether barbarous method of warfare', although he then added that 'the essence of war is violence, and moderation in war is imbecility'.

Churchill, ever anxious to demonstrate pugnacity, queried some of Fisher's assumptions:

> There are a few points on which I am not convinced. Of these the greatest is the question of the use of submarines to sink merchant vessels. I do not believe this would ever be done by a civilized power. If there were a nation vile enough to adopt systematically such methods, it would be justified and indeed necessary, to employ the extreme resources of science against them; to spread pestilence; poison the water of great cities, and, if convenient, proceed by the assassination of individuals.
>
> These are frankly unthinkable propositions and the excellence of your paper is, to some extent, marred by the prominence assigned to them.

Churchill's view, seemingly, was that if, for instance, German U-boats sank merchant ships, Britain had free rein to spread pestilence throughout the Black Forest, pour cyanide into the River Spree and send teams of crack assassins to Potsdam. The Geneva Convention outlawed plague, poison and murder as acceptable policies, although subsequent politicians have expressed a wish to abandon the only rules that make warfare's horrors even vaguely acceptable to those who fight them.

The Admiralty drew precisely the wrong interpretation from Fisher's outburst: if a submarine used barbarity as its only resort, clearly it had no place in naval warfare.

The 1909 Declaration of London, a document that attempted to civilise the whole business of blockading, supported this comforting thought. It attempted to lay down some rules of civilised behaviour. Merchant ships openly flying an enemy flag were legitimate targets. They could either be seized as a prize or scuttled. The crew became prisoners.

Neutral ships were a three-way problem. 'Absolute contraband' covered goods used exclusively for war and consigned to an enemy port. Outright seizure was authorised.

'Conditional contraband' described cargoes which might or might not be used for warlike purposes. Food, animal fodder, oil, petrol and coal were examples. These could be seized only if clearly consigned to the enemy via an enemy-held port. They could not be taken if destined for a neutral port even though they could be shipped onward.

The third category was 'free goods', items that were not contraband in any way. Examples of this innocuous group included copper, iron ore, wool, cotton, flax, rubber, a whole variety of raw materials, machinery and various manufactured items, none of which had any possible use in such activities as making munitions.

As a final blow, the Declaration decreed that blockade should only apply to enemy coasts, a condition that rendered the whole document meaningless.

Clearly, a blockade required ships to be stopped, manifests to be scanned and decisions taken. Seized neutrals went to a home port under a prize crew. Cargoes were compulsorily purchased, the crew repatriated. Inconvenient, certainly. Without doubt, annoying. But not lethal. And not something a submarine could do.

Admiral Sir Percy Scott, one of the finest gunnery experts the Royal Navy ever produced, did little to quell unease when he wrote to *The Times* in June 1914. Firmly of the opinion that capital ships were doomed dinosaurs, he suggested that no more should be built. The money for them should go on aircraft and submarines. With some foresight, he prophesied that capital ships at sea would be in grave danger of torpedo attack from submarines. If war came, the big ships on both sides would retreat to safe anchorages. Submarines, he declared, could deliver a deadly attack in broad daylight. If they patrolled off the British coast, they would destroy everything they found.

He attracted criticism, not least from the patrician Admiral Lord Charles William de la Poer Beresford, who nursed a fierce dislike of the plebeian Percy. Beresford loathed Fisher and his entire coterie, of which Scott was a member. In a Royal Navy split by cliques and cabals, whose labyrinthine convolutions rivalled any modern television series of betrayal and deceit, enmities died hard.

Scott, as commander of the 1st Cruiser Squadron, served under Beresford as part of the Channel Fleet. The second son of the 4th Marquess of Waterford harboured a dark suspicion that the solicitor's son reported secretly to 'Chinese Jack'. Scott, in turn, nursed a low opinion of Beresford, both professionally and as an individual.

An extra twist of the knife came in 1907. Scott sent one of his cruisers back to port. His order, read by every ship in the area, contained the acid comment that 'Paintwork appears to be more in demand than gunnery, so you had better come in, in time to make yourself look pretty by the 8th', a reference to a forthcoming visit by the Kaiser with which Beresford was much concerned. When Beresford heard of this ripe piece of sarcasm, he sent an abusive signal round his command, designed to humiliate Scott.

The following year, at sea, Beresford signalled a manoeuvre that would have caused a collision. Scott ignored the fluttering flags until Beresford cancelled the signal. At which point, Scott acknowledged the order, an action which emphasised his disdain.

Beresford, displaying his characteristic refusal actually to consider the facts, stated without preamble that submarines could operate only in daylight – a restriction placed on them during exercises – and that a few rounds from a machine gun put them out of action.

Even Bacon joined in. He expressed astonishment that Scott, a gunnery specialist, published views on matters about which he was no expert. Bacon, himself retired after a number of bruising disputes with his seniors, alleged that it was extremely difficult to navigate a submarine, a strange claim given Bacon's own extensive seagoing experience.

Press and experts alike rushed to join the debate. Percy Scott found himself in a definite minority. His self-evident point that enemy submarines were a threat to British naval supremacy sank from view. The debate rumbled on as Britain slipped nearer to the First World War.

If war did come, neither the Royal Navy nor the Kaiserliche Marine contemplated more than a few months of conflict. For the British, the programme was simplicity itself. The fleet would sally out to inflict a crushing defeat on the enemy. After that, the Navy would blockade enemy ports. Six months would see the end of the affair.

Berlin agreed that the conflict would end swiftly. The mailed fist of the German army would scatter opposition to the winds. If the British were involved, an unlikely prospect, the 'beefeaters' had few options. Their negligible army would not trouble Germany. The Royal Navy would do what it had always done and blockade the coastline. Single ships on patrol, unsupported, would prove easy pickings for hit-and-run attacks.

July days passed in a haze of heat. In Britain, Irish Home Rule dominated the headlines. Nobody was much concerned about events elsewhere. The kerfuffle in the Balkans would blow over. It didn't concern anybody but central Europeans.

Then it was August 1914.

THREE

QUIT YE LIKE MEN. BE STRONG

The first two soldiers killed on the Western Front died on 2 August 1914. A French corporal and a German lieutenant fought each other thirty hours before the war officially began. They met on the sun-baked dusty road to Faverois in the sleepy village of Joncherey, close to the French border with both Germany and Switzerland.

Caporal André Peugeot of the 44th Infantry Regiment and Leutnant Albert Mayer of the Jäger zu Pferd Regiment Nr 5 died a little after ten o'clock on that hot summer's day. Rich, yellow stooks of wheat dotted the fields. Spots of blue marked cornflowers basking in the warmth. A few lazy birds wheeled across a cloudless sky. Nothing much happened in Joncherey on a Sunday.

Peugeot and his four-man section passed an idle morning. The post orderly had just collected their letters home when a scream cut across the air. A village girl, crossing the road to fetch water, saw horsemen – in black helmets and dark-green uniforms.

'The Prussians are here!'

Peugeot advanced, rifle at the ready. The riders came closer.

'Halt! Halt!'

The riders charged. Mayer, in the lead, fired his revolver one, two, three times at the man in a dark-blue coat and red trousers who stood in his way. Peugeot managed a single shot before he crumpled. His men joined the sudden unexpected skirmish. French rifles cracked angrily. Mayer swayed in the saddle, galloped on for a few yards and then slid to the ground. His sweating horse, its saddle bloodstained, became the first booty of the war. The German patrol retreated.

A French corporal, 19 years of age. A 20-year-old German lieutenant. They were the initial dead, victims of two revolver shots fired far away in that obscure Balkan town of Sarajevo.

While Peugeot and Mayer bled in the hot sun, Britain enjoyed the start of the August Bank Holiday. At seaside resorts, excursionists relished the sunshine. Bands played, flags fluttered. Ice-cream sellers rejoiced. In the towns, the poorest sweltered in cramped rooms; children played in the street, the lucky ones splashing in park lakes. Newspapers mentioned that Russia had mobilised its army to protect her frontiers.

Germany mobilised in return, a move that prompted France to do the same. Enthusiastic hordes cheered Kaiser Wilhelm when, in full Guards uniform, he drove in an open carriage from Potsdam to Berlin. As German warriors strode through the streets to the waiting trains, excited onlookers threw roses. The troops tucked them into pockets, poked them down rifle muzzles.

France mobilised. Red-trousered soldiers marched to the railway stations. Loud cheers and spirited renderings of 'La Marseillaise' urged them on their way. It was all far away and little to do with Britain. The *Manchester Guardian* commented that 'we care as little for Belgrade as Belgrade does for Manchester'.

For the British public, for most of its politicians, the prospect of conflict in Europe concerned them as much as an uprising in Outer Mongolia. Secure behind the grey steel shield of the Royal Navy, confident that no nasty Continental obligations ensnared the Empire, happy crowds basked in summer sunshine.

Everything changed within days. The network of alliances under which Russia supported Serbia against Austro-Hungary, Germany upheld Austro-Hungary against Russia, while France backed Russia against Germany, unravelled. Rather than keep the peace, they led to war.

German plans insisted that the only way to beat Russia was to remove France from the board. The quickest route to Paris went through Belgium. On Bank Holiday Monday, 3 August 1914, news filtered through that Germany demanded permission for its soldiers to march through Belgium. The Belgians refused, and asked for diplomatic intervention by Britain. The British government sent a polite message to Berlin. They asked that Belgium be left alone. It arrived several hours after the first cavalry units trotted down the road from Aachen to enter their neutral neighbour.

By midnight, Britain was at war for one single purpose. To remove the Germans from Belgium. With France as an ally, it would not take long. Everybody knew that the war would finish within months.

Thanks to the practice mobilisation, the Royal Navy was ready. Churchill, indeed, jumped the starting blocks. As Army officers took their swords to the armourers to be sharpened, as reservists piled back to regimental barracks, as harassed quartermasters presided over rapidly dwindling stocks of boots, entrenching tools, jackets, puttees, trousers, caps, mess tins, ammunition pouches, both left and right, haversacks, belts, badges, braces, rifles and the myriad of other items a soldier needed, the Grand Fleet rode serenely and safely in its war harbour at Scapa Flow.

Not all of the Royal Navy watched the sea, the sky, the clouds, the rain and the three types of birds that sailors could identify – big jobs, little jobs and seagulls – that were the free amenities at Scapa Flow. At ports and harbours around Britain, the Royal Navy prepared for war.

The blind goddess of chance, be it the Greek Tyche, the Roman Fortuna, or any other from the pantheon of the world's deities, threw lives like dust into the air to watch them drift in the winds of war. Across the world, men and women left tiny villages or great towns to undergo mighty adventures. Men who had never ventured more than a dozen miles from home sailed across vast seas. They marched or rode through foreign lands to places they knew only from the Bible or wall maps in school. Jerusalem. Messines. Cairo. Bombay. Baghdad. Singapore. Riga. Caperneum. Salonika. Ypres. Villagers who had heard blackbirds sing from English trees listened to the sound of pi-dogs yapping in dusty streets. Men from the grimy slums of Hamburg saw spring flowers bloom in Anatolia. Chance chooses at random. Fame or ignominy. Life or death. Medals or maiming. Perhaps both.

At Devonport, Lieutenant Gordon Campbell, 28 years old, in command of the elderly Avon Class destroyer HMS *Bittern*, waited for orders. A Londoner by birth, the ninth son and thirteenth child of sixteen, Campbell grew up in genteel poverty. His father, Frederick, served in the New Zealand War of 1865 as a junior artillery officer. He left the Army soon after. He joined the Volunteers, eventually to become a lieutenant-colonel. The 14-year-old Campbell left Dulwich College to follow an elder brother into the Royal Navy. He entered HMS *Britannia* in September 1900 and passed out as a midshipman in January 1902.

His career followed the pattern of a hardly well-connected, middle-class Navy officer. He joined HMS *Prince George*, a seven-year-old Majestic Class battleship, in the Channel Fleet. By his own account, barely a week went by without his falling foul of authority. Most officers believed that midshipmen improved mightily if caned for misdemeanours. Campbell received twelve strokes at regular intervals.

After a short period with the Mediterranean Fleet, Campbell returned home. An old rugby injury suffered at Dartmouth came back to plague him. After a cartilage was removed, he eventually returned to duty after six months on the sick list.

Promoted, after examination, to sub-lieutenant, he served with HMS *Arun*. Once he became lieutenant, in October 1907, he went to HMS *King Alfred*, the flagship of the China Station.

Campbell came back to England in April 1910. After another short hospital stay, he ended up in Devonport, at HMS *Impregnable*. Not a dreadnought battleship, not even a cruiser, but almost a 'stone frigate'. The honoured name was the training ship for boy ratings.

Service appointments are roughly 'career-enhancing', 'marking time' or 'backwater'. All three are essential. Counting blankets in the Hebrides may not be the most glamorous job but it must be done. That such work does not thrust one under the benevolent gaze of an influential senior officer is simply another hardship of the service.

It helped not one iota that Campbell showed an independent spirit within weeks of his arrival. He decided to wed. His new commanding officer had other ideas. In the arcane world of the pre-1914 military, 25 was the minimum age at which an officer could marry without formal permission. Even then, matrimony was not a sensible career move for a junior officer.

Eight days after his 25th birthday, Campbell married. He believed that the Navy had no claim on his private life. As he did his duty efficiently, there could be no argument. His commander promptly asked for the removal of the rebellious new arrival. Only a time-honoured arrangement saved Campbell. The commandant of the boys' school, usually an inflexible officer on his last appointment, received promotion to flag rank on retirement. The admiral's flag arrived before officialdom acted.

After a little more than two years, Campbell took his first command, HMS *Ranger*. She formed part of the Devonport local defence flotilla. Its job was to patrol off the harbour and support local defences in the event of an enemy attack. The Royal Navy had three fleets. The First Fleet, which became the Grand Fleet in time of war, used the most modern ships, staffed with the officers deemed most likely to succeed. The Second Fleet's ships spent most of their time in harbour with maintenance crews. The Third Fleet, of which the local defence flotillas were part, employed the oldest warships still floating. And officers who were not expected to shine.

A leftover Victorian relic from 1895, the Opossum Class destroyer was at least a ship. Six months later, Campbell moved to HMS *Bittern*, also part of the Devonport fleet. Like *Ranger*, she was no longer young. Launched in February 1897, she was, nonetheless, a fighting craft; and there was a war to be fought. Young ship's captains have ambition; young ship's captains dream of glory.

The news of the German invasion reached Charles George Bonner, an officer on a Johnston Line steamer, at Antwerp. He was born in 1884 at Shuttington in Warwickshire. His family moved to Aldridge in Staffordshire soon after his birth.

Bonner left school in 1899 to join the merchant training ship *Conway*, moored off Rock Ferry Pier in the Mersey. The Board of Trade accepted the two-year training course as equivalent to four years at sea for aspiring Merchant Navy officers. Every cadet absorbed the ship's motto: 'Quit ye like men, be strong'.

Cadet Bonner left *Conway* in 1901. He served his apprenticeship under sail in *Invermark*, a steel barque of Colonel George Milne's Inver Line. Generally reputed to have the finest fleet of windjammers anywhere on the world's oceans, the Inver Line worked between Australia, New Zealand and Great Britain. Charles Bonner became a master mariner by his 21st birthday.

For Lieutenant Commander Godfrey Herbert, the war presented a golden opportunity. He was ginger-haired, a muscular 13st. Acquaintances described him, not always kindly, as 'the life and soul of the wardroom'. He enjoyed parties, told jokes well, encouraged confidences from others. He was brave. He was unconventional. He could be ruthless. He gambled with a cold eye for his chances. Some called him bombastic. Others thought him a poseur.

The son of a solicitor, Herbert entered the Royal Naval College in 1895. His first appointment was to the battleship HMS *Resolution*. Once promoted to sub-lieutenant, Herbert joined the cruiser HMS *Blenheim*. In a steady progression to smaller craft, he moved to the destroyer HMS *Fervent*.

Big ships, all spit and polish and fixed routine, bored Herbert. Smaller ships were better, although they lacked excitement. When the chance came, in 1905, to volunteer for the new submarine branch, Herbert grabbed it.

His first commission was as first lieutenant on *A4*, under the command of 22-year-old Lieutenant Martin Nasmith. He very soon showed his personal coolness under pressure. In October 1905, *A4* took part in signalling trials. An anchored dinghy with an underwater bell bobbed at a distance. The *A4* signalled if the sound of the bell reached them. To do this, a ventilator shaft remained open. A sailor pushed a flag, attached to a boathook, up to the surface each time he heard the bell.

On 15 October, in the open sea, the experiments went well. The next day, rougher weather kept *A4* inside the breakwater. Nasmith used his previous trim settings. The water inside the breakwater had less salt in it. The more salt, the more buoyant the water, as the Dead Sea proves. The submarine sank. The sea poured through the open ventilator shaft to swamp the unfortunate *A4*.

She grounded 90ft down, a mere 10ft less than her designed safe limit. In darkness as black as Irish stout, with water flooding into the hull and chlorine gas seeping through the boat, Herbert stayed ice-calm. He groped his way to the blowing controls. Between them, Nasmith and Herbert restored power. They took the boat to the surface after four long, frightening minutes.

The inevitable court martial found Nasmith guilty of default. It acquitted him of negligence. Both officers received plaudits for their bravery and coolness. Herbert looked set for a promising career as a submariner. Some months later, he took command of *A4* himself.

When he finished his tour, Herbert went to the China Station, to the battleship HMS *Monmouth*. To relieve the tedium, he spent happy hours designing a one-man midget submarine-cum-torpedo. Its crewman steered the projectile close enough to the target to ensure a hit before he went over the side.

Herbert named the project 'Devastator'. He offered it to the Admiralty who rejected it on the interesting grounds that when other navies learned the details, they would simply copy the idea. The device thus nullified the advantages of a big fleet. As a sop to humanity, they also felt that it would be 'too dangerous to the operator'.

The spurned inventor approached the Japanese navy. A swift, sharp rebuke thundered down from Whitehall. Herbert learned, with no room for doubt, that the Admiralty's refusal was not an invitation to hawk the idea to a foreign power.

During the Second World War, Herbert's former commanding officer, Martin Nasmith, wearing admiral's rings and a Victoria Cross, revived the idea. Midget submarines finally appeared on the Navy's inventory.

Herbert returned to Britain in 1911. He took command of the 300-ton, 140ft-long *C36*. Designed as a 'coastal defence' submarine, Herbert's boat, in company with *C37* and *C38*, stunned doubters by sailing 10,000 miles from Portsmouth to Hong Kong. It took eighty-three days, albeit with stops along the way.

A further clash with authority occurred. Herbert devised a 'Messiah on the Water' practical joke. Clad in a white sheet, he lashed himself to the top 6ft of the boat's periscope. Entering Kowloon Harbour, *C36* would submerge gently to leave Herbert apparently walking on the surface. Superstitious onlookers believed they witnessed the Second Coming, especially as some alleged that *C36*'s captain proclaimed the fact in his stentorian voice. The admiral failed to see the joke.

When war began, Herbert commanded the submarine *D5*. Diesel-powered, with a crew of twenty-five men, armed with six torpedoes, she had three torpedo tubes from which to fire them. One was at the stern; her bow held the other two. She reached her war station at Harwich and waited. Like every other man in the Royal Navy, Herbert hoped that glory was in store.

For New Zealander William Sanders, first mate on the barque *Joseph Craig* in August 1914, the war was far away. Three days after the news reached him, his ship was wrecked inside the Hokianga Bar, 140 miles north of Auckland. Sanders grabbed a boat and steered alone through a dangerous sea to summon help.

Sanders, generally known as Willie, was born in Auckland on 7 February 1883 to Edward Charles Herman Sanders, a bootmaker, and his wife Emma. Edward had arrived in New Zealand at the age of 9 with his parents. Emma, another immigrant, was the daughter of Captain William Wilson, a master mariner. He was part of the family that founded the Wilson Line, the largest privately owned shipping fleet in the world.

Genes and a sense of adventure led Willie to a sailor's life. He left school in 1897 for an office job. All of his spare time, including his midday break, was spent at Auckland Harbour. He made friends with many of the ships' crews. In February 1899, when he had just reached his 16th birthday, his chance arrived.

An officer of the Coastal Shipping Company offered Willie the job of cabin boy on the *Kapanui*, a pygmy steamer of about 80 tons. Willie went to sea on the ship that served the river harbours of the North Auckland area. He stayed with *Kapanui* until he was 20 years old.

He then transferred to the SS *Aparama*, the training vessel of Union Steamships.

By 1906, Willie was on a New Zealand government ship, the SS *Hinemoa*. He joined as an ordinary seaman, grasping every chance to gain experience as he studied for his master's certificate. The *Hinemoa* delivered provisions to government lighthouses and maintained, built and supplied castaway depots in the southern islands.

In 1908, Sanders moved on. He joined the J.J. Craig Company, whose sailing barques roamed the southern waters. He went to the *Marjorie Craig* and followed it up with the *Louisa Craig*, before finishing with the *Joseph Craig*. The shipwreck became an omen. The Great European War needed him. He volunteered for the Navy.

Thomas Crisp was at sea when war came. Skipper of a company fishing smack, the 61-ton wooden ketch *George Borrow*, he worked out of Lowestoft. At 38 years of age, Crisp was well respected, with an intimate knowledge of the waters he worked. He needed it. Skippers who did not find fish soon found themselves on the beach.

Crisp was not a wealthy man. Fishermen, even skippers, who worked for wages rarely were. Scarcity commands high prices. Fish were no rarity in East Anglian seas. Four days on the water, one at home, month in, month out, year in, year out, produced a modest wage to sustain an equally modest life.

Tom Crisp never wished to be anything other than a seaman. Born on 28 April 1876, he had four brothers and two sisters. As with many children brought up in seaports, the quayside proved a magnet. Tom skipped lessons to roam the waterfront, a practice that led to his summary transfer to a school that was a decent distance from the bustle of the dock.

As soon as he left school, Tom Crisp went to sea. He began on a drifter that fished the Irish Sea. After a few years hauling in mackerel and herring, he took a job as third hand on a Lowestoft sailing smack.

Wider horizons beckoned. Tom Crisp became a blue-water man. He sailed the Atlantic run between London and New York for two years before marriage called. On shore leave, he met Harriet Elizabeth Alp, a fisherman's daughter from Aldeby, a small village on the Norfolk Broads. In 1895, they married and settled at Burgh St Peter, 6 miles across the marshes from Lowestoft. Tom returned to the sandbanks and their tricky currents. He became a mate, then gained his skipper's certificate. Every trip, he trudged 6 miles to work. At its end, he plodded 6 miles home for a single day off.

In 1902, he joined the Chambers company as skipper of their newest boat, *George Borrow*. In 1907, the Crisp family moved to Lowestoft, moving every couple of years as their fortunes slowly improved. By 1914, the family lived unpretentiously with the help of a small extra wage. Crisp's eldest son, also Tom, served as a 15-year-old apprentice alongside his father on *George Borrow*.

Harold Auten of the Royal Naval Reserve was gazetted as sub-lieutenant a mere two months before the German armies crunched into Belgium, Luxembourg and France. He was born on 22 August 1891 in Leatherhead, Surrey. After formal education at the much-respected Wilson's Grammar School in Camberwell, the 17-year-old joined the Peninsular and Oriental Line as a cadet in 1908.

The 'Exiles' Line', as Rudyard Kipling called it, monopolised the lucrative trade to India. They had the government contract for first- and second-class passages. No third-class or steerage traffic sullied P&O cabins. They carried suave diplomats, anxious missionaries, bland civil servants, nervous subalterns, choleric majors, ascetic bankers, wide-eyed world travellers, the occasional maharaja and, at regular intervals, unmarried ladies. The last, collectively known as 'the fishing fleet', went to hook a husband in the bachelor wilds of the Raj. If they failed to catch one, they were less affectionately called 'returned empties' on the homeward leg.

Like other major British shipping lines, P&O modelled its uniforms on those of the Royal Navy. Merchant officers and seamen could, at a quick glance, be mistaken for their regular equivalents. The companies encouraged their officers to join the Reserve. Membership added a decent social cachet, always welcome on expensive liners. P&O, in particular, considered itself a most superior line. Its captains were generally reckoned to be responsible only to God and the company directors, although not necessarily in that order.

Auten became a midshipman in the RNR in 1910, the year in which he graduated from his cadetship with P&O. By 1914, he was a deck officer. Then came the war.

William Williams was an Anglesey man. He was born on 5 October 1890, at Amlwch Port, his father a dock worker and fisherman. Neither job paid well. William grew up in a family where money was always short. Educated at the local school, he escaped as soon as he could to go to sea.

Williams served on two three-masted schooners, the *Camborne* and *Meyric*. Neither was large. *Camborne*, built at Amlwch, displaced a mere 108 tons. Williams sailed in her under the command of Captain Thomas

Morgan. *Meyric* was the bigger ship, coming in at 253 tons. With her, Williams went to Rio Grande in Brazil. Confusingly, but not surprisingly on an Anglesey vessel largely crewed by local men, the captain was also a William Williams.

Williams, 6ft tall, strong, a hard worker, earned his rating as a thoroughly reliable and totally satisfactory seaman. He was at sea when the war started. He knew where duty led him. He went to the Royal Naval Reserve as a seaman.

Shore facilities at Scapa Flow hardly existed. The shore canteen, popular rumour claimed, owned one trestle table, ten wooden chairs and three barrels of beer. For men and officers, life on board or ashore proved monotonous. Petty Officer Ernest Herbert Pitcher, serving in the dreadnought battleship HMS *King George V*, part of the Grand Fleet, considered life should offer more to a career sailor.

Pitcher was born on the very last day of the year in 1888 in Cornwall. His father, George, served in the coastguard. Ernest was still an infant when George and his wife Sarah moved to the coastguard station at Swanage in Dorset.

After the usual round of lessons at the local board school, Ernest satisfied the examiners that he could read, write and calculate simple sums to the required standard. Armed with his school-leaving certificate, he joined the Royal Navy as a boy on 22 July 1903 to become a gunner. When *King George V* cleared for action against the High Seas Fleet, Ernest Pitcher would be an integral part of her fire-power. In the meanwhile, he watched the gulls and hoped for battle.

Ronald Neil Stuart was a deck officer with the Montreal Ocean Steamship Company, generally known as the Allan Line, in 1914. Born on 26 August 1866, he was the only son of Neil Stuart, a master mariner, and his wife, Mary, herself the daughter of a master mariner. He had five sisters. As the only boy in the family, he was fussed over at every opportunity.

His father had sailed the Australia route from England. The first child was born in Quebec and, after a series of occupations, the family returned to Britain, where they settled in Toxteth, Liverpool. Neil Stuart set up as a grocer with a line of 'prize teas'. Mariners and shop counters are rarely a successful amalgam. Neil decided to return to sea but died in an accident before he took up his appointment.

The family suffered in genteel poverty. Ronald left school for a hated office job with dismal wages. He loathed both his job and Liverpool.

Salvation came from an aunt who helped him gain a maritime apprentice-ship. In 1902, Ronald Stuart, son and grandson of master mariners, went to earn his living on great waters.

He joined Steel & Company's barque *Kirkhill*. The seas introduced themselves forcibly in 1905 when *Kirkhill* argued with a rock off the Falkland Islands. The barque went down and Stuart lost every possession he had. Not long afterwards, he endured another shipwreck, in which his vessel capsized in fearsomely bad weather near Florida. Seafaring is not for the timid.

His apprenticeship served, Ronald changed employers. He went to the Allan Line, a Scottish-Canadian company with a thriving immigrant trade between Scotland and the Dominions. With them, Ronald Stuart sailed the world. In August 1914, he decided that he must join the Royal Navy.

The Royal Navy had plenty to do. Although the Grand Fleet, snug in its northern fastness, manoeuvred, exercised, and prayed for the High Seas Fleet to offer battle, the remainder of the service had its hands full as Britain went to war.

On 12 August 1914 the British Expeditionary Force began its move. For eight days ships ferried troops, guns, horses, wagons, lorries, fodder and rations to France. The Royal Navy guarded the Channel Approaches against German destroyers, German battleships, German cruisers and German U-boats as the British Expeditionary Force went to France. It was a job they would have for four long years.

The new concept of distant blockade allowed the Royal Navy to claim one particular distinction. An unknown gunlayer on HMS *Lance*, a spanking new destroyer that entered service in February 1914, fired the first shot in anger from the British side.

The war, for the British, officially began at 2300hr on 4 August 1914. Even before the Whitehall ultimatum expired, *Königin Luise*, a German auxiliary minelayer, left Emden under the command of Korvettenkapitän Karl Biermann for the mouth of the Thames. She had clear orders. 'Make for sea in Thames direction at top speed. Lay mines near as possible English coasts, not near neutral coasts, and not further north than Latitude 53°.'

A former excursion steamer on the Hamburg to Heligoland run, *Königin Luise* received a hasty conversion for her wartime role. Time ran out before her main armament was in place. Similarly, her promenade deck still boasted huge glass windows through which happy holidaymakers had gazed at rolling waves. Two raked masts, two raked funnels gave the steamer a look very similar to a Great Eastern Railway ferry on the Harwich to Hook of Holland route. Hastily applied good German paint, black on the hull, buff on the upper works and yellow topped off with black on the funnels, matched the standard GER scheme.

The first morning of the war, misty, damp, cold, saw a swarm of Royal Navy destroyers sweep north from Harwich. Their task was to harry any German shipping they might find. HMS *Amphion*, an Active Class light cruiser, led the flotilla from Harwich towards Heligoland.

A British fishing boat alerted a destroyer to some strange behaviour. An anonymous steamer was 'throwing things overboard' about 20 miles north-east of the Outer Gabbard, a position conveniently close to the Harwich to Hook of Holland route.

At 1025, *Amphion* sighted the unknown through dull rain. She sent the two Laforey Class destroyers HMS *Lance* and HMS *Landrail* to investigate. The *Königin Luise* made off at a handsome 20 knots, disappearing briefly with the help of a sudden rain squall. At 1030, *Lance* opened fire. Minutes later, *Amphion* joined the fight.

Biermann had no reply worth considering. A solitary pair of 3.7cm pom-poms failed to deter two hungry destroyers and an eager cruiser. The Germans fired helpless rounds from revolvers and rifles to no avail. His ship hit time and time again, Biermann decided to scuttle rather than surrender. At 1222, *Königin Luise*, on fire, damaged, rolled over to port and went down, the first casualty of the war. Some 46 of the 100 crew on board survived.

Amphion and her followers continued their hunt. They soon sighted another steamer, almost identical in appearance to their first victim. The destroyers wanted more flesh, a desire much increased when they saw an enormous German flag fluttering from the new target.

Fortunately for the German Ambassador, Prince Karl Max Lichnowsky and his entourage, Captain Cecil Fox of the *Amphion* recognised the vessel. She was the *St Petersburg*, a GER steamer, taking the diplomats back to their homeland.

Fox called off the destroyers that had already opened fire. Their blood was up. They ignored the signals from their leader. Fox hastily put *Amphion* between them and *St Petersburg*. Even the most ardent destroyer captain took heed of that manoeuvre.

At 2100, *Amphion* and her flotilla turned for home. At 0645, the cruiser hit one of the mines laid by *Königin Luise*. The explosion broke the ship's back. The mine almost completely destroyed the bridge, and devastated the forecastle and messdecks. Men died at breakfast, including most of the twenty-one prisoners the *Amphion* had taken on board.

Fox stopped engines. Fighting the raging fires that raced through the forward part of the ship proved a hopeless task. Down by the bows, the *Amphion* was a dead vessel. Cecil Fox ordered his men to abandon ship. The destroyers hurried to collect the boatloads of survivors. Although Fox had stopped engines, ships have no brakes. *Amphion* continued to move in a circle, striking another mine as the last sailors scrambled clear. Her magazine went up in an expanse of yellow flame. The remains of HMS *Amphion* slid under the water at 0705. Her sinking claimed the lives of 151 men.

Staff Paymaster – the equivalent of a lieutenant commander – Joseph Theodore Gedge attracted the sombre credit of being the first British officer to die in the war. Over the next days, telegrams expressing the Admiralty's deep regret went to Mabel Tolcher in Plymouth, now the widow of her leading seaman husband; to the parents of 17-year-old Private Jerome Cann, a Marine, who joined from the tiny village of Trevena, in Cornwall. Boys on Post Office bicycles delivered telegrams to Newton Abbot, to Argyll, to Ballymena, to Birmingham. War's sacrifices came early to some.

No German vessels attempted to interrupt the flow of men and supplies during the heady days of August when the British Expeditionary Force crossed the seas to France. Nobody believed that the Germans would attack unarmed transports. That was the mark of the barbarian. Henry V may have slaughtered unarmed prisoners at Agincourt but that was after the French had attacked the old men, women and boys who worked the baggage train. Oliver Cromwell, it was true, had slit tongues, hacked off ears and noses of similarly unfortunate wagon drivers and wives. But that was all a long time ago. Civilisation had advanced since those days of barbarity. A few more imaginative souls did see periscopes behind every wave top, but the U-boats were not there. The speed of the British deployment had caught Berlin by surprise. It also caught out the German field commanders. They believed that the BEF was still assembling on the very day that the first field-grey patrols met men in khaki.

Like the Grand Fleet, the High Seas Fleet moved to its war deployment before hostilities began. The Germans had the advantage of foreknowledge. On 30 July 1914, the Erste Unterseebootflottille followed the giant battleships through the Kiel Canal. The nine boats of the First Flotilla sailed directly to Heligoland. On 31 July, *U 5*, *U 7* to *U 10*, *U 15* to *U 18* began to patrol. They did not go far. In the daylight hours, they anchored among the sandbanks to the east of the island. Each evening, they returned home. Their sole duty was to give warning of the anticipated mass onslaught by the Grand Fleet.

For the German navy, the recently adopted British scheme of distant blockade came as a surprise. When no grey silhouettes appeared on the horizon, thoughts turned to the U-boats. They could make a reconnaissance with every chance of evading detection.

On 6 August 1914, ten U-boats set out to find the Grand Fleet. They left Heligoland at 0430 Berlin time, twenty-six hours after British submarines left Harwich to probe the defences of the High Seas Fleet.

The German boats, under the command of Kapitänleutnant Helmuth Mühlau, were the most aged in the U-boat fleet. *U 5*, *U 7*, *U 8*, *U 9*, *U 13*, *U 14*, *U 15*, *U 16*, *U 17* and *U 18* were the pioneers. Shepherded by the light cruisers SMS *Hamburg* and SMS *Stettin* and two destroyers, *S 99* and *S 135*, which acted as wireless relay centres, the ten boats travelled 80 miles into the wastes of the North Sea before their escorts bade them 'Gute Reise und viel Glück!' The escorts turned for home. The boats went on.

Simplicity dominated the plan although it was divorced from reality. As with the German air service, the U-boat planning came from staff officers who had yet to understand the limitations of the men and machines of the new technology. The boats were to go north, line abreast, 7 miles between each boat, as far as a line drawn on the chart between Scapa Flow and Hardanger Fjord in Norway.

What is perfectly feasible on the unruffled surface of a maritime chart is less so in wind, rain, darkness and enveloping cloud. Navigators on U-boats had little experience in the use of chronometers for celestial position-finding. Bad weather toppled gyrocompasses. Needles swung wildly on magnetic compasses. Maintaining a predetermined course and speed became impossible.

After two days, Kapitänleutnant Otto Weddigen in *U 9* turned back with a faulty clutch on one engine. A defective compass caused some excitement when *U 9* found herself 220 miles adrift of track off the Jutland peninsula instead of at Heligoland.

Kapitänleutnant Johannes Lemmer of *U 5* hobbled home, his mission unaccomplished. With one engine out of action, he retired to Heligoland at low speed.

Kapitänleutnant Richard Pohle found himself, after two days at sea, off Fair Isle. His boat, *U 15*, was over 100 miles west of the planned position. Three British battleships, the dreadnought HMS *Ajax* and two super-dreadnoughts, HMS *Monarch* and HMS *Orion*, engaged in gunnery practice, were within range. Pohle dived, stalked *Monarch* and fired a torpedo. It disappeared into the white caps of the ocean but the lookouts saw it. The three massive ships, each costing a fraction under £2 million to build, left hurriedly. Pohle, back on the surface, presumably checked his position, for he was well to the east the next morning.

Mist lay across a gently swelling sea when HMS *Birmingham* saw a U-boat on the surface at 0340hr. *U 15*. Hammering sounds drifted across the water as mechanics tried to right a fault. Pohle was helpless as *Birmingham* first opened fire with every gun she could bear and then turned, her funnels belching, as she went to maximum speed. She caught Pohle's boat squarely in the middle to slice her soul in two. Eight weeks earlier, the 5,440-ton *Birmingham* was a welcome guest at the Kiel Regatta. *U 15*, a mere 512 tons, died. Pohle and all hands perished. Friends in peace, friends for ever.

The remaining boats, having seen nothing of the Grand Fleet, eventually turned for home. One vanished. The unfortunately numbered *U 13*. Kapitänleutnant Hans Artur, Graf von Schweinitz and his men never returned. *U 13*, sister boat to *U 15*, came from the same Danzig yard. The dead from the 2 boats were the first of 4,716 men to die in the Kaiserliche Marine's underwater arm.

A loss rate of 20 per cent is hardly good news, but they were old boats, powered by the less-than-perfect Körting engines. When four MAN-diesel boats went out on 8 August to seek a mythical collection of British capital ships covering an even more mythical landing of the BEF at Calais, Dunkirk, Ostend and Zeebrugge, each one returned home safely.

The mere appearance of U-boats caused consternation at Scapa Flow. The 'War Harbour' had no defences against underwater attack. Jellicoe fretted about the chance of a U-boat sneaking into Scapa to play havoc with his dreadnoughts. Driftwood, floating bottles, a thoughtless seabird, all set alarms ringing. U-boat warnings became a regular feature in the northern waters. On one occasion, Jellicoe moved the whole fleet to Loch Ewe on the north coast of Scotland. It returned almost at once because of another false alarm, this time that the Germans were about to invade Britain.

By the end of August 1914, the Royal Navy had every reason to feel smug. A venture into the Heligoland Bight was a triumph. Harwich destroyers under Roger Keyes joined Vice-Admiral Sir David Beatty's battlecruisers from Rosyth to hunt the enemy. Three German light cruisers, *Mainz*, *Ariadne* and *Köln*, were sunk. Poor communications, the curse of the Royal Navy, nearly caused disaster, but the propaganda value of a victory in the enemy's back yard convinced the public that the Navy had the measure of the Germans.

Whitehall unilaterally made alterations to the Declaration of London. On 20 August 1914, an Order in Council flatly abolished the different categories of contraband. The same order introduced the concept of 'continuous voyage'. All prohibited goods destined for enemy countries, in neutral ships bound for neutral ports, became contraband. Seizure became the order of the day. Germany promptly replied that she would abide by the Declaration of London. As a countermove, she laid mines along the shipping routes to Britain's east-coast ports.

The Royal Navy's distant blockade enjoyed immediate success. The High Seas Fleet skulked behind its defences. The war was as good as won. Churchill, in typical fashion, wrote that 'the German Navy was indeed muzzled. Except for furtive movements by individual submarines and minelayers, not a dog stirred from August until November.'

The German Naval Staff was also reasonably pleased. The High Seas Fleet remained in being. German armies were within days of Paris. Once that city fell, the generals would deal with Russia. Not that they need hurry: the German Eighth Army had annihilated the Russian Second Army and thrashed their First and Tenth Armies in the forests and lakes of East Prussia. The war was as good as won.

Although the U-boats failed to find any sign of the Grand Fleet on missions into deep water throughout August, prudence dictated more mines in the Heligoland Bight to deter any further British raids. The Staff concluded that no worthwhile targets were in range of the U-boats. As a result, U-boat activity could cease until the Royal Navy came closer to German waters.

The heady days of August 1914 ended in a haze of golden sunshine. Soon, the leaves would turn from green to yellow, brown or red. By then, the war would be over. Everything would be back to normal by Christmas.

FOUR

A WEAPON TO TURN THE TIDE

The steady tramp through France of advancing German army boots came to an unscheduled halt in September 1914. In a welter of confusion, rumours spread throughout the German army's High Command. On 5 September, Oberstleutnant Richard Hentsch on the staff of the Oberste Heeresleitung, or Supreme Command, delivered an ominous, albeit inaccurate, assessment to Generaloberst Alexander von Kluck, commanding the First Army: 'The news is bad. The Seventh and Sixth Armies are blocked. The Fourth and Fifth are meeting with strong resistance. The English are embarking fresh troops continuously on the Belgian coast. There are reports of a Russian expeditionary force in the same parts. A withdrawal is becoming inevitable.'

Von Kluck, on the right flank of the advance, had seriously over-extended his army. They had marched the furthest and the fastest in response to the Generaloberst's fierce desire to seize the glittering prize of Paris. Orders to von Kluck to close the gap between himself and the Second Army had exposed its flank to the enemy. Even as Hentsch delivered his dispiriting words, the French Sixth Army was moving to attack.

The Battle of the Marne exposed a collective loss of nerve that gripped OHL ever more firmly as the days passed. The Germans retreated to the line of the River Aisne. The Schlieffen Plan, designed to conquer France within forty days, had failed. The war, it seemed, would not be over as quickly as promised by the Army. Hopes of a fast, decisive victory in the west died.

On 5 September, the same day that OHL's messenger spoke to von Kluck, Kapitänleutnant Otto Hersing of *U 21* put a torpedo into the 2,940-ton HMS *Pathfinder*, a light cruiser. She sank inside four minutes. Of the 268 officers and men on board, only 12 survived. In the Admiralty, the loss of *Pathfinder* created alarm. The cruiser was hit in home waters, at the very entrance to the Firth of Forth.

Two weeks later, on 22 September, Kapitänleutnant Otto Weddigen nailed home the lesson that U-boats were a serious weapon.

Weddigen's *U 9* left Heligoland on 20 September on war patrol. He had orders to attack British transports approaching the Belgian coast. The strict morality of not hitting unarmed ships had already slipped. Two days later, *U 9* ambled serenely on the surface to the west of the Hook of Holland. She was 50 miles out of position, thanks to a faulty gyrocompass. Oberleutnant zur See Johannes Spiess, the first officer, or 'Heinrich', had the watch. 'Heinrich' was a pleasantry in the Imperial U-boat arm, used by the captain to his second in command. It came from a quotation wearily familiar to every German schoolchild, from Goethe's *Faust*: 'Heinrich, mir graut's vor dir', which loosely translates as 'Henry, I have a horror of you'.

Weddigen and his chief engineer strolled casually on the narrow deck, enjoying the fresh air after a night on the seabed. The Körting engines pushed a plume of telltale white smoke skywards as *U 9* recharged her batteries.

Spiess, mildly distracted by the white smoke, stiffened when a shape jumped into the view of his Zeiss binoculars. A mast. Dark smoke. A patrolling British warship. Weddigen submerged. The batteries were not fully charged but that could wait.

The mast became upperworks. Not one ship but three, all with four funnels. Four funnels. Weddigen knew they were a feature of the Birmingham Class, so he identified them to the attentive Spiess. Weddigen watched the shapes grow in the attack periscope. With luck, sweet revenge for *U 15* hovered.

Four funnels were not unique. Cressy Class cruisers, built at the turn of the century, also had them. In Weddigen's sights were HMS *Aboukir*, HMS *Hogue* and the class name-ship, HMS *Cressy* of the 7th Cruiser Squadron. They came on, steaming at a steady 9 knots, in line abreast, 2 miles apart. The three 12,000-ton ships should not have been sandwiched in the waters between the Dutch coast and a German minefield. With no escorts, steaming at a dangerously low speed, the pre-dreadnoughts were hideously vulnerable. The 7th Cruiser Squadron enjoyed the nickname of the 'live-bait squadron', a phrase that came to Churchill's ears. He had ordered them out of the narrow seas but events conspired against him.

Weddigen waited. His boat was not the most modern in the Kaiserliche Marine, but he compensated for its deficiencies by remarkable skill and determination. In prewar manoeuvres, Weddigen had regularly 'sunk' his targets. Now it was for real.

At 0620 British time, *Aboukir* was 500m from *U 9*. A single bow torpedo bubbled towards her. Weddigen immediately dived, down to 15m. Porpoising was a fault of early U-boats. When the torpedo launched, the boat's bow broke the surface. The crew acted as mobile ballast. They pelted forward to keep the trim even. As seawater gurgled in to compensate for the loss of weight, they scampered aft.

Weddigen brought *U 9* to periscope depth. He stared through the sight, waiting, counting the seconds. After half a minute, the torpedo struck. A fountain of water, smoke, a flash, followed by a dull thud, a crack of sound. *U 9* shuddered as the blast pushed through the water. *Aboukir* settled wearily, stern first.

Aboukir's commander, Captain John Drummond, decided that his ship had struck a mine and called for help. *Hogue* and *Cressy* rushed to aid their sinking sister. At 0640, *Aboukir* turned turtle and went to the bottom.

Fifteen minutes later, *U 9* fired two bow torpedoes, ten seconds apart, at *Hogue*, stationary in the water as she picked up survivors. Both torpedoes struck. The *U 9*'s crew galloped aft and back. Weddigen ordered one motor full astern as *U 9* nosed towards her huge target, close to collision with the steel monster.

When the second torpedo struck home, *Hogue* started to heel over. One of her officers recalled:

Within three minutes of the first torpedo hitting, the list had increased to about 40 degrees, and realising that her end was very near all hands began to tear off their clothes and crawl down the high side or jump overboard to leeward. To add to the general confusion the stokehold crowd suddenly poured up on deck, their blackened faces dripping sweat and tense with apprehension. It was now a case of every man for himself, and tearing off my boots and clothing and then fastening to my wrist by its chain, my gold watch, which I greatly prized, I walked down the sloping deck into the water and struck out for dear life.

As British sailors struggled to survive, Weddigen moved into position for a third attack. The chief quartermaster on the diving planes was grey with exhaustion. Weddigen nodded encouragement for him to carry on. The chief engineer, as engineers are wont, winced at the captain's abuse of much-loved machinery. The batteries, he believed, were exhausted. 'How much longer', he demanded, exasperated, 'are we doing this?' He received a curt reply: 'We are going to attack.'

At 0717, two torpedoes from U 9's stern tubes sped towards *Cressy*, 1,000m away. A lookout caught a glimpse of U 9's periscope as she fired. Captain Robert Johnson called for full speed. The engines worked up. Seconds ticked by. It was too late. One torpedo caught her. Weddigen finished her off with a bow shot. All torpedoes were gone. So had the Royal Navy's belief in its invincibility. In less than an hour, one obsolescent U-boat sank three admittedly aged cruisers. Technology that started before Nelson's victories had reached fruition. A vessel, inferior in size and armament, destroyed an infinitely more powerful opponent before vanishing beneath the waves.

Some 63 officers and 1,397 ratings of the Royal Navy died. More telegrams. Of the survivors, one midshipman, Kit Wykeham Musgrave, achieved a remarkable treble. When *Aboukir* sank beneath him, he swam towards *Hogue*. Pulled on board, he soon found himself back in the water. He swam to *Cressy*. After she sank, he hardly believed it when he was pulled aboard a ship whose crew spoke a guttural language. Resigned to becoming a prisoner, he then discovered his rescuer was the Koninklijke Nederlandsche Stoomboot Maatschappij ship *Titan*.

Outrage. Disbelief. Anger. The British public felt all three. Rumours abounded. Many believed that such desperate damage could be done only by a whole fleet of submarines. The realisation that it was the work of a single U-boat was hard to bear. Although the loss of three veteran ships had not destroyed Britain's overall naval supremacy, this did not appease press and public.

Commodore Roger Keyes chose to ignore Weddigen's undoubted skill when he later wrote that the exploit 'in the early days of the war . . . was about as simple an operation for a submarine captain as the stalking of tame elephants, chained to trees, would be to an experienced big-game hunter, who wished to kill them unseen and unsuspected'. Keyes did not apply his strictures to his own commanders. Max Horton received generous approval when he despatched the antiquated 2,000-ton armoured cruiser *Hela*, whose main claim to fame was that she was often the escort to Wilhelm's yacht.

The Kaiserliche Marine considered options. Clearly, the Army had failed to deliver a knockout blow. The war would probably drag on, even into 1915. Hersing and Weddigen had laid bare the weakness of British naval power. Formidable on the surface, vulnerable beneath it. The U-boats had a task to perform. Admiral Reinhard von Scheer commented in 1920: 'Weddigen's name was on every lip, and for the Navy in particular, his exploit meant a release from the onerous feeling of having done so little in this war in comparison with the heroic deeds of the army. But no such victory was necessary to totally reveal the value of the U-boat for offensive operations, especially after it had given such unanticipated and convincing proof of its ability to remain at sea.'

In Britain, the Admiralty wondered how to counter the threat. The committee that studied anti-submarine warfare was disbanded when the war began, a decision that is hard to grasp. The Navy itself was totally unprepared. No depth charges to destroy an underwater enemy, no hydrophones to hear submerged U-boats were in service. Anti-submarine detection simply did not exist.

Fantastic proposals flowed into the Admiralty throughout the war. One suggested that seagulls could be trained to hunt U-boats. All this required was a British submarine to cruise back and forth with its periscope smeared with fish oil. At regular intervals, the crew would release titbits. The gulls would quickly associate periscopes with food. When a U-boat appeared, the birds would congregate around it. The Navy could do the rest.

A similar plan suggested using seals and sea lions. This scheme's proposer felt that they could be trained to bark when the sound of U-boat diesels reached them. Admiralty desperation accordingly led to the expensive hire of several sea lions from an astute trainer. Like their feathered comrades, they failed to understand the problem. The U-boats remained safe from detection by British fauna.

Jellicoe recorded that he received a letter that earnestly suggested that the Royal Navy fill the North Sea with effervescent salts. The resulting bubbles would lift lurking U-boats to the surface, where they could be picked off at leisure.

The Navy pinned its hopes on its anti-submarine picket boats, a motley collection of yachts, trawlers and motor launches that patrolled the coastal waters. Their equipment to fight U-boats consisted of a canvas bag and a heavy hammer. When a periscope appeared, the intrepid crew would slip the bag over it, then smash the glass with the heavy hammer.

Hardly more effective was the other method of attacking Weddigen and his comrades. In an adaptation from an equally optimistic method of minesweeping, two ships, well apart, towed an explosive charge between them at slow speed. If a U-boat got in the way, it would detonate the explosive. To be really effective, this method required the cooperation of the U-boat. It either had to poke up its periscope or fire a torpedo. After a year, this cumbersome procedure gave way to the high-speed sweep of the paravane with an explosive charge of 400lb. This, too, failed to yield the results for which its users hoped.

The British blockade of Germany caused great resentment in Berlin. The Royal Navy's command of the sea automatically cut off Germany from most of the world when war began. German access to the oceans was from her North Sea ports. Ships could then go south, through the Channel, or between the Shetland Islands and Norway to reach the Atlantic.

It was easy to police the Straits of Dover. They were no more than 21 miles wide, and passage was restricted even more by a minefield. All surface vessels were forced into a narrow seaway between the Kent coast and the Goodwin Sands. To evade the ships and vessels of the Dover Patrol was a virtual impossibility.

The northern route was a different proposition. At 150 miles, it was substantially wider. Moreover, the long, neutral Norwegian coast offered sanctuary to ships avoiding interception. As an additional drawback for the British, lengthy northern winters made the waters some of the stormiest in the world. Long nights, appalling weather, seemingly incessant gales and driving snow when the rain stopped made the Northern Patrol a grim test of endurance for the blockaders.

One sea alone was outside British control. The Baltic. Danish minefields effectively blocked its entrance. The ramshackle Tsarist navy had little success in imposing a blockade. As a result, Germany enjoyed easy access to Swedish iron ore and other goods. Only the arrival of British submarines countered German trade.

For Germany, the only way she could continue to trade was to sink the Grand Fleet or, at the very least, confine it to port. As long as the Royal Navy controlled the North Sea, the Dover Patrol and the Northern Patrol could do what they wished, confident in the protection of Jellicoe's dreadnoughts.

German inability to deny that protection justified every last penny spent on the Grand Fleet. For Berlin, angry at the almost total effectiveness of the Royal Navy's blockade and an almost equal inability to harm the Grand Fleet, something else was needed. A weapon to turn the tide. In short, das Unterseeboot.

Otto Weddigen and U 9 continued their winning ways on 15 October 1914. HMS *Hawke*, an Edgar Class cruiser of 7,735 tons, went down in eight minutes with the loss of 524 men. Reservists and young trainees made up much of the crew. The popular press questioned whether they should have even been at sea. The agitation grew. *Amphion, Aboukir, Cressy, Hogue, Hawke*. Someone was responsible, had to be responsible, for these disasters.

That someone was the First Sea Lord. Prince Louis of Battenberg. Born in Austria, Ludwig Alexander von Hesse was the eldest son of Prince Alexander of Hesse and Countess Julia Theresa von Haucke. His mother was a firm friend of Princess Alice, one of Queen Victoria's daughters, who had married Prince Louis of Hesse. This close relationship with the British royal family changed Ludwig's life. He moved to England when young. He changed his name to Louis and took British citizenship. Finally, Prince Louis Alexander entered *Britannia* as a cadet in 1868. He turned into an extremely competent naval officer, with the added advantage of highly desirable social connections. For the seekers of a sacrificial goat, Louis Alexander was ideal. He was clearly as German as leberwurst and sauerkraut and no doubt sent messages to Berlin in invisible ink by messenger pigeon. Vociferous 'patriots', spurred on by the newspapers and magazines that pandered to them, demanded his scalp. His position rapidly became untenable and he resigned on 29 October 1914.

Churchill recalled Jackie Fisher as First Sea Lord. Nobody had the nerve to suggest that 'Chinese Jack' took the Kaiser's gold.

Apart from Weddigen's trophy, 20 October 1914 witnessed the first sinking of a merchant vessel by a U-boat. Six days later came the first attack without warning. Even more disturbing was the report of a U-boat at Loch Ewe, the alternative anchorage favoured by Jellicoe. If the enemy could get there, nowhere was safe.

Berlin dearly wished to strike at the British. The Royal Navy was not prepared to fall in with German hopes by mounting a mighty attack on the Heligoland Bight. In turn, the High Seas Fleet, at least in the early days of the war, needed to keep a beady eye on the Baltic. If the Army went astray on the Eastern Front, command of the Baltic would be essential. A foray in strength to meet the Grand Fleet was not possible.

In particular, the Kaiser would not approve. But, however the Staff looked at the problem, one fact was crystal-clear. Germany had to break the British blockade.

On 2 October 1914 the Admiralty advised the world that a 1,365-square-mile area of the Channel was mined. The only safe passage was through British territorial waters.

One month later, on 2 November 1914, the Admiralty issued a further proclamation. The whole of the North Sea was declared a war zone. Any ships that crossed it on routes other than those laid down by the Admiralty did so at their own risk. Mines were laid. Any ship outside the prescribed routes was liable to interception and seizure. Germany seethed. Something had to be done.

The first retaliatory shot came from Admiral Friedrich von Ingenohl, Jellicoe's opposite number. The Commander-in-Chief of the Hochseeflotte delivered a broadside. In a closely argued submission, he pointed out that submarines were used by every state. This alone gave Germany the right to use U-boats in the manner to which they were best adapted. They could appear unexpectedly, cause fear and panic. They could escape by diving. U-boats were ideally suited to attacking merchant shipping. If crews and passengers on merchant ships ignored German warnings, so be it. They were no different from those who took passage in a ship that dared British minefields.

England, von Ingenohl and his supporters claimed, was trying to destroy German trade. Germany had exactly the same right as her enemy to declare a blockade of Britain.

On 7 November 1914, Admiral Hugo von Pohl, Chief of the Naval Staff, submitted the formal proposal to Theobald von Bethmann-Hollweg, the Chancellor. His recommendation was simple. There must be a U-boat blockade of Britain.

The proposal met with immediate opposition. The Chancellor was a shrewd politician. He knew that von Pohl's proposal, which presumed sinking without warning and without surfacing, would outrage world opinion. Neutral shipping would be in danger. Of the world's neutrals, the most important was the United States. Already, some neutral vessels tried their luck against the blockade, among them US-registered ships. Dodging the gentlemanly British was one thing. Running the risk of a German torpedo was another entirely.

The admirals pressed their case. Nobody could deny that the U-boats could destroy enemy shipping. Already, Britain had lost 60,000 tons in

August 1914, half as much again in September, to mines and surface raiders. Add in the U-boats and the English would be in a world of nightmare. They had proved that they sank ships. *Pathfinder, Hogue, Cressy, Aboukir,* and *Hawke* gave ample proof of their abilities. If the U-boat men were let loose to turn their attention from warships to cargo vessels, they could win the war. Britain had no answers to the hidden killers in the depths of the sea. As a footnote, by the end of the year the U-boats had sunk three merchant ships for a mere 2,950 tons. Things would change.

Opposition to the Naval Staff came from the Kaiser himself as well as the Chancellor. And, perhaps surprisingly, from the head of the U-boat arm, Fregattenkapitän Hermann Bauer, Senior Officer of the U-boat Flotilla since March 1914. At the outbreak of war, Bauer acquired the title Führer der U-booten, abbreviated to 'FdU'. His staff for this new appointment and responsibility was a solitary Kapitänleutnant whose duties included keeping the FdU war diary. With no secretary, the diary was written in longhand, a practice that possibly accounts for its brevity.

Bauer explained that Germany possessed less than thirty U-boats. For various reasons, it was hard to maintain more than four on patrol. And, he emphasised, a prewar study by an experienced U-boat captain, Korvettenkapitän Otto Blum, concluded that an effective blockade of Great Britain required precisely 222 U-boats.

As the German Naval Staff wondered how to break the blockade, a blockade that became more effective day by day, the Admiralty considered the problem of destroying U-boats. Not, some thinkers noted, preventing their onslaughts, but destroying the attackers.

It took no genius to realise that the first priority was to find the prowling killer. Enormous metal nets, supported by buoys and laced with mines, in strategic locations were one answer. Minefields provided another.

The greater problem lay in the miles of open sea. Mines failed to discriminate between friend and foe. Patrol boats were a limited answer at best. Any halfway competent U-boat commander could see them and escape by diving. With neither depth charges nor sound detection equipment to worry about, a submerged U-boat was as safely bedded as in dry dock at Kiel.

With no technical aids, Admiralty minds cast around for other means, any means, to bring U-boats to book. Merchant shipping was suffering. What was more, the U-boats by and large, observed the rules. They stopped ships flying the Red Ensign. They allowed the crew to take to the lifeboats. The U-boat then either sent a boarding party to scuttle the victim or the deck gunners spent a happy time aiming at a real target. Neutrals, too, were treated in accordance with recognised procedures.

Thus the weakness in the U-boat's armour was found. It is impossible to pin down who first suggested the idea of a decoy, a snare for the U-boats. Some officers had served on Arab dhows in the Indian Ocean and the Red Sea, dhows that not only carried a local crew, but a naval one as well. Their business was to wipe out pirates and slave raiders who infested the coasts. A fat dhow, sailing comfortably along a pirate coast, invited attack. When the raiders struck, they were met by a 3-pounder and a machine gun.

Clearly, the principle could be moved from the Indian Ocean to the Western Approaches and the English Channel. Decoy dhows changed into decoy merchant steamers. When the U-boat surfaced in accordance with the Prize Regulations, hidden guns would blast her to eternity.

Decisions came quickly when reports arrived of periscopes sighted near Le Havre. On 26 November 1914, a signal chattered across the ether from Whitehall Wireless, the Admiralty's transmitting station, to the Commander-in-Chief, Portsmouth. He was to fit out a ship with concealed guns. She was to cruise off Le Havre in the guise of a merchant ship.

SS *Victoria* had a brief career as a decoy. Sent to sea, her guns screened by crates of vegetables, she failed even to sight a U-boat. Unserviceability struck. On 9 December 1914, the C-in-C Portsmouth wrote to advise that she had been paid off.

In Germany, the argument for a wider use of the underwater arm gathered strength. Stalemate beckoned on the Western Front. The offensive at Ypres, designed to capture the Channel ports, had failed. Long casualty lists gave a grim reminder of the human cost of modern war.

Elation in November, when news came that von Spee's Ostasiengeschwader had destroyed Admiral Sir Christopher Cradock's elderly West Indies Squadron off the coast of Chile, vanished a few weeks later. SMS *Scharnhorst, Gneisenau, Nürnberg, Dresden* and *Leipzig* met HMS *Invincible, Inflexible, Cornwall, Kent, Carnarvon* and *Glasgow*. The Royal Navy's two battlecruisers, three armoured cruisers and one light cruiser, under the command of Vice-Admiral Sir Frederick Doveton Sturdee, massively outgunned the two armoured cruisers and three light cruisers of the Kaiserliche Marine. Admiral Maximilian, Graf von Spee and his two sons, Heinrich and Otto, perished. The isolated Germans' outstanding gallantry could not compensate for inferior machines in the new era of mechanised warfare. *Dresden* alone escaped.

In January 1915, Beatty's battlecruisers failed to crush a German force in the Battle of the Dogger Bank. Appallingly bad gunnery and ambiguous signals allowed the Kaiserliche Marine to avoid a shattering defeat. For German admirals, the affair reinforced their professional opinion. The damnable English still controlled the seas. Only Unterseeboote could redress the balance. The Kaiser, alarmed at the possible fate in store for his beloved big ships, reluctantly agreed.

On 4 February 1915, the German government issued its own declaration of a war zone:

1. The waters around Great Britain and Ireland, including the whole of the English Channel, are hereby declared to be in the War Zone. From February 18 onward, every merchant ship met with in this War Zone will be destroyed, nor will it always be possible to obviate the danger with which passengers and crew are thereby threatened.
2. Neutral ships, too, will run a risk in the War Zone, for in view of misuse of neutral flags by the British Government on January 31, and owing to the hazards of naval warfare, it may not always be possible to prevent the attacks meant for hostile ships being directed against neutral ships.

The acid reference to 31 January concerned Admiralty advice to ship owners. Their Lordships pointed out that the hoisting of a neutral flag was a perfectly acceptable ruse of war. Previous wars had seen its use. It breached no international conventions as long as no hostile act took place under the cover of the neutral ensign.

This, in due course, became the policy for Q-ships. As long as they did not fire until the British flag fluttered in the breeze, no breach of international law occurred. The Germans did not agree. The use of the neutral flag to disguise a warship, crewed by sailors in plain clothes, until it could surprise an enemy was a breach of accepted conventions.

On the same day as Germany declared its war zone, the SS *Lyons*, under the command of a prickly, slightly dubious, hastily commissioned officer, Lieutenant Commander C.A.P. Gardiner, became a decoy. In

August 1914, the Admiralty requisitioned the salvage vessel *Lyons* for service with the Royal Fleet Auxiliary, complete with crew. She came from a Poole company, the National Salvage Association. Its managing director was a certain Charles Alfred Parfoy Gardiner. *Lyons* was the company's major, if not sole, asset.

A snowstorm of vitriolic paperwork filled the files as Gardiner and the Admiralty crossed swords. His initial instructions were a mixture of hope and wishful thinking. Worse followed.

Lyons collected her concealed guns and other decoy gear in a secluded spot at Poole. The engineering company that modified her came under the ownership of a Charles Alfred Parfoy Gardiner. An invoice duly found its way to Whitehall. *Lyons* also acquired a venerable Maxim machine gun, thirty-six rifles and a selection of revolvers, with stocks of the appropriate ammunition. Whether the small arms were to round up surrendering German prisoners or to sink U-boats is not clear.

Gardiner's orders instructed him to hurry to an attacked ship to help survivors. He learned that a ship under submarine attack 'will hoist her largest flag half-mast at foremasthead or on triatic stay, and make calls with her syren [sic]; if fitted with wireless she will make "S O S" followed by a repeated letter S.'

Even before *Lyons* went to hunt U-boats, another decoy ship was in the offing. An attack on the Great Eastern Railway's ferry *Colchester* on 11 December 1914 probably suggested that a similar packet ship, sufficiently armed, might tempt an unwary U-boat. In January 1915 the mills of the Admiralty ground into action.

The ideal ship was, like *Lyons*, already in naval hands. Again leased for the Royal Fleet Auxiliary, the 1,800-ton SS *Vienna* came from the Great Eastern Railway. Pressed into service as officers' accommodation at Harwich, she still wore GER colours of black hull, white upperworks and buff funnels. She had plodded regularly across the North Sea for years. On her return to seagoing duty as a Q-ship, still in her distinctive livery, it took no great effort to change her name from the capital of a foe to *Antwerp* as a graceful tribute to a gallant ally.

Even more fortunately, a man to captain her kicked his heels in that same port of Harwich. It was, for the Admiralty postings staff, akin to a marriage made in heaven.

Using decoys remained secret. Not even all members of the Board at the Admiralty knew of these tentative steps. On 3 February 1915, the Fourth Sea Lord, Cecil Foley Lambert, wrote to the First Lord, Sir John

Fisher. The Fourth Lord explained that he attached no little importance to the use of merchant ships, armed with hidden guns, to trap U-boats. They could, he suggested, cruise in areas where submarines lay in wait. When challenged, they should stop and allow the U-boat to send a boarding party. They could then sink the U-boat with gunfire. The boarding party would become prisoners or casualties if they tried to escape.

Lambert was not naive. Although sinking without warning became a parrot cry in the British press, the facts tell a different story. Just one-fifth of sinkings by U-boats in the months to follow ignored the accepted code of behaviour. U-boats stopped ships, checked papers, allowed crews to row away before sinking their prey.

But during those months, the Q-ships began to roam.

FIVE

BOIL PRISONERS IN OIL – IF YOU TAKE ANY

Lieutenant Commander Godfrey Herbert's war had been less than successful by the time he boarded his first Q-ship in late January 1915. Command of the submarine *D5* wrote an inglorious chapter in his chequered career. During the early days of the war, as the British Expeditionary Force crossed to France, Herbert patrolled the Channel, alert for any ambitious German destroyer. He repeated his 'Messiah' act with serious intent. Minus the white sheet, he took the post of lookout. A heavy boot stamped signals to the crew below.

While the BEF marched north to Belgium, *D5* headed for German waters. Off Denmark, Herbert's luck was in. On 21 August 1914, SMS *Rostock*, a Karlsruhe Class cruiser, 139m long at the waterline, appeared in Herbert's sights. One of the most modern warships in the Kaiser's fleet, she entered service a mere six months earlier at a cost to the German taxpayer of a trifle over 8 million marks.

From 600yd, Herbert knew he could not miss. A gambler by instinct, he decided to make doubly sure. Although Admiralty orders prohibited the simultaneous firing from the bow tubes of two expensive torpedoes, Herbert knew the chance to send 4,900 tons of best Solingen steel to the bottom of the sea more than justified a minor breach of a rule dreamed up by Whitehall.

D5 crept into position. *Rostock* and her destroyer escort steamed on, oblivious. Herbert rapped out firing orders.

'Fire one!'

'Fire two!'

Both torpedoes headed directly towards the enemy cruiser. Herbert counted the seconds before they turned the German ship into a costly collection of scrap metal.

The torpedoes serenely sped a few feet underneath *Rostock*'s keel. Herbert, sure he was on a winner, discovered only later that the live missiles weighed 40lb more than training dummies. They ran deeper than he calculated. *Rostock* sailed on while her attendants, like maddened hornets, homed in on the telltale wakes. It took three hours for Herbert and *D5* to lose their pursuers.

Back at Harwich, Herbert confessed to Commodore Keyes. Two torpedoes fired simultaneously, two torpedoes that both missed. Keyes always forgave much of brave men. In his opinion, Herbert showed plenty of dash and spirit, was gallant, determined. He would undoubtedly do better in the future. And that was the end of the matter.

Opportunity beckoned once more for *D5*. On 4 November 1914, Konteradmiral Franz von Hipper's battlecruiser squadron of the High Seas Fleet, *Seydlitz, Von der Tann, Moltke, Blücher*, with four light cruisers, *Stralsund, Strassburg, Graudenz, Kolberg*, dashed across the North Sea to England. The heavy ships were to shell the coast while the light cruisers laid mines off Lowestoft and Yarmouth.

As dawn crept across the water, Hipper's ships were at Yarmouth Bay. A relic of Queen Victoria's Navy, HMS *Halcyon* blinked a challenge with her Aldis lamp when she spotted two four-funnelled ships, 5 miles distant. Once a torpedo gunboat, now converted to a fleet minesweeper, *Halcyon* had the dreary job of clearing the coastal shipping lanes. She was no match for cruisers.

Two miles astern of *Halcyon*, in drifting mist, two time-weary destroyers, HMS *Lively* and HMS *Leopard*, trudged along on their own routine patrols.

Strassburg and *Graudenz* unambiguously answered *Halcyon*'s query. Gunnery officers snapped out range, elevation. Gun muzzles swung into line. The British ship found herself in the middle of cascading water spouts. Shells crashed into the sea around her.

Hipper, fearful that his two light cruisers might stray into a known British minefield, ordered them to cease fire. *Seydlitz* alone would deal with the upstart.

Seydlitz spoke. The other battlecruisers, anxious not to miss their chance, joined in without orders. Their gun crews, keyed up by the knowledge that they were deep in English waters, wanted to grab the chance to sink an enemy. Enormous splashes engulfed *Halcyon*. Fire control officers on the big ships swore as *Halcyon* vanished in walls of spray.

Lively hurtled up towards the sound of battle, her four funnels billowing smoke. *Leopard* closed to the action, wireless room stuttering urgent Morse.

Fifteen minutes passed before Hipper called off the fight. Acutely aware of the danger of entering a minefield, he ordered his ships back to deep water. At 0740, the departing battlecruisers hurled a few shots in the general direction of Yarmouth. The shells landed on the beach to make a collection of craters for the curious to admire. And all the while, *Stralsund* laid a 5-mile trail of mines off Yarmouth Bay.

Halcyon escaped nearly unscathed. One German shell had hit her bridge. It wounded three crew and damaged a quickly repaired wireless room. As Hipper's ships vanished, the old ship spread the alarm. *Leopard* and *Lively*, joined by another veteran, HMS *Success*, shadowed Hipper's fleet as it retreated eastward.

Excitement ran high at Yarmouth as news of the German incursion raced round the port. Three off-duty destroyers hastily raised steam. The submarines *E10*, *D3* and Herbert's *D5* hurried out to sea. A chance, however slender, to sink a capital ship, was not to be ignored. Triumph was promotion, medals, fame.

Herbert pushed *D5* along at her top surface speed of 14 knots – 16 miles per hour. Diesel engines clattered. *D5* headed towards the action. Expectation ran through the crew. One opportunity, one strike, the destruction of a major enemy ship, would make heroes of them all.

Herbert was on the bridge when *D5* hit a mine, possibly a drifting British one. If it were British, his luck was truly out, for they were often temperamental about exploding. More probably, *Stralsund* had claimed a victim. In the days that followed, a series of fishing smacks and foreign merchantmen suffered the same fate.

Nineteen died as the submarine went under the water. Herbert himself, with six others on the bridge, struggled in the cheerless sea. Two trawlers, *Homeland* and *Faithful*, finally came to the rescue. Only Herbert with two others remained alive. The bitter North Sea claimed the rest.

Back on shore, Herbert learned he had no instant new command. Moving officers, submarine captains in particular, like pawns on a chessboard, to accommodate one unfortunate lieutenant commander, was low on the Admiralty's list of war-winning priorities. Even so, despite his reverses, Herbert had his value as a recognised expert in the submarine world. In December 1914, he received his next appointment.

He went to the French navy's *Archimède*, based at Harwich, as liaison officer. He knew little French but experience outweighed linguistics.

An engineering monstrosity, a retractable funnel, distinguished *Archimède* from other submarines. Her designers considered steam engines ideal for surface use. Submerging became a leisurely process as the funnel was first lowered, then secured under a watertight hatch.

On 14 December 1914 *Archimède* and her British companions, *E10*, *E11* and *E15* of the 8th Flotilla, left Harwich. Keyes commanded the group from the destroyer *Lurcher*. Orders sent them to patrol a line 30 miles NNW of the island of Terschelling off the Dutch coast. Room 40, the Admiralty's code-breaking office, had deciphered German wireless messages. Hipper intended to raid once more.

Keyes was to prevent any attempt by German ships to reach the English Channel. The small flotilla waited patiently without result. A further instruction ordered Keyes towards the Heligoland Bight. Anxious to preserve their code-breaking secret, the Admiralty's wireless messages often lacked specifics. Keyes detached *E11* to the area of the Elbe and Weser. The three remaining submarines stayed to guard the Channel approach. They spent the night of 16 December resting peacefully on the ocean floor.

Winter gales the next evening whipped the sea into a fury. *Archimède*'s captain decided to submerge to escape the battering by the wind and waves. The funnel had other ideas. Damaged by heavy seas, it refused to lower fully. The watertight hatch stayed open. Every billow that washed across the vessel poured water into the hull. *Archimède* wallowed heavily in the restless seas. A bucket chain tried to bale her out. The situation worsened. Her captain, Lieutenant Deville, decided to head for the Netherlands and internment.

Herbert disagreed. After some stimulating dialogue between the two, in a mixture of French and English, the bucket chain baled harder than ever, buoyed by Herbert's wisecracks and enthusiasm. *Archimède* laboriously lurched back to Harwich at a steady 10 knots. It took two days.

Herbert's career as a tactful connection between two proud navies abruptly ended when Deville reported to his seniors. The lieutenant commander returned to the depot ship, HMS *Maidstone*. Disconsolate, he suspected that the Admiralty viewed him with disfavour. His gallantry was undoubted, his professional ability profound. He was not, though, a lucky officer. Luck often made careers.

Nevertheless, he knew submarines and submariners. He understood the psychology of men who served under the waves. He was flamboyant, inventive, a man with ideas, a man who thought for himself. He was the ideal type of man to command the secret new weapon against the U-boat.

At the end of January 1915, Lieutenant Commander Godfrey Herbert took command of the Royal Navy element aboard SS *Antwerp* – one sub-lieutenant, one petty officer, eight seamen and twelve Royal Marines. The ship remained under the control of her merchant captain, who retained his ordinary crew. He would, however, steam wherever Herbert instructed, rather in the manner of an old-time sailing-master.

Antwerp had two 12-pounder guns, hidden from view. In her GER livery, she plodded her familiar path between Harwich and the Hook of Holland. Herbert, determined to fool even the keenest eyes that peered through a periscope, regularly adopted a disguise on the bridge. In hat, overcoat and untidy blond wig, he had no doubt that he passed as a Dutch pilot.

To no avail. *Antwerp*, the former *Vienna*, sailed back and forth, totally unmolested. The reason was, almost certainly, a complete lack of security. A report from the Continental Manager of the GER in Rotterdam pointed out that '*Vienna* is well known in Rotterdam and therefore in Germany.' He explained that her civilian crew gossiped with their friends from other ships. They, in turn, repeated the news to people they met. As a clincher, he drew the Navy's attention to the simple fact that 'all the G.E.R boats have had their appearance altered . . . so that *Vienna* stands alone in the original appearance of a Great Eastern steamer.'

After six weeks of mind-numbing lack of action, Herbert started to patrol between Southampton and Le Havre. Not a single contact appeared. He received orders to work in company with the opportunistic Lieutenant Commander Gardiner and SS *Lyons*. Both were to patrol the Irish Sea and the Western Approaches, a killing ground for determined U-boat captains.

The sharp-featured Otto Weddigen was one. He and his crew all received the appropriate class of the Iron Cross. The Kaiser was said to be 'in seventh heaven' after the destruction of *Aboukir*, *Cressy* and *Hogue*. His navy had shown his dead grandmother Victoria, his dead uncle Edward and his very much alive cousin George that their vaunted navy had an equal.

The blue-enamelled cross of the Pour le Mérite now dangled at Weddigen's throat for further valuable services to the Fatherland. Spiess, the 'Heinrich', took command of his own boat.

Promoted, with a fresh vessel, *U 29*, Weddigen left Ostend on 10 March 1915. In the next forty-eight hours, he sank two merchantmen,

SS *Headlands* and SS *Indian City*, close to the Scilly Isles. Wireless messages alerted *Antwerp*, cruising hopefully some 60 miles north of the sinkings. Herbert hurried south.

Some 10 miles west of the Scillies, 12 miles north of the Bishop Rock lighthouse, *Antwerp* closed on a sailing ship. On board huddled the survivors of Weddigen's latest victim, SS *Andalusian*, a 2,349-ton steamer from the Ellerman and Papayanni Line. Weddigen had scuttled the ship but she still floated sluggishly, low in the water, when *Antwerp* arrived. A wary 4 miles distant, *U 29* watched.

Herbert kept up the pretence of a peaceful merchantman. He transferred the survivors to *Antwerp*. Then he turned towards the German to offer himself as a target. Weddigen was not tempted. *Antwerp* raised speed, her nose pointed towards the U-boat. *U 29* observed. Before Herbert was even close, she dived.

Weddigen probably had his suspicions about *Antwerp*. She was clearly a railway ferry, still in the colours of the GER. The Western Approaches were an unlikely spot for a North Sea packet ship. When she steamed towards *U 29* instead of hurrying away like a prudent merchantman, Weddigen's suspicious instincts probably sharpened. He may well have heard of Captain Charles Fryatt, commanding a genuine Great Eastern steamer, SS *Brussels*, on the Rotterdam route. On 3 March 1915, Fryatt dodged a U-boat attack with a spirited display that won him a gold watch from the owners.

U-boat captains were well informed about ships, civilian and military. They sailed with a collection of documents ranging from *Lloyd's Register of Shipping* to *Jane's Fighting Ships*. Captain and crew were mariners. They knew ships. Some had served in the British Merchant Navy. As the Senior Naval Officer at Queenstown explained to an enthusiastic Q-ship captain later in the war: 'I sometimes think that you gentlemen in Q-ships do not quite realize that you are up against the best brains in the German Navy. Pray give the commanders of German submarines credit for possessing as much common sense as you have yourself – or even a little more.'

Weddigen never did explain his doubts about *Antwerp*. He chose to go home the long way, up the Irish Channel, past the Isle of Man and round Scotland. By 18 March, he was in the Pentland Firth between the Orkney Islands and the Scottish mainland, the 8-mile-wide channel that connects the Atlantic Ocean with the North Sea.

The Grand Fleet was out. A series of sitting ducks for a determined U-boat skipper. Weddigen fired a torpedo at HMS *Neptune*, a dreadnought battleship. It vanished into the distance. Close behind *Neptune* steamed the 4th Battle Squadron. Too close for Weddigen.

On HMS *Dreadnought*, the lookout raised the alarm. 'Periscope, 20 degrees off the port bow!' On the bridge, Lieutenant Commander Basil Piercy demanded full speed. The battleship's 27,500hp drove her 17,900 tons of steel directly at the 65m length of *U 29*. The Danzig-built boat broke in two. The entire crew, thirty-two officers and men, perished.

Herbert had no chance of recruitment as a sunbeam when he returned to shore. In a service phrase, he ticked like a runaway clock. 'This . . . ship', he grumbled, 'is too fast . . . *or* she is known to the enemy, although in the latter case he would simply have tried to attack me, diving on sighting me.' Nonetheless, Herbert could claim one tiny footnote in the annals of naval warfare. The encounter, abortive though it was, was the first meeting between Q-ship and U-boat.

Herbert's superior was Captain Henry Grant, Assistant Director of Operations at the Admiralty. Grant ensured that Herbert's opinions rapidly reached Fisher. The First Sea Lord summoned Herbert to London. The commander's name was not unknown in the rarefied wood-panelled atmosphere of the Admiralty. Apart from his earlier exploits, Herbert had flooded the Admiralty with proposals on how to make Q-ships more lethal. He overwhelmed Grant with a series of suggestions.

Herbert had already earmarked a tramp steamer berthed at Portland as a likely vessel. Mercantile Fleet Auxiliary No. 5, serving in an unheroic but vital role as a squadron supply ship, was another vessel commandeered from civilian service. She came from the same group of companies as the luckless *Andalusian*, this time from Ellerman and Bucknall. Displacing 4,192 tons, with a single funnel, SS *Baralong* was an unremarkable cargo steamer. She was a 'three-island' vessel, a phrase that simply means her bridge, engine room and cabins were in the centre, while the front and rear contained the cargo holds.

Fisher listened. Fisher considered. He then gave the lieutenant commander a free hand. He could choose his ship. He could name his own crew. He could roam the sea as he pleased. As long as he destroyed U-boats.

Nor was that all. Henry Grant was also impressed by Herbert's stream of plans. Without a single destroyed U-boat to give it credence, Admiralty Operations authorised, in February 1915, the fitting out of two more 'special service' ships. They were to operate under Herbert's control.

Neither the 1,459-ton SS *Peveril* nor the 1,198-ton SS *Princess Ena* were particularly suited to their new roles. *Princess Ena*, indeed, was a fruit boat from another railway company, the London & South Western, originally intended to run between the Channel Islands and Southampton.

Slow, lethargic, *Peveril* lasted only a few weeks as a Q-ship before returning to normal service. She was, nonetheless, recommissioned as a Q-ship in February 1917. A U-boat sank her off Gibraltar in November of the same year.

Herbert moved *Baralong* to Pembroke Dock in Wales for fitting out. The two 12-pounder guns that had graced *Antwerp* moved to the new ship. Mounted on the front deck, they both fired to either side. A wooden cover, looking like an animal pen, hid a third gun on the stern. The grubby freighter had fangs.

Herbert picked his crew. Along with the 12-pounder guns came his second in command from *Antwerp*, Sub-Lieutenant Gordon Steele. Third officer on the Anchor Line's SS *Caledonia* when war began, he was a rare bird among RNR officers. He had served in a submarine. For five months, he was aboard *D8*, only leaving when she went into dock for a lengthy refit. Chief Petty Officer Dickinson also joined *Baralong* from *Antwerp*, together with the senior Royal Marine, Corporal Frederick Collins of the Royal Marine Light Infantry.

Steele was an outstanding cadet at the Merchant Navy training ship *Worcester*. He won a P&O scholarship at the completion of his training. He had courage, and later won the Victoria Cross during the British intervention in Russia in a suicidal attack on the Red Fleet in Kronstadt.

Apart from these three stalwarts, Herbert retained most of the *Baralong*'s crew. Her master, George Swinney, stayed on board as the navigating officer after he obligingly joined the RNR. Of the sixty-six others, nineteen were regular Navy men, nine were merchant seamen and the remainder were RNR or Marines. This was twice the number normally needed to run a vessel of *Baralong*'s size. Half would fight the ship when they met a U-boat.

Much of the detailed supervision of *Baralong*'s conversion to a decoy was left to Gordon Steele. Herbert himself had two more immediate concerns.

First, he wanted to improve *Baralong*'s buoyancy. If she was to fight after being attacked, she had to stay afloat as long as human ingenuity could devise. He therefore requisitioned 2,680 empty casks from Devonport. *Baralong* had four holds. Casks would fill the forward hold, number 1, and the after hold, number 4. Coal would occupy the other two. The engines and boiler room were in the middle of the ship. As Herbert explained with an accompanying sketch to Captain Grant, himself no mean seaman, if the ship were holed anywhere as far aft as number 3 hold, her trim would not greatly alter. Hit elsewhere she would survive because of the empty casks in numbers 1 and 4 holds.

Second, Herbert laid down ground rules for his crew. *Baralong* would not pass muster as a scruffy tramp steamer if the visible crew marched around like regular sailors. It was not enough simply not to wear uniform. Everyone, from Herbert downwards, must look and act appropriately for the more slovenly end of the mercantile marine.

Herbert banned the use of regular naval terms. A loose word in harbour could spill the *Baralong*'s secret. The wardroom turned into the saloon. Ranks and trades went out of the window. Herbert became the master, not the captain. Stokers lost their ranks to become firemen. The Royal Marines gritted their collective teeth when they yielded up their uniforms. King's Regulations and Admiralty Instructions as to the appropriate dress of the day no longer existed. Sub-Lieutenant Steele alone was later authorised to wear 'some sort of uniform' to help maintain a semblance of discipline. The 22-year-old thoughtfully used his old P&O midshipman's kit. Even more pensively, he purchased a pistol in Portsmouth. Mutiny by the ill-assorted crew was not far from his mind.

Watch changes happened out of sight. Nobody ran anywhere. Rubbish was thrown over the side. Herbert encouraged the off-duty stokers to lounge around on the deck when *Baralong* entered or left harbour. They smoked. They spat. They whistled at any woman they saw.

Away from curious eyes, Herbert brought his gun crews up to standard. Some were positioned close to their action stations, pretending to do odd jobs. Others remained hidden. *Baralong* could not be seen with a rash of men on board. As the wives of merchant skippers were not unknown on board, Herbert even tried to have one of the crew dress as a woman. Captain Henry Grant stepped on that idea with a certain firmness.

Captain Fryatt of the *Brussels* did not help the Q-ship concept when he decided to ram a U-boat. On 28 March 1915 Fryatt saw one on the surface. He considered that it was about to fire a torpedo. He turned his ship and went to full speed to try and ram her. The U-boat crash-dived. Fryatt received another gold watch, this time from the Admiralty. His picture appeared in papers that crossed the North Sea. German anger flared. Merchant captains were not combatants. If they behaved as such, they deserved retribution.

At the end of March 1915, *Baralong* was ready. Her first port of call was Devonport to load her barrels. Herbert's instructions from the Admiralty were concise and clear. His normal cruising area was the English Channel. He must not pass Folkestone or the western limit of the Scillies. If U-boats operated off Queenstown, however, he could extend his patrol.

Herbert now had *Lyons* and *Princess Ena* under his command. The former fruit boat, although relatively fast, was out of place in the Irish Sea. Herbert ordered her to seek the enemy in the English Channel. She had hardly more luck than the wretched SS *Victoria* with her display of vegetables. *Princess Ena* did manage to sight the enemy in the distance when she dashed to the aid of SS *Anglo-Californian* on 4 July 1915.

The 59-year-old master of the *Anglo-Californian*, Frederick Daniel Parslow from Islington, stubbornly refused to leave his command at *U 39*'s behest. Resolute, under withering fire from Kapitänleutnant Walther Forstmann's boat, Parslow continually changed course, circled, dodged and weaved his way across the water. He died on his shattered bridge. The traditional gold watch for gallant Merchant Navy captains, such as Fryatt received, seemed an inappropriate gesture for such defiance. Difficulties arose with finding a suitable decoration. Merchant Navy men were civilians. They did not qualify for military awards that were, except in two clear cases, only for the living. In addition, German anger about mercantile captains who resisted U-boat commands partly inhibited the authorities. His widow finally received the Victoria Cross he won from the sovereign's hands at Buckingham Palace in May 1919. It took an amendment to the Royal Warrant in 1918 before Parslow became the first Merchant Navy officer to gain the decoration. Parslow's son, on board the ship as second mate and helmsman throughout the action, received the DSC for his part in it.

Princess Ena, alerted by Parslow's distress signals, hurried towards the action. Official sources declared that her opening shots – fired from some 5 miles away – drove off the enemy.

Lyons spent much time in the Irish Sea. She cruised the shipping lanes between Liverpool and the southern coast of Ireland. Her chances of intercepting a U-boat were slim. She was slow and stolid. A salvage tug stubbornly insists on looking and behaving precisely as a salvage tug should.

Further, Gardiner suffered a stream of Admiralty orders, requests and instructions which complicated his patrols. The chief culprit was Rear Admiral Henry Oliver, who detested amateur officers, rarely delegated any task to his juniors, seldom changed his mind, and was easily aroused to fury.

Querulous orders came thick and fast. *Lyons* was to remain available for salvage work although all her gear vanished when she became a decoy. Gardiner should pick up survivors from stricken vessels. He was to escort important passenger ships into Liverpool. *Lyons* was to intercept suspicious surface ships, for the Admiralty was convinced that a U-boat supply vessel operated in the area.

On top of these demands, Gardiner received details of an enemy minefield he had to clear. The minefield was probably the result of fevered speculation and *Lyons* was not a minesweeper. Gardiner, for once, did not argue. He bloody-mindedly pursued the order in exact detail, despite his normal inclination to question any instruction from higher authority as absurd, impracticable or lacking in vision. Finding the area awash with debris, Gardiner and his crew spent a pleasant time as they machine-gunned and sniped at all the wreckage they saw in case it hid mines.

Gardiner, at 52 years of age, remained undaunted by their Lordships' testy calls. He replied in kind with a stream of memoranda, suggestions, letters, proposals and complaints. In due course, *Lyons* ceased to be employed on special duties. She sailed to Kirkwall with the acid comment of an Admiralty minute bouncing off her hull. 'Lieutenant Commander Gardiner has given trouble before,' wrote the exasperated officer, 'and appears unable to accept an order without questioning it.' The sentiment was echoed by the short-tempered Oliver who observed: 'The captain of *Lyons* had a very free hand to catch submarines for over six months, he has been well tried at the work and not made good, and has been a source of trouble owing to his disinclination to do as he is told and to always make excuses to refit and stay in harbour.'

At the end of the year, Gardiner and his ship went back to Poole. Six years later, his shipbuilding and engineering company went into liquidation through a pressing lack of funds. The former lieutenant commander, who had ambitions of standing for Parliament, revived his fortunes with a profitable line in gun-running as well as a variety of other distinctly unethical ventures.

Herbert and *Baralong*, the flag of the United States of America at the stern, spent the first two weeks of April slogging along St George's Channel, the strait which separates south-east Ireland from Wales and joins the Irish Sea to the Atlantic Ocean. For fourteen days, she plied between the Scilly Isles, Smalls, Queenstown and the Fastnet. Nothing happened. No, periscopes appeared. No U-boats surfaced. Herbert became bored and steered his ship to Jersey on 14 April. She spent the next night at Falmouth. On 17 April, Torquay was close to hand, followed by Swanage the following day. On 18 April, Herbert ended his diversionary cruise at Portland.

Two weeks of idleness without the sniff of action did little for crew morale or discipline. Herbert's casual approach, that worked well with small numbers of regular ratings in the cramped and dangerous confines of submarines, had less success with the mixed complement of SS *Baralong*. Discipline wavered. Herbert's habit of inviting the chief engineer and his acolytes into the saloon for drinks did not help.

Steele was disconcerted. Merchant officers generally supposed their Royal Navy counterparts to be at least archangels if not minor deities. The captain of *Baralong* scarcely fitted the mould of the Dartmouth-trained permanent officer. Steele's doubts increased when Herbert announced a new identity. Henceforth he was Captain William McBride, a ruse, he explained, to mislead any casual listener.

For the same reason, Herbert followed Admiralty instructions to employ harbour pilots as little as possible. The fewer people who boarded *Baralong*, the fewer people to be curious about her. In some ports, the captain or navigating officer collected an appropriate fee if no pilot was used. Herbert turned matters to his own advantage. *Baralong* frequented ports where a pilot was not mandatory. Herbert conned the ship himself and pocketed the proceeds.

April became May. Herbert kept *Baralong* at sea for long stretches. The ship entered harbour only to take on coal and supplies. In part, this was to head off even greater trouble from the motley crew. Herbert finally banned shore leave for both disciplinary and security reasons. At Dartmouth, his men wrecked a public house in an orgy of fighting and drunkenness. Arrests followed. Herbert stood bail. At the magistrates' court the next morning, not a single sailor answered his name. *Baralong* had weighed anchor and skipped during the dark hours.

At various times, some of his merchant seamen simply swam ashore to get drunk. Three deserted.

Baralong saw no U-boats. On 7 May 1915, as she patrolled the waters off Jersey, her wireless room picked up an urgent cacophony of Morse code. *Lusitania*, sinking, cried for assistance. A single torpedo strike from *U 20*, under the command of Kapitänleutnant Walter Schwieger, sealed the great liner's doom.

The tramp's engines went to full power as Herbert headed for the Old Head of Kinsale. They arrived too late to help. *Lusitania* sank in less than eighteen minutes, taking with her 1,250 boxes of field artillery ammunition, eighteen boxes of percussion fuses that contained fulminate of mercury, a potently explosive material, and most of the souls on board. Of 1,957 passengers and crew, 1,198 lost their lives. Men, women, children, infants. 1,198 casualties of war.

Three weeks later, Herbert and his men paced angrily between the rows of bodies laid out at Queenstown. In an era accustomed to atrocities, wearily familiar with a world in which cluster bombs never kill children or pregnant women but simply cause collateral damage, it is almost impossible to recapture the feeling of shock, of anger, of rage which the sinking created. To most men raised in Victorian and Edwardian England, the killing of non-combatants was anathema, a convincing proof of barbarity. The realities of industrial warfare, of mechanised slaughter, had not hit home.

The depressing truth was that the *Lusitania* sinking proved that warfare had changed for ever. Civilians were no longer sacrosanct in times of conflict although, in truth, they never had been. In earlier years, the killing was usually close-up and personal. The advent of the torpedo, the aerial bomb, long-range artillery and the mine allowed slaughter to be conducted from afar. And mines, shells, torpedoes and bombs did not discriminate.

Germany had already accepted the brutal realism that total war was just that. Any ship could carry munitions, articles to aid the prosecution of the war, a word and a phrase that resembled Auntie Mabel's fabled knicker elastic. It went not merely twice round the dining table but stretched to take in a sideboard, four chairs and a Welsh dresser. Anything that helped the enemy's cause was a target.

The logic was inexorable, inescapable. The banker who financed a factory making Army boot laces, the theatrical producer presenting morale-lifting stage shows, old ladies knitting socks, sister Suzie sewing shirts for soldiers, the crew and the ship carrying comforting letters and parcels to the troops. They all were as much a target as soldiers in the front line.

Although Schwieger claimed that he did not know the identity of his victim before he sank her, this was a touch of Teutonic sophistry. A mere handful of enormous four-funnelled passenger liners plied the world's oceans. Schwieger knew that it was either the *Lusitania* or her sister, *Mauretania*, in his attack periscope. He had no doubts that he attacked a legitimate foe. There was no debate, no searching of conscience. She was, as *Jane's Fighting Ships* and *Lloyd's Register* made clear, an armed merchant cruiser and a legitimate target.

Despite, or because of, widespread condemnation of Schwieger outside Germany and her associates, few tears were shed when he was killed in command of *U 88*. Fate tossed an ironic smile in his direction for his boat went down when it struck a newly laid British mine near Terschelling on 5 September 1917.

To Herbert, to his men, to much of the world, the sinking of passenger ships was an atrocity. It mattered not a jot that *Lusitania* was technically an auxiliary cruiser. Everyone knew she was really a passenger ship. The German claim that she carried munitions for the Western Front, that there were soldiers on board, was enemy propaganda. That the great liner flew the neutral Stars and Stripes from her jack rather than the Red Ensign signified nothing. It was a sensible precaution in dangerous waters. The Germans had shown themselves to be barbarians, killers of women and children, not worthy of respect. Torpedoing passenger liners was at one with raping Belgian women, butchering babies, executing innocent villagers, using poison gas and routinely crucifying prisoners. The destruction of the *Lusitania* proved the essential evil of the Second Reich and Kaiser Wilhelm II personally.

A coin and medal designer in Munich, Karl Goetz, offered the Allies an unexpected propaganda coup. He produced a commemorative piece. On one side, *Lusitania*, her deck crammed with armaments, sank stern first. On the other, Death sold tickets to a queue of passengers. Above ran the slogan, in German, 'Business Above All'. Goetz made his medal as a vicious satire on the hypocrisy and money-grubbing antics of Cunard. They used innocent people to disguise the 'Lucy's' true role as a military transport and charged them for the privilege.

Goetz took the details from his local newspaper. That gave the wrong date for the sinking. Goetz copied it. 5 May 1915, two days before Schwieger's attack: Britain and others briskly produced thousands of copies. Proof inescapable that the Kaiser and his minions planned mass murder by sinking innocent liners.

Jackie Fisher considered the whole business an inescapable fact of war. The admiral had startled delegates to the 1899 Hague Peace Conference when he suggested that common sense meant it was reasonable to 'hit your enemy in the belly, and kick him when he is down, and boil his prisoners in oil – if you take any – and torture his women and children. Then people will keep clear of you.'

Herbert's first lieutenant, Gordon Steele, later recalled the high emotion which ran through *Baralong*'s crew:

> It was just the culminating point of a long series of minor violations of war, and inhuman practices . . . it just required the sight of those silent figures of drowned children from the *Lusitania*, as they were laid out on the front at Queenstown in a temporary mortuary to rouse the deepest hatred in the *Baralong*'s crew, composed as they were of a mixed collection – naval, mercantile and marine ratings – who had never so hated before.

At an impromptu meeting, the crew agreed to show no mercy to any U-boat man who fell into their hands.

Herbert was left in no doubt what to do if he engaged a U-boat. 'The *Lusitania*', he learned from Captain Herbert Richmond, who had joined Grant at the Admiralty, 'is a shocking business and our unofficial answer is – take no prisoners from U-boats.'

This was simple and direct. All *Baralong* had to do was to find her quarry.

SIX

AND THE SEA TURNED RED

Q-ship commanders, like every other seagoing officer in the Royal Navy, yearned to destroy a U-boat. Unlike their contemporaries in the 'Grey Funnel Line', however, they positively invited U-boats to attack them. They had only sharp eyes aided by the best binoculars the Admiralty could beg, borrow or buy, and wireless distress calls to help them hunt U-boats. To find the enemy needed that capricious ally, good fortune. As May turned to June, Herbert and *Baralong* tramped the waters of the Channel and the Western Approaches with growing frustration.

For seven weeks, until 29 May 1915, not a single merchant ship was sunk by a U-boat in the English Channel. In the Western Approaches, the Kaiser's U-boats spent their days despatching a small collier here, a three-masted schooner there, with an apparent disregard for larger targets.

A spell of fearsome weather hindered the decoy's chances. Grey skies, howling winds, slate-grey seas added to Herbert's annoyance. When blue skies returned, *Baralong* still failed to find the enemy.

Herbert snarled his opinion of uncooperative U-boat captains in a report on 12 June 1915 to the long-suffering Henry Grant at the Admiralty. 'If they will persist', he wrote, 'in sinking things like Plymouth schooners, with 150 tons of coal aboard, when the ocean is thick with large steamers, I can't help it.' Ten days later, his frustration mounting, he complained again. He was, he felt, destined to suffer ill luck. *Baralong* had steamed nearly 18,000 miles without sighting a U-boat.

Grant dealt relatively patiently with Herbert's stream of reports, comments and suggestions. He rejected a request for *Baralong* to have her own seaplane. He adamantly refused to provide a motor boat for Herbert's use. Either would destroy *Baralong*'s guise as an unloved tramp steamer.

Grant was equally unsympathetic to another request on 27 July 1915 when Herbert bluntly asked for promotion to acting commander 'in view of the fact that I have got two ships beside my own? Of course I shouldn't expect to keep the rank as soon as I go back to submarines, but just while I have command of this show I thought possibly the extra "guns", so to speak would be an advantage.' Anticipating a refusal, he continued, 'I am reluctant to make such a suggestion, not having scored a hit up to date. . . . I hope you will forgive me suggesting it, but I see fellows junior to me holding acting ranks and wondered whether my job is worth it.'

A touch disheartened, a little disgruntled, Herbert carried on. On the morning of 19 August 1915, *Baralong* patrolled the Western Approaches. She played the part of a conspicuous neutral who had taken unmistakable precautions in perilous waters. The flag of the United States fluttered from her stern and masthead. On each of her sides, 16ft by 12ft boards proclaimed she was *Ulysses S. Grant*. Each board carried the letters 'USA', reinforced by a painted 'Old Glory'.

Sunlight sparkled off a gentle swell. A blue sea, its waves capped with white foam, a sharp horizon, perfect weather, with not a U-boat in sight. Just wreckage or smoke in the far distance as another freighter met her doom. Lifeboats with desperate survivors were ignored. Rescued, they might discover *Baralong*'s true purpose. Personal belongings, floating, abandoned, forlorn. And sometimes bodies of seamen like themselves. Herbert and his crew developed a hatred of U-boats and all who sailed in them. Wreckage, unending wreckage.

For word had gone out. To Kiel, Cuxhaven and the Baltic ports, to Heligoland, to Bruges and the Flanders Flotilla. U-Boote heraus! Gegen England! Fregattenkapitän Hermann Bauer, in charge of the U-boat arm, issued a typically aggressive order.

The boats were there. Hunting. Searching for rich pickings. Supplies flowed across the Atlantic from America. Weapons, shells, animals, food. Troop ships left Liverpool and Southampton for France and the new battle front at the Dardanelles, for Egypt and India. Britain's lifelines were strings across great waters. U-boats could slice them in two.

In the Western Approaches, three of the Kaiser's determined U-boat captains were ready. Kapitänleutnant Max Valentiner with *U 38* from II Flotilla. Kapitänleutnant Rudolf Schneider in *U 24* of III Flotilla; IV Flotilla's Kapitänleutnant Barnard Wegener with *U 27*. All three were good, very good, at their job.

Chance had given Wegener mostly military targets. He torpedoed a British submarine, the *E3*, on *U 27*'s maiden voyage. For the first time one submarine destroyed another. For good measure, he subsequently sank HMS *Hermes*, a venerable cruiser converted to a seaplane carrier, as she crossed from England to France. He later destroyed HMS *Bayano*, a banana boat pressed into service as an armed merchant cruiser. He torpedoed her as she sailed to Liverpool from Clyde to take on coal. Wegener was not totally scrupulous, as *U 27*'s log of the incident shows: '0500 March 11 1915 Large blacked-out steamer – initially mistaken for a warship – sighted from a coastal inlet. Target engaged. Bow torpedo struck steamer for'ard. Range 2–300 metres, vessel about 8,000 tons. Steaming under blackout. Nationality unknown. Steamer went down by the head in about 10 minutes. Three life boats with flares on the water.'

Schneider was heartless. Any ship, military or civilian, that flew an enemy flag was fair game. He was the man who first attacked a merchantman without warning on 26 October 1914. He torpedoed the French ship *Amiral Ganteaume* in the Channel. She did not sink, and was towed to safety. The 2,000 Belgian refugees on board were confirmed in their hatred of Germans.

Of the three, Valentiner, proved to be most ruthless. From the later months of 1915 onward, he terrorised the Mediterranean. In all, 300,000 tons of enemy shipping fell to *U 38*'s shells and torpedoes. To the British, he became a war criminal. The Germans saluted him as a hero. Valentiner could claim that he had done no more than his duty. Admiral von Ingenohl had himself declared in 1914 that 'we should free ourselves from all scruples which certainly no longer have justification'.

After the war, Britain accused Valentiner of fifteen war crimes. He never faced trial. Allegations are easily made; proof is another matter.

On 13 August 1915, *U 38* met *U 27* off the Welsh coast, close to the Liverpool sea lanes. Valentiner and Wegener studied their orders, made decisions. The Wilhelmstrasse wanted massive attacks on enemy shipping. Additionally, a chance existed to pick up three escapers: Kapitänleutnant Heinrich von Hennig and two other Kaiserliche Marine officers, who had escaped from Dyffryn prisoner-of-war camp. If all went to plan, the trio would be on the beach at Great Ormes Head.

A well-experienced submariner, a prewar instructor at the Kiel U-boat school, Valentiner took the job of making the rendezvous. Wegener was to head towards the Scillies. Schneider would join them after he created

The Kaiser's Heroes.
Kapitänleutnant Otto
Weddigen and the crew of
U 9 after the sinking of
HMS *Cressy*, HMS *Aboukir*
and HMS *Hogue*, 1914. (*RN
Submarine Museum*)

Lieutenant Commander
Godfrey Herbert and crew
of HM Submarine *D5*, 1914.
(*RN Submarine Museum*)

Sir John Arbuthnot Fisher – 'Chinese Jack' – First Sea Lord, 1904–10. He was recalled by Churchill to replace Prince Louis of Battenburg in October 1914. (*Royal Naval Museum*)

Winston Leonard Spencer Churchill, First Lord of the Admiralty, 1911–15. (*Royal Naval Museum*)

Sir John Jellicoe, Commander-in-Chief of the Grand Fleet, on board HMS *Orion* with Vice-Admiral Arthur Cavenagh Leveson, Scapa Flow, 1914. *(Royal Naval Museum)*

Oberleutnant zur See Iwan Crompton, hero or villain of the second *Baralong* incident, 1915. *(Private Collection)*

A ship's lifeboat alongside an inquisitive U-boat. (*Private Collection*)

Sinking a steamer. A U-boat gun crew in action. (*Private Collection*)

Never mind the weather – a U-boat's gun in heavy seas. (*Private Collection*)

The Flanders Flotilla. A UB I Class boat in Ostend Harbour. (*Private Collection*)

Deception is all. A gun position on a
Q-ship. (RN Submarine Museum)

Cold, wet, vigilant. The life of a U-boat
lookout. (RN Submarine Museum)

A gallant patriot to the British, a franc-tireur to the Germans. Captain Charles Fryatt, master of the SS *Brussels*, 1915. *(Imperial War Museum)*

Admiral Reinhard von Scheer, Commander-in-Chief, High Seas Fleet, 1916. *(Imperial War Museum)*

Lieutenant Commander Gordon Campbell. (Times History of the War *via S. Snelling*)

Lieutenant William Bonner. (*the late David Harvey via S. Snelling*)

Lieutenant Neil Stuart. (*via Canadian Pacific Archives*)

Petty Officer Ernest Pitcher. (Times History of the War)

Able Seaman William Williams. (*Private Collection via S. Snelling*)

Skipper Tom Crisp. (*Private Collection via S. Snelling*)

Lieutenant Commander Willie Sanders. (*Private Collection via S. Snelling*)

Lieutenant Commander Harold Auten. (Times History of the War)

U 93 at sea, 1917. (*Private Collection*)

Kapitänleutnant Adolf Karl Georg Edgar, Freiherr von Spiegel und Peckelsheim, commander of *U 93*, 1917. (*Private Collection*)

Taken from USS *Noma*, this shows HMS *Attack*'s attempt to save Q-ship HMS *Dunraven*, 8 August 1917. (*US Naval Historical Center*)

On patrol. A U-boat's bridge crew. (*Private Collection*)

The turning tide. An SS Zero Class airship patrols over a convoy, 1918. (*Author*)

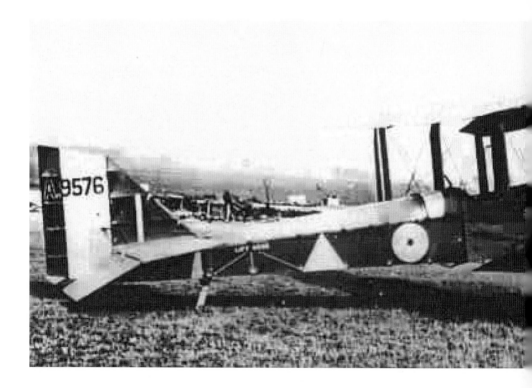

Above: Five tons of peril for the U-boats. A Felixstowe F2A flying boat. Its long range and heavier bomb load prophesied the shape of things to come in the Second World War. *(via Peter London)*

Left: The DH6, underpowered, unreliable, unloved by its crews. It still managed to deter U-boats. *(Private Collection)*

Oberleutnant zur See Wolfgang Steinbauer, commander of UB 48. (*Courtesy of Horst Bredow, Deutsches U-Boot Museum, Cuxhaven-Altentruch, Germany*)

'The U-boat War'. A mid-1918 German poster. The enemy's average monthly shipbuilding – 270,000 tons. Sunk by U-boats, 600,000 tons. The balance is in Germany's favour . . . (*Private Collection*)

The last victim of a Q-ship. J6 in port, 1918. *(RN Submarine Museum)*

End. Surrendered U-boats at Harwich, 1918. *(RN Submarine Museum)*

Kapitänleutnant Klaus Hansen and some of the crew of *U 41*. All submariners have their photograph taken by the conning tower, much as aircrew stand in front of aeroplanes. (*Private Collection*)

tremors of panic by shelling oil tanks near Whitehaven. Wegener left. Valentiner waited.

For three successive nights *U 38* nosed to within 300m of land. For three successive nights, at the agreed time, a lamp flashed briefly towards the dark shore. For three nights, keen eyes with powerful binoculars scanned the beach for a reply. Nothing.

Meanwhile, 500m away, on a different beach, hidden from *U 38* by a jumble of rocks, the hungry escapers blinked a signal out to sea. For three nights. Nothing.

Valentiner finally gave up. Von Hennig, captured in an attempt to take *U 18* into Scapa Flow, and his companions would have to surrender to the Tommies. A disappointment, but war was full of hardships. *U 38* surged south.

Towards Herbert and *Baralong*.

Captain William Finch, master of the White Star Line's SS *Arabic*, bound for New York from Liverpool, was a careful captain. His ship, 50 miles off the Old Head of Kinsale at 0930 on that bright August morning, was ready for a torpedo strike. Watertight doors firmly closed, stores checked in the lifeboats, 600 lifebelts placed throughout the ship for the 186 passengers and the ship's crew. *Arabic* ploughed through the sparkling water at a steady 16 knots, zigzagging to confuse an attacker.

On the bridge, Finch saw a freighter ahead, on his right. Her head was down as she sank into the Irish Sea. Nearby, two small boats, sails set, headed for Ireland. Finch ordered a change of course to starboard to take *Arabic* across the bows of the steamer. *Arabic* slowed, although Finch did not intend to stop. He studied the sinking ship. No distress call but that was not unusual. Tramp steamer companies considered wireless a luxury.

Arabic click-clacked a message on behalf of the merchantman. As Finch inspected the freighter, the 4,930-ton SS *Dunsley*, a sleek, grey shape, dripping water, surfaced from behind the sinking ship.

Rudolf Schneider had come to call.

U 24 fired a single torpedo. Someone shouted a warning as bubbles raced across the water. Finch rang for emergency power. The wheel spun to put the helm hard to starboard.

Large liners move slowly. Small torpedoes move quickly. Schneider's aim was good. His shot tore into *Arabic*, 30m from her stern. The explosion destroyed the wireless room. *Arabic*'s own SOS calls died in the air. The 15,801-ton liner slowed, listed, settled, started to sink. Eight minutes after impact, her bows rose in the water, the stern dipped under the waves and she plunged to the ocean floor.

Schneider blandly claimed later that not only did he believe the liner to be a troopship but that her erratic course suggested she was attempting to ram him. Captain Charles Fryatt's antics in the North Sea had something to answer for. Some 18 of the 186 passengers, along with 21 crew, died.

Baralong heard the two cries for help. They galvanised Herbert into action. With Swinney beside him, Herbert quickly calculated they were a mere 25 miles away. Hectic work with the coal shovels could place the *Baralong* on the scene within two hours. A U-boat captain who waited to see his victims sink might still be there when *Baralong* arrived.

Elation ran through the ship. The enemy was near. Steele and his gunners lounged conveniently close to the fore deck. Corporal Collins and his Marines took up post. Lookouts gazed ahead, eager for the first sign of the enemy. On the bridge, Herbert and Swinney checked the time. Seconds became minutes. The minutes became an hour, then more. The sea stayed empty.

Seven miles from *Arabic*'s reported location, Herbert slowed his ship. If the U-boat was close by, it might try its luck. Closer still. Nothing. Not a single plume of smoke. No lonely lifeboat. Nothing.

Herbert stood down the crew from action stations. Once again, they were too late. Herbert had no idea where the U-boat might be. He set course eastward. One direction was as good as another. What Herbert didn't know, as *Baralong* slowly steamed towards the Scillies, was that Leonard Batchelor, *Arabic*'s 21-year old wireless operator, had keyed the wrong position. Herbert's choice of course took *Baralong* towards Kapitänleutnant Wegener and a mule transporter named SS *Nicosian*.

At 1505hr, 80 miles west of the Scilly Isles, 100 miles south of Queenstown, the loud chatter of Morse in his headphones nearly deafened *Baralong*'s wireless operator. The sender was about 20 miles away, if experience was any guide. Indelible pencil scribbled frantically. 'SOS. Am being chased by enemy submarine.' A messenger ran to the bridge to thrust the paper into Herbert's hand.

As Herbert read the words, a shout alerted the bridge. Steam from a freighter's funnel. To the south-west, apparently making a radical change of course. Topmasts appeared in Herbert's binoculars, perhaps 10 miles distant. Less than an hour away.

Another message timed at 1508. 'Captured by enemy submarine. Crew ready to leave. Latitude 50.22N, longitude 3.12W.'

Word rattled around *Baralong*. There was a chance for revenge, after all. Revenge for the *Lusitania*, revenge for the drowned women, the innocent children, revenge for the dead sailors whose grave was the unforgiving sea. Revenge for the *Arabic*. It seemed certain the U-boat was the same killer, who had moved on to another victim. A third message at 1515. 'Crew nearly all left. Captured by two enemy submarines.'

It was almost a year to the day that Herbert had missed his opportunity to sink *Rostock*. Now he had two chances to destroy a pirate of the seas. He called for every last ounce of speed. In the engine room, sweating stokers frantically thrust more coal into the furnaces.

Five long minutes ticked by. *Baralong* shuddered her way through the waves. Every minute that passed was one minute closer to destroying a bunch of Hun baby-killers. A hasty message: 'Main fuses blown.' Another five minutes paced by. *Nicosian's* final signal, spluttered out on the emergency transmitter. 'Help, help. For God's sake, help.'

Baralong pounded towards the lone plume of steam on the horizon. A single funnel. Masts. The Red Ensign at her stern. Herbert assessed the scene. *Nicosian* sat at right angles to him, her stern to port. Further left, about 900yd away, the low silhouette of a U-boat, men clustered around her forward gun. In front of the steamer's bows, a gaggle of lifeboats pulled clear.

Herbert swung his binoculars towards the sinister, stark black outline against the bright horizon. The U-boat's bridge came into focus. An officer in the conning tower gazed back through Zeiss lenses. Herbert ordered a turn to starboard to show the United States markings on the side and the Stars and Stripes at the stern. Long moments of waiting before the U-boat sidled towards her victim. Her deck gun fired. *Nicosian* and her cargo of mules had little time to spare.

Herbert snapped an order. Bunting, a red cross on white, a yellow flag with a black ball in its centre, coloured stripes, crosses, followed each other up the *Baralong* halyards. The International flag code. V I C Q R A. 'To save life only'. The U-boat continued to close on the far side of *Nicosian*. Herbert headed towards the lifeboats. Within minutes, the doomed freighter would be between him and the enemy. The sound of a shell echoed across the morning. On board the *Nicosian*, a mule screamed.

Herbert rang down to the engine room. *Baralong* lost way precisely like a would-be rescuer. *U 27* continued the business of sinking an enemy freighter. Within moments, the bulk of the *Nicosian* shielded the decoy. At which point, *Baralong* shed her disguise to become a ship of His Majesty's Royal Navy.

'Clear away guns!'

Three black muzzles appeared. The US colours vanished. The White Ensign rippled out from stern and masthead. Collins and his men peered along rifle barrels. Gunners waited to open fire.

'Marines! Concentrate on the forward gun. Twelve-pounder crews! Aim at the conning-tower and hull!'

Baralong moved clear of the mule-ship. Seconds later, U 27 was visible, 600yd away. Collins grunted the command. 'Fire at will!' A dozen rifles spat bullets.

The gunlayer fell first. His crew ran towards the conning tower. The Marines continued to fire, picking their targets in the bright air.

At the 12-pounder gun on the port side of *Baralong*, Gordon Steele yelled his firing orders. The gun banged. A miss. Again. Another miss. A third try. Silence. A breech jam.

If regulations meant anything, they were specific about misfires. No matter what the cause, electrical, percussion or the personal interference of the Almighty, nobody touched the breech mechanism until thirty minutes passed. As gunners wryly observed, removing a temperamental round was bad enough after the allotted time. Shells were capricious creatures with a nasty habit of exploding without warning. If someone was foolish enough to pull it out before thirty minutes and it detonated, the miscreant faced a court martial. Piece by individual piece.

Steele did not hesitate. He warned his gun crew to get back, wrenched open the breech, pulled out the round, ran to the rail, heaved it as far as he could. The shell splashed docilely into the water. By the time Steele re-joined his gun, another round was already in the breech.

While Steele took his chances, the other guns dealt U 27 its death blow. The periscope and black-crossed Ensign vanished on the second salvo. A third shell crashed into the conning tower. The fourth hit the pressure hull amidships. More shells rained on the boat. Survivors abandoned the sinking wreckage. Most struggled free of their green leather clothing before they jumped clear.

U 27 heeled over. Months of careful work by the men of the Imperial Dockyard at Danzig sank beneath the water. Two huge bubbles of air escaped to the surface to mark her passing.

Cheers rippled along the *Baralong*'s decks. More cheers came from *Nicosian*'s lifeboats. On board the Q-ship, the jubilation lasted only a few seconds before Herbert shouted more orders. The section of his official account that dealt with the next events was a trifle skimpy:

The *Nicosian*'s boats were now called alongside and whilst clearing the boats, I observed about a dozen Germans who had swum from their boat swarming up ropes' ends and the pilot ladder which had been left hanging down from the *Nicosian*. Fearing they might scuttle or set fire to the ship with her valuable cargo of mules or fodder, I ordered them to be shot away; the majority were prevented from getting on board, but six succeeded.

As soon as possible I placed my ship alongside and put a party of marines on board under Corporal Collins, RMLI, warning him to be careful of snipers in case they had found the rifles which I was informed by *Nicosian*'s captain had been left in the charthouse.

A thorough search was made which resulted in six of the enemy being found but they succumbed to the injuries they had received from Lyddite shell shortly afterwards and were buried at once.

No. 17036 Corporal Frederick Collins, a long-time Marine, told a different story nearly fifty years later. His testimony, preserved, insisted that Herbert's instructions ended with the firm injunction, 'Don't forget, Collins – no prisoners aboard this ship. Get rid of them.' His statement continues:

I sent a couple of parties to each hatchway to start with. Then I told three men to search the upperworks. We searched the boat decks and the bridge. I heard someone scuffling down below and a shot was fired. We never discovered who fired that shot. Then the marines went down each hatchway to the next deck, which was the cabin deck. After this, the marines just shot them.

After I got down below I heard the shots and turned to go aft and on the after deck I saw somebody disappear through an alley and into a cabin. I kicked the door open, the bloke shouted out and I shot him. He toppled over the side the moment he was shot. Herbert was standing on the bridge and saw him floating past. Herbert had a revolver in his hand and threw it in the face of the man in the water and said, 'What about the *Lusitania*, you bastard?' I don't know about any of them being shot in the water swimming.

No. 16021 Marine Thomas Henry Haywood had no qualms about the action. He recorded the events in his diary, written that evening:

Rifles opened fire and cleared the Germans from the Guns, our second shell hit the Conning Tower and blew it into scrap Iron everything sunk in 4½ mts. We then picked up the *Nicosian*'s lifeboats, meanwhile the Huns were doing their best to get aboard the liner by climbing the lifeboats falls. We fired 2 shells and hit a few of them. We then ran up to *Nicosian* and shot all of them in the water and the Sea turned red. Next the 10 Marines were ordered to fix bayonets and search the liner for any Huns that were aboard her so we got aboard and found 5 and shot them but it was a pitiful sight to see the Mules who had got wounded by the Shell fire.

Baralong's log laconically noted the event: '4.10 Submarine sunk. 4.20 took crew from lifeboats. Captured vessel proved to be SS *Nicosian*'.

With no prisoners to concern him, Herbert concentrated his efforts on *Nicosian*. He had either forgotten, or dismissed, the story that the mule-ship's captain claimed she was captured by two U-boats. His hour of triumph would have been severely marred if a torpedo had sent *Baralong* to the bottom of the sea.

The master of the *Nicosian*, Captain Charles Manning, and a scratch crew returned to their ship. The holes could be patched enough to allow a tow. The pumps would clear the 20ft or so of water from number 1 hold, which had been badly hit. The long journey from New Orleans might end with a certain lack of dignity but his ship was saved.

Herbert's report to the Admiralty continued: 'The *Nicosian* had two shot holes in No. 1 hold below water line, and several above water line further aft, also one boiler damaged. I took her in tow at 6.20 p.m., and as she made no more water, though No. 1 hold was flooded, headed for Avonmouth, for which port she was bound, reporting same to Admiralty, via Land's End.'

The tow parted the next morning. Manning decided that his command could reach Avonmouth under her own power. The remainder of *Nicosian*'s men rejoined their ship to commence the dismal task of clearing the mess of slaughtered mules, urine, dung and blood in the stables. Twenty-four animals were dead. Another six were shot. Others were injured but could be treated.

Herbert became aware that some of the *Nicosian*'s crew were Americans. A few were working their passage to Europe to join the war.

Although undoubtedly sympathetic to the Allied cause, they saw the use of their country's flag. They witnessed apparent civilians sink the U-boat from a ship flying the White Ensign. They noticed the disguised guns. They discovered the *Baralong*'s name, for it showed through a hastily applied coat on the bows.

Under his assumed rank and name of Captain William McBride, Herbert asked Manning to speak to his crew and urge them to remain silent. Manning agreed in a polite letter addressed to 'Captain William McBride'.

And that would have been the end of the matter except that the Americans and British talked anyway. They spoke of what they had seen, the tales becoming more lurid with every recounting. Some accounts were fantasy. Others had an uncomfortable ring of truth.

By September, the stories reached the American press. The American crewmen expanded on their experience. The *Baralong* had not replaced the Stars and Stripes with the White Ensign. The struggling swimmers were used as target practice. The British shot men trying to surrender. The muleteers, stewards, stokers had all heard *Baralong*'s captain order his men to take no prisoners. The U-boat captain had surrendered when he was gunned down. The name of the ruthless master, Captain William McBride, went round the globe.

Outrage shook Germany. Military honour demanded that enemies be properly uniformed. Men in civilian clothes with guns were francs-tireurs.

Karl Goetz produced another commemorative medal. On one side, King George and Queen Mary presented an award to a sailor. On the other, a hand with a Union Jack cuff held a dagger. The legend, BARALONG MOERDER '19 AUG 1915 U27' completed the decoration.

This time, nobody copied it.

SEVEN

A BLACK AND BLOODY OCEAN

In response to the fierce demand from Berlin for an explanation of the *'Baralong* Affair', the British counterattacked by reciting a list of German misdeeds. In both diplomacy and war, attack is often the most effective defence. Whitehall firmly believed that the mote in the British eye was nothing compared to the beam in the German one.

Fortunately, the British press and officialdom agreed that nothing would be gained by telling the public about the controversy. The papers stayed silent. Four months passed before the first information appeared. The British government released a White Paper: *In Regard to Incidents Alleged to Have Attended The Destruction of a German Submarine.*

By that time, the furore had washed through London, Berlin, Washington and most other cities of the world. The German propaganda machine took very good care to pass on the gory details, true or false, to more than 1,000 papers and journals across the globe.

Ninety years on, sifting the fanciful from the likely becomes a thankless task. Steele, near the end of his life, confirmed that he heard Herbert give the instruction to take no prisoners. Corporal Collins was positive about his orders. Certainly, every man on board *U 27* perished.

Herbert fudged the course of events when he claimed the men who boarded *Nicosian* 'succumbed to Lyddite shell injuries'. Bizarrely, he also assured the Admiralty that he had never adopted the name and identity of 'Captain William McBride'.

To Berlin, Herbert was a murderer. Wegener became a slaughtered hero. After the Second Reich passed into history, when a new, perverted regime held sway in Germany, Hitler's Kriegsmarine named its VI U-boat flotilla 'Flottille Wegener' to commemorate the officer killed by the treacherous William McBride.

Herbert received the DSO for his exploit. To preserve the secret of the Q-ships, a fraudulent citation accompanied the announcement of the award. That it was for services in the Dardanelles was the official explanation.

Rumours persisted. Writing after the war, a former RNVR lieutenant from the 10th Cruiser Squadron recounted the full-blown legend that was the bitter business of the *Baralong*:

One account depicts a terrible scene when the British Marines rushed at the Germans with iron bars, and in more than one case strangled the murderous Germans who had so wantonly fired on a defenceless passenger steamer. The ghastly fight continued in the tunnel leading from the engine room to the stoke-hold, where the doors were thrown open, and the Germans pitched headlong into the flames. Another account describes the British Marines discovering the German sailors in the *Nicosian*'s engine room drying their wet clothes over the hot steam pipes, and before they could escape, fired into them at close range, until every German had paid the penalty for their murderous crime.

Given that men swimming in the water can hardly raise their arms in surrender; given that once the survivors had reached the *Nicosian* they could have made positive signs of submission; given that some of the stories are fanciful – there is a certain unlikelihood about the Marines finding the survivors in the engine-room drying their clothes – it is hard to resist the conclusion that, in strict terms, Herbert's men committed a war crime.

It is too easy to forget that such transgressions regularly happened on the Western Front. A British private, tossing a Mills bomb into the middle of capitulating prisoners with the kindly instruction that they share it among themselves; a German machine-gunner, stitching bullets across a group of Tommies without weapons, running back to their own lines; a pilot shooting down an enemy with a jammed gun. Not every act observed the strict limits of the Geneva Convention.

Warfare is a brutal and degrading business. Those who fight the wars, who slaughter with bombs, with bayonets, with torpedoes, with bullets, make compromises. Only those who have faced the situation can sit in judgement.

The story of *U 27* crackled through the closed world of the U-boat crews. In the officers' clubs and seamen's bars, a new word passed from mouth to mouth. The 'beefs' used decoys. Trapships. The word was muttered, considered, repeated. U-Boot-Falle. One must be careful. Shoot first, if need be. Ask questions afterwards.

Herbert left *Baralong* to take command of the new British submarine *E22*. Gordon Steele went with him as the first lieutenant. *Baralong* acquired a new skipper and a new identity. Lieutenant Commander Arthur Wilmot-Smith, a regular officer, took command. *Baralong*'s name was obliterated. A new name would be decided later. In the meantime, she would sail with no indication of her previous identity. Wilmot-Smith promptly dropped the Admiralty and Foreign Office into a new squabble.

On 23 September 1915, Kapitänleutnant Claus Hansen and *U 41* despatched three freighters within twelve hours. At 0945, after checking the manifest and ordering the crew to their lifeboats, Hansen torpedoed the Sligo Steam Navigation Company's 4,792-ton SS *Anglo Columbian* with its cargo of 800 horses. The boyish-faced commander used an expensive torpedo rather than an economical deck gun, for he wanted the animals to die quickly.

At noon, the SS *Chancellor*, 4,586 tons, with a mixed cargo, met her end. She was one of twenty-seven ships of the Harrison Line to be lost during the war. A few hours later, as the light faded from the sky, the 3,363 tons of SS *Hesione*, owned by the Houston Line, crammed with motor vehicles, became the third victim. Frantic wireless messages from the three ships reached Falmouth. *Baralong*, now anonymous, left harbour for the scene.

An ochre-yellow sky hung over *U 41* at 0800hr the next morning. In the distance, dark blue-grey clouds raced towards the boat. Oberleutnant zur See Iwan Crompton, the U-boat's first watch officer, the 'Heinrich', handed over his duties and thought of breakfast. A buzz of well-being had run through the boat as she lay on the surface the previous evening to recharge the batteries. *U 41* had destroyed 12,000 tons of enemy shipping during a single day. The boat was on course for a record-breaking commission. Not that anybody in Germany knew of her successes. *U 41*'s wireless couldn't transmit that far. Nor receive. Claus Hansen and his men were blissfully unaware of Berlin's instructions to suspend all offensive operations in British waters.

Hailstones, the size of pigeons' eggs, battered *U 41* when the black clouds arrived. They bounced off the conning tower and steel hull. In the conning tower, the rattling sounded like the efforts of a demented drummer.

The hail went as quickly as it arrived. The wind freshened. The bridge sounded the alert. Another steamship, the Wilson Line's

SS *Urbino*, bound for England with a mixed cargo. Once her crew were in their lifeboats, *U 41* shelled 6,651 tons of merchantman to send her under the waves. Satisfied that she was doomed, Hansen gave the order to submerge. *Urbino*'s shipwrecked sailors would attract the next passing steamer. If she was an enemy, she would increase their tally.

'Auf Tauchstationen! Tauchtanken ausblasen. Auf zwanzig meter gehen.' The U-boat slid under the surface.

Urbino, listing badly and close to sinking, duly enticed another steamer. She came up at about 10 knots, the Stars and Stripes at her stern. A line of washing fluttered in the breeze. A typical 4,000-ton tramp, a mercantile workhorse.

'Auftauchen!'

U 41 surfaced. Hansen, Crompton, the chief engineer, Oberleutnant zur See Julius Schneider, and the helmsman, Steuermann Franz Godeau, climbed the steel-runged ladder, through the deck hatch, into the tower and on to the bridge. Crewmen doubled to their positions at the 88mm forward gun.

Hansen turned to Crompton. 'Notice anything special about her?'

'No.'

She was an obvious neutral. The flag of the United States adorned boards on each side of her grubby, black hull. On deck, a handful of sailors, in the usual shabby seamen's attire, lounged around.

Hansen hoisted a peremptory signal. The black and yellow flag of the International Code rattled up the halyards.

'Stop your vessel immediately.'

The new arrival lost speed.

'Bring your papers on board.'

The merchantman replied. 'I see your signal but do not yet understand its meaning.'

U 41 motored forward slowly. The steamer hastily swung to give a lee to the men who clumsily started to lower a boat. A menacing U-boat with a manned deck gun allowed no ambiguity. Especially at a range of 300m.

The men on the bridge watched the bumbling efforts with wry amusement. Yankee sailors were no seamen.

Without warning, the ship changed appearance. Men emerged from hiding. Men with rifles. Guns menaced *U 41*. Big guns. Which fired. *Baralong* was back in business.

The first shell smashed into the flimsy panelling of the forward dive tanks. Hansen screamed orders. 'Vorderes Geschütz Schnellfeuer! Beide Maschinen äusserste voraus!'

The deck gun barked. Below, the 850hp Germaniawerft diesel engines fought to drive *U 41* forward at full throttle.

An explosion near the forward gun. Godeau yelled at the crew to keep firing as Obermatrose Dieckmann toppled into the water. The helmsman jumped from the bridge to help the gun crew.

Baralong smacked another shot into the forward deck.

'Schnelltauchen!' The alarm bell shrilled throughout the hull. Only a crash-dive could save *U 41*. Compressed air bubbled out of ballast tanks. Godeau heard the clanging, shouted the order to the gunners. 'Alles auf Tauchstation! Schnelltauchen!' They ran, under fire, to the conning tower. The sooner they got below, the sooner their boat was out of peril.

All three guns on *Baralong* fired as fast as they could. A shell thumped into the conning tower. Crompton felt searing pain. Shards of metal and glass splinters from the periscope ripped into his head. He fell, barely conscious, down the ladder, through the hatch, slammed on to the deck of the conning tower well. He grabbed the periscope casing, clung on desperately as darkness overwhelmed him.

U 41 went down into the water, seeking safety in the depths. Oberleutnant Schneider clattered into the control room to his diving station. Godeau, the last man down the ladder, slammed shut the watertight hatch as the waves closed over *U 41*'s nose. Oberleutnant Crompton's body, huddled by the wrecked periscope, needed no second glance. If not already dead, it was merely a matter of time.

Five, ten, fifteen metres deep. The bows dropped, dropped fast, dropped more than the diving planes could counter.

Hansen called for damage reports. They were grim listening. The living quarters in the front section were taking in water. The auxiliary pumps struggled to keep the level from rising. The watertight doors prevented its spread but the weight dragged *U 41* steadily downward. The forward batteries, essential for underwater movement, were out of action. If the sea slopped over them, a new horror would stalk the boat. Chlorine. Poison gas.

Hansen blew the ballast tanks. It did not matter if he used all of the compressed air she had as long as the descent stopped. *U 41* continued to plunge towards the bottom. Her bow was down at a 30-degree angle. The depth-gauge needle quivered as it moved across the white clock face. Thirty metres. Forty.

Extreme dangers call for extreme measures. When Death's pinched fingers reach out to grasp a prize, it is better to try anything rather than simply submit.

Hansen gambled.

He left the control room, slithered down into the bilges where iron trim weights kept the boat on an even keel. A desperate solution to stave off disaster.

'Klar bei Sicherheitsgewichten!' Every man available would take as much ballast trim weight as he could carry.

'Alle Mann nach achtern!' Everyone aft. Weight the stern, bring up the bow. With luck.

'Pressluft auf Tank 6 und 7!'

The last of the compressed air hissed into the forward tanks. Anything to bring up the bow. Anything to stop the inexorable descent. Otherwise, *U 41* was their coffin.

Godeau, tight-voiced, called out the depth as *U 41* floundered.

'Funfzig Meter!' Fifty metres down. Her design depth. The hull creaked, a warning that Death was impatient. The needle moved on.

'Sechzig Meter!' Sixty metres.

'Siebzig Meter!'

'Achtzig Meter!'

'Dreiundachtzig Meter!' Eighty-three metres down.

U 41 steadied, stopped. Hung in the water.

'Noch Achtzig Meter!' Back to eighty metres. A faint note of hope in Godeau's voice.

Sluggishly, *U 41* rose. Slowly. The bow came up. Twenty degrees. Ten degrees. Horizontal. Closer to the surface. Forty metres, thirty, twenty. The problem, the big question was where the enemy were. They could be close. They could be in the distance. They might have left the scene altogether, confident that the U-boat was finished.

Ten metres. The air vents for the diesel engines would soon clear the surface. Once started, they could drive the main pumps, clear the remaining water from the dive tanks. With power, the boat could be controlled. Without it, the boat was helpless. Not even the periscope could be raised. Not that it any longer served a purpose. It was twisted metal and smashed glass.

Hansen needed a pair of eyes. A sharp order. Godeau climbed the ladder past Crompton's still body. Blood splayed across the floor. The helmsman opened the hatch, climbed on to the deck, peered out through the thick glass of the conning tower. *Baralong* was 3,000m distant, heading away from *U 41*. Even better, the diving tanks were just clear of the water. The diesels would work.

'Ausblasen mit Gebläse!' Hansen was now convinced that he could control the boat, at least on the surface. And with a working gun on the after deck, the trapship would discover that *U 41* still had a bite.

She broke into the fresh air and sunlight. Level. As Hansen uttered the command to start the engines, a wave broke over the bow. Directly over the living quarters. Enough water to bring disaster, to upset the trim, to destroy the hard-won buoyancy in a fraction of a second. The hungry sea rushed to claim its prize. The stern climbed high, its two screws, clear of the water, turned uselessly. The ocean stampeded in, through the damaged tanks. *U 41* plunged towards the seabed. Water drove the boat's air before it, compressing it just as it had in *Brandtaucher* years before. With the same result. The only way out was through the conning tower hatch. Like glugging bubbles from a bottle tossed into a pond, the air rushed to the surface, taking Oberleutnant zur See Iwan Crompton with it.

The cold water dragged him back to consciousness. Spluttering, coughing, bruised, battered, blind in his left eye, his wound a searing pain through his brain, instinct saved him. He swam towards the only ship he could see. The U-Boot-Falle, according to Crompton, turned away. For the first time, he claimed, he saw the White Ensign at her stern. Throughout the action, he later maintained, the decoy flew the Stars and Stripes.

Crompton's accounts of his experiences are those of an embittered young man. Both of his published works, in 1917 and 1941, bear the aroma of propaganda. Even so, much of his account is reinforced by others.

Supported by his lifejacket, Crompton floated in the water. The Q-ship returned. He raised his arms in a desperate signal for help. She swept past at speed. The crew jeered and cat-called, he claimed, although the identical allegation was made about the behaviour of the *U 41*'s crew by Captain Allanson Hicks when he and his men rowed away from the sinking *Urbino*.

Crompton had decided he was done for until his single eye saw a lifeboat. Empty, rolling gently in the swell. From the *Urbino*, left to drift by the rescued occupants. With a final effort, he struggled aboard. A cry for help drifted across the water: Franz Godeau. He, too, went through the conning tower hatch. He, too, was the target of jeers, whistles and cat-calls from the men of the *Baralong*. They had thrown anything to hand at him as they passed. Godeau believed the ship had tried to run him down.

Crompton held out his arms. Godeau grabbed them. With pushing, pulling, panting, the helmsman managed to get into the boat. Godeau, exhausted, sprawled at the bow end. Crompton crumpled in the stern.

Baralong returned. The two Germans managed to stand. They waved their arms. They must, they thought, have been mistaken earlier. It was impossible that the ship's captain would deliberately run them down. As they beckoned, the ship changed direction to head directly towards their boat. They saw a man in the bows who seemed to direct a sailor at the helm. She appeared to gather speed.

'Der will uns rammen!'

Godeau and Crompton tumbled over the side into the water. Crompton yelled to Godeau to make for the bow wave which would take them clear of *Baralong*'s screw. Both men went under, surfaced, spluttered, forced tired muscles to swim back to the lifeboat that bobbed furiously in the wash from the speeding vessel. They grasped its wooden sides, too weary to get back on board. Crompton could think only that it was a miracle the sea was so calm that he was able to cling on. Godeau finally hoisted himself back into the boat. Slowly, painfully, he summoned up the strength to help Crompton to climb in.

Baralong came back again. Her engines thudded less loudly. She slowed. A rope snaked down. The Germans were pulled to safety.

Wilmot-Smith, triumphant at his success so soon after taking command, ordered Corporal Collins to confine the prisoners in the sheep pen on the upper deck. This was sometimes used by crew members who couldn't sleep in the hot, confined messdecks below. With no doctor on board, no first aid was offered.

Collins, rightly or wrongly, believed the captain did not care if the prisoners died. The corporal had no great love for the enemy but there was a world of difference between hunting down the men who climbed on board *Nicosian*, men he believed were baby-killers, slaughterers of women, murderers, and two helpless prisoners.

The corporal did his best to make them comfortable. He offered cigarettes, fetched hot Bovril from the galley, made bandages from some clean shirts. He bathed Crompton's fearsome head wound, spread Vaseline on it and bound it up. As a final gesture, he curled up alongside the German officer to protect him from the chilly night.

At 2300, the first lieutenant woke Collins with a message from the captain.

'Is that German dead yet?'

'No, but he soon will be if he doesn't have any treatment.'

'Well, the skipper isn't going to take him into port. If he's not dead by midnight, you've got to shoot them both.'

Collins bridled. 'I can't do it, sir,' he answered firmly. He paused. 'What's more, I shan't give the order to any of my men.' Collins knew Royal Marines always listened to their own corporal before they took notice of a naval officer.

The lieutenant left. At midnight, he returned. 'It's been decided to take them into Falmouth.'

Marine Haywood noted:

2 am anchored outside Falmouth in Thick fog. 2 trawlers arrived with 40 cots for Wounded men and Seemed quite Disgusted that we only had one.

8 am Fleet Surgeon arrived and patched up the Germans.

12 noon all the shipwrecked crew disembarked and gave us a good cheer. 1240 entered Falmouth Harbour.

4 pm Cptn Filmore [sic] RN Cpt Trench RM and Lieut Com Brandon came on board and questioned prisoners.

Captain Valentine Egerton Bagot Phillimore, of Naval Intelligence, informed Wilmot-Smith that *Baralong* was henceforth *Wyandra*. Commander Vivian Brandon and Captain Bernard Trench would interrogate the prisoners. The captain's cabin was the most suitable place for the business.

Collins first escorted Steuermann Franz Godeau down below. 'Godeau', the corporal remembered, 'thought he was going to be shot because a marine was standing guard outside the cabin with a rifle and fixed bayonet.' With that prospect in front of him, the helmsman willingly answered every question put to him. Every detail. Every crew member.

Crompton was a different matter. Collins first asked the captain if he could borrow the captain's bath to wash off the caked blood, the caked salt, from Crompton's body. He received a short answer.

'That bloody German's not going to use my bath.'

A determined Collins proceeded to wheedle permission from the chief engineer to use his bath. A clean Crompton steadfastly refused to give any details other than his name and rank. Oberleutnants zur See, officers of the Kaiserliche Marine, did not cooperate with those who sent francs-tireurs to trap honourable warriors.

Crompton's ongoing story is a claim of primitive medical treatment, unsympathetic guards and all-round misery. He wrote to the US Embassy in London to protest about the misuse, as he believed, of the American flag. No reply came for, he alleged, the Embassy apparently did not receive his letters.

The matter was known in the Admiralty, however. Another *Baralong* incident. Fortunately, it could be kept under wraps. Until, that is, Crompton was repatriated as unfit. He arrived in Switzerland on 4 November 1916 and lost no time in telling his story.

Another German note. More outraged German papers. More ill feeling. And the specific charge from Berlin that the Royal Navy had orders not to rescue the crews of sunken U-boats.

The Admiralty flatly denied it. The war of words continued. Wilmot-Smith, decorated with the DSO for the destruction of *U 41*, submitted a report which skipped lightly over most allegations: 'Unfortunately . . . not knowing if they were to be trusted we had to pick them up; they could not have been left . . . in case they were picked up by a neutral ship.' And on the charge that *Baralong* deliberately tried to swamp the lifeboat, he wrote:

On approaching this boat my attention was temporarily distracted from the work in hand and I suddenly realised the ship had too much weight on. I immediately reversed engines, at the same time putting the helm hard a port. The boat was not struck by the ship and came past along the port side. The prisoners, however – when the boat in which they were – was some twenty yards from my bows, both dived overboard. The boat was in no way damaged.

Wilmot-Smith insisted that the two survivors were treated reasonably, given comfortable beds, with plenty of blankets, were issued with dry clothes and left alone. Nobody asked Corporal Collins for his version.

Baralong's log did not even mention the sinking.

The war went on. Some U-boat men decided that any trapship crews they caught would pay the price there and then. Q-ship men heard about the threats. Some carried poison in case they faced capture.

The Q-ships continued to duel with the Kaiserliche Marine. To the bitter end.

EIGHT

THE ACE IN THE HOLE

On 4 February 1915, the day after Cecil Foley Lambert suggested the use of decoy ships, Rear Admiral Henry Oliver, Chief of the Admiralty's War Staff, minuted the file:

One steamer is already operating on the Harwich, Hook of Holland route: she was finished fitting out about a week ago. A second steamer is being fitted out with guns now to commence duty in the English or Irish Channel. About two months ago a steamer was fitted out at Portsmouth and worked off Havre but it was evident she was not being run on the proper lines and she was paid off. There should be little difficulty in getting four more small steamers, the greatest difficulty is to get the right sort of Commanding Officer for an enterprise of this kind. The Commanding Officer in the steamer fitting now has been engaged in mine laying and blockade running, and is an enterprising man who will probably be a success.

Oliver's summary covered the dismal career of SS *Victoria*. The steamer on the Harwich route was, presumably, *Antwerp*, once *Vienna*. The ship 'fitting now' was apparently *Lyons*. Opinions changed about Gardiner, although he certainly showed enterprise both during and after the war.

The Admiralty had much to concern it in February 1915. The U-boat problem, essentially no more than a minor headache, came well down the list. The Grand Fleet, with its myriad requirements in personnel, fuel, rations, training and 24-hour readiness took highest priority, closely followed by the threat of hit-and-run raids in the Channel, now that the enemy occupied Zeebrugge. Zeppelin raids, the need for a myriad of small vessels for minesweeping and coastal patrols, a supply of ships and munitions to force the Dardanelles, the ongoing demands of the distant blockade, the Dover Patrol, mined steel nets to protect the Grand Fleet in harbour, all clamoured for attention. And, much as the Navy needed resources, the demands of the Army on the Western Front took precedence. Wars create priorities. Flanders came first.

The Admiralty largely discounted sustained U-boat attacks on merchant shipping. The Kaiserliche Marine had too few boats. They had done little damage to the British merchant fleet. Set against the available tonnage, the amount destroyed in the first six months of the war scarcely registered.

Mercantile trade would continue no matter how much the German wolf huffed and puffed. A State Insurance scheme, introduced at the start of the war, that paid compensation for goods and vessels lost to enemy action kept ships on the trade routes.

The Admiralty and the British government failed to realise that Germany had changed her mind. Once the ideal of a swift victory vanished, a new realism gripped the German military mind. Ruthlessness. Ruthlessness not merely against the obvious enemy but to embrace the neutral accomplices in Britain's cowardly attack on German trade.

Three factors determined whether the Kaiser's navy would win the battle of the high seas. The first was obvious. The U-boats must sink so many ships that Britain starved. The second component was morale. The risk of sudden death by explosion, of a slower death by drowning or exposure in open lifeboats or on life rafts, would deter men from sailing as merchant seamen. Without men, the ships stayed idle. Third, and most important, was world opinion, especially that of the United States. If the damage inflicted on the British outweighed the hostility of nations outside the conflict, the campaign could succeed.

In the last two weeks of February, the unrestricted campaign despatched thirteen ships. One a day. By the end of April, the handful of U-boats at sea had launched fifty-seven torpedo attacks without warning on merchant ships. Of these, thirty-eight brought sinkings, four severely damaged the target, and fifteen ended with the intended victim escaping unscathed. A further ninety-three ships came under surface attack. Forty-three escaped.

These losses did not alarm Whitehall. New ships on the slipways easily made up the deficit. Only a few noted the statistics. In the ten weeks or so of the campaign, five U-boats perished. But German yards also thrived. Another twenty-five U-boats joined the Kaiserliche Marine during the period. One hundred ships sunk, against five U-boats destroyed. Not the best of odds.

Decoys became the Admiralty's secret ace in the hole.

Logic suggested that a single authority should control decoys. This did not happen. Admirals proved touchy about their authority. Decoys in their area must report and belong to their command.

London showed some dismay when U-boats attacked the North Sea fishing fleets. Fish was a staple for many people. Cheap, nutritious, plentiful, with a range of helpful by-products, any interruption to supplies caused fierce annoyance. Trawlers and drifters proved easy prey for prowling U-boats.

The grey steel shape would rise from the depths. The deck gun menaced the unarmed fleet. Shouted orders led to abandoned boats. After helping themselves to fresh fish, the U-boat crews then sank the helpless targets. That some U-boat men asked the dispossessed fishermen to pass on greetings to friends and even family in England was a final thumb to the nose.

Armed trawlers appeared among the fishing vessels. On 5 June, *U 14*, under the command of Oberleutnant zur See Max Hammerle, attempted to sink *Oceanic II* near Peterhead. Unfortunately for Hammerle and his crew, the target returned fire. Surprised, Hammerle screamed for an emergency dive. In the ensuing panic, nobody flooded the forward tanks. *Oceanic II*, joined by another armed trawler, moved in for the kill. Hammerle went down with his boat. The gathering trawlers picked up the rest of the crew.

A more elaborate scheme originated in Beatty's 1st Battle Cruiser Squadron at Rosyth. His secretary, Paymaster Frank Spickernell, suggested that a trawler tow a submarine, the two in contact by a telephone cable. When a U-boat surfaced, the trawler would inform the submarine of the course and behaviour of the enemy. The British submarine would then slip the tow and sink her enemy.

Beatty was enthusiastic. With him, enthusiasm reaped results. He placed the submarine *C24* under the control of Admiral Sir Stanley Colville, the Admiral Commanding Orkney and Shetland. Colville was already busy fitting out a personal fleet of decoys. Like Beatty, he seized upon the paymaster's idea with relish.

A genuine Aberdeen fishing boat, the *Taranaki*, set out with *C24*. On 23 June, about 50 miles off Aberdeen, Kapitänleutnant Gerhard Fürbringer and *U 40* sighted the tethered goat. Complex tricks sometimes have problems. *Taranaki* told *C24* of the new arrival. The submarine found herself unable to slip the tow. In desperation, her commander told the trawler to cut the cable at her end.

Yard upon yard of cable and telephone cord swirled in the water. *C24* struggled to maintain her trim as the wires came close to fouling her screws. Luckily, Fürbringer and his companions on the bridge were distracted by reactions on board *Taranaki*. *C24* neatly put a torpedo into *U 40*'s hull, just beneath the conning tower. Fürbringer and the bridge watch were the only survivors.

Less than one month later, on 20 July 1915, the trawler and submarine combination struck again. *Princess Louise* and another C Class submarine, *C27*, met *U 23* at 0755hr, close to Fair Isle. Oberleutnant zur See Hans Schulthess opened fire from about a mile as he took his U-boat across the trawler's bows. *Princess Louise* warned *C27*. Seconds later, the telephone wire snapped. *C27* released the tow and surfaced. She fired a single torpedo at *U 23*. Without success.

On *Princess Louise*, a panic party pretended to abandon ship. As the boat swung out on its davits, a second torpedo from *C27* scored a bull's-eye, a few feet aft of the U-boat's conning tower. Four officers and six men of the Kaiserliche Marine survived, Schulthess among them.

Despite two successes, the decoy trawler and submarine ploy had limited use. Seaworthiness proved a major problem. A submarine tow needed calm seas. Despite the size of the Royal Navy and the relative obsolescence of C Class submarines, demands for their services were legion. Further, the trick had a limited life. Genuine trawlers hauled in their nets every two hours or so. Decoys could not both fish and tow at the same time. After a couple of narrow escapes, U-boat captains studied their target extremely carefully. No fishing meant a trapship.

With Beatty's support and Colville's enthusiasm, decoys, proper Q-ships that operated on their own, soon roamed the seas. In the north, armed trawlers patrolled. *Quickly* and *Gunner* met a U-boat. Despite apparently being hit by some 12-pounder rounds, and the dropping of an explosive charge, the U-boat escaped. *Quickly* was commanded by Captain James Startin, RNR, the Senior Naval Officer at Granton in the Firth of Forth. Startin was a former vice-admiral who cheerfully dropped several notches in rank to come back into service.

On 20 July 1915, Colville sent a 370-ton collier, *Prince Charles*, to look for U-boats. She carried a naval crew of one officer, one petty officer and seven ratings in addition to her regular merchant seamen. Her captain, Lieutenant William Mark-Wardlaw, had precise, particular orders from Sir Stanley:

The object of the cruise is to use the *Prince Charles* as a decoy, so that an enemy submarine should attack her with gunfire. It is not considered probable, owing to her small size, that a torpedo would be wasted on her. In view of this I wish to impress upon you to strictly observe the role of decoy. If an enemy submarine is sighted, make every effort to escape. If she closes and fires, immediately stop your engines and with the ship's company except the guns' crews who should most carefully be kept out of sight behind the bulwarks alongside their gun (and one engineer at the engines), commence to abandon ship. It is very important if you can do so to try and place your ship so that the enemy approaches you from the beam. Allow the submarine to come as close as possible, and then open fire by order on whistle, hoisting your colours. It is quite probable that a submarine may be observing you through her periscope unseen by you and therefore on no account should the guns' crews on watch be standing about their guns.

Mark-Wardlaw observed his instructions to the final full stop. Near North Rona Island in the Outer Hebrides, *Prince Charles* met *U 36* on the surface, close to a hove-to coaster in Danish markings. In a textbook display, Mark-Wardlaw pretended to notice nothing amiss. *U 36* fired a warning shot. Mark-Wardlaw stopped, blew three blasts on the ship's whistle, ordered his panic party away and stood by. Kapitänleutnant Ernst Graeff came closer. At 600yd from *Prince Charles*, he turned broadside on to sink the collier at leisure.

Mark-Wardlaw opened fire. His two guns, one 6-pounder and one 3-pounder, both missed with their first salvo. The German gunners ran for safety as *U 36* tried to crash-dive. The second shots hit the mark, some 20ft aft of the conning tower. Graeff's escape attempt resulted only in the U-boat presenting her other side as a target. *Prince Charles* steamed towards *U 36* in high excitement, firing all the while. The U-boat lifted vertically out of the water, hung motionless for a moment, then slid to the bottom of the sea.

Fifteen of the crew, including Graeff himself, were rescued. Mark-Wardlaw received a DSC, subsequently upgraded to a Distinguished Service Order. The crew received a bounty of £1,000 to share among themselves.

The *Prince Charles* flew the Red Ensign during the engagement. In purely technical terms, she was thus a pirate as she was not commissioned as a warship.

But all that really mattered was success. On 15 August, the armed trawler *Inverlyon* met *UB 4* off Yarmouth. The U-boat came from the Flottille Flandern, based at Zeebrugge. Oberleutnant zur See Karl Gross commanded a boat designed for coastal attack rather than deep-sea killing. He had only two torpedoes. *Inverlyon* let him come to within 30yd before she showed her teeth in the shape of a single 3-pounder gun.

A few days earlier, on 11 August 1915, a similarly disguised trawler, the 61-ton *G&E*, saw off *UB 6*, another Zeebrugge-based boat. Oberleutnant zur See Erich Häcker and his crew escaped with a shaking.

When *Baralong*, in her turn, sent *U 27* and *U 41* to the bottom, the Admiralty congratulated itself. The U-boat menace was on the wane. Attacks tailed away although that had nothing to do with the Royal Navy's endeavours.

A shortage of U-boats and crews slowed the campaign just as politics intervened. World indignation at the *Lusitania* sinking increased when news of the *Arabic* encounter, suitably filtered, reached the papers.

Bethmann-Hollweg, never a supporter of the U-boat offensive, was in cahoots with Admiral Georg von Müller, the Chief of the Naval Cabinet, who served as the normal conduit to Wilhelm II for the Kaiserliche Marine. Müller, a total abstainer, considered himself something of an artist. He also enjoyed the company of pacifist-minded friends. He was thus no crony of Tirpitz.

The pair worked on the Kaiser. The Unterseeboote may have sunk ships but the results were less impressive than hoped. Worse, all-out U-boat action badly hurt Germany in the diplomatic war. Their efforts met success. On 27 August 1915, Kaiser Wilhelm II ordered that, in future, passenger steamers were to receive a warning. They could be sunk only if passengers and crew were not in danger.

Lack of boats and crews. Political pressure. The two factors forced the U-boat offensive to a crawl from a canter. In June 1915, fifteen boats were at sea. By the end of August, it fell to eight. Five raiders went on patrol in September. During October, the North Sea and Flanders Flotillas mustered only four boats at sea. The next month, they had three. In December, four boats went out. They all came from Zeebrugge.

Things would change. The din sounded day and night as the shipyards in Kiel, Bremen, Hamburg and Danzig moved into top gear. In the Wilhelmstrasse, a mood of determination ran through the German Naval Staff. Bethmann-Hollweg and von Müller were old women. The

U-boats were Germany's maritime steel fist. Steel fists delivered knock-out blows.

If the war began to go against Germany, if some desperate throw of the dice were needed to knock out one of her potent enemies, the U-boat campaign of 1915 pointed firmly in one direction. Enough U-boats, given free rein, would decide the war.

By autumn 1915, the Royal Navy believed it had the measure of the U-boat with its decoy ships. The Admiralty pressed ahead with more trapships. The expansion needed commanding officers of quality, together with dedicated crews. This was a problem. Whatever the War Staff might demand, the administrators of appointments and postings worked to their own arcane rituals. A quick skim through an officer's file revealed whether he would be happier away from the flinty gaze of authority.

For Gordon Campbell, the call came in the nick of time. His tenure as a destroyer captain did not go well once the war began. His command of the elderly HMS *Bittern* was limited to a dreary round of escort duties and routine patrols. The 225 destroyers of the Royal Navy all worked hard. Most were relatively modern but even the ninety-eight that were more than a decade old possessed a nifty turn of speed. Their engines, though, did not retain a fierce reliability.

Campbell discovered this in September 1915, when he pursued a mysterious ship that ignored his signals. *Bittern*'s engines, pushed to their limit, gave up the fight. She hobbled back to harbour at a miserable 4 knots. No consolation came with the revelation that the stranger was a British seaplane carrier.

A bored Campbell, having reached his time advancement to lieutenant commander, wanted excitement before the war finished. He volunteered for a Persian Gulf gunboat command to support the Indian army in its disorganised Mesopotamian campaign. When that failed, he asked for an appointment to a Harwich-based destroyer. They, at least, had a chance of meeting the enemy when they patrolled the bleak waters of the North Sea. Gunboats and modern destroyers were not on the Admiralty's agenda for the lieutenant commander. His career had not sparkled. His service record held some unfavourable comments from his seniors. They were not necessarily fair comment, but fairness is not a word always found in military dictionaries.

The Admiralty plucked Campbell, his deputy, Lieutenant W. Beswick, RNR and other officers from their files. 'Special service' beckoned.

It promised, the selected few learned, action, adventure and glory. Campbell went to London for an interview about his mysterious new duty.

He was to serve under Vice-Admiral Sir Lewis Bayly at Queenstown in the south of Ireland. The Queenstown ships patrolled the Western Approaches, the vital seaway between the Atlantic and the Irish Sea. Bayly had no doubts about the value of decoys. Sailing ships or steamers both had their uses:

> I entirely agree with the principle of disguising armed ships as the best means of sinking submarines. The armed yachts, sloops and trawlers are excellent for protection of trade, rescuing crews and passengers, escorting etc., but except in thick weather or at night, their chance of getting close to a submarine is small. What at first is not apparent, though very real, is that the appearance of our sloops, armed yachts, and trawlers very often frighten the submarines away from the area in which they are working, and save the ships which are in, or approaching, that area, though none except the submarine knows or will know that such a thing has happened.

Bayly was content that U-boat crews knew that decoys existed. That knowledge alone deterred attacks. Few U-boat captains used several thousand Reichsmarks' worth of torpedo on a sailing ship or a small steamer. They were prey for deck guns. If decoys were known to be on patrol, enemy skippers would hesitate to attack. The innocent would escape.

The admiral, like many senior officers, had no time for those he considered fools. Neither did he hesitate to slice his way through thickets of inconvenient regulations. He also, like many an admiral or general, had his blind spots. Campbell took meagre comfort from another officer's comment that Bayly would either make him or break him.

By mid-October, Queenstown – or 'Q', as it was known to the Navy – supported several decoys. *Glendevon* and *Chevington*, both colliers of around 4,000 tons, converted to transports, ploughed up and down the Irish Sea. These two new arrivals, like their predecessors, carried a merchant crew and navigating officer who served under a commanding officer appointed by the Admiralty. Regular or reservist ratings made up the gun crews.

Queenstown probably gave its name to the decoys it served. Q-ships became a quick and easy way to refer to the jumble of steamers that always anchored in remote parts of the harbour. No proof exists, although the Services' common use of abbreviations makes a strong case as to its origin. In due course, the Admiralty gave known decoys Q-numbers, a relatively short-lived system.

The two colliers had little success. They sailed a fixed route, already well guarded by Bayly's regular patrols.

The Admiralty, in contrast to Bayly, felt that the highest secrecy should attach itself to Q-ships and their doings. Captains received stern warnings that their crews, both Service and mercantile, should say nothing about any combats with U-boats. The less the enemy learned about decoys, the more they might speculate. If U-boat captains became wary of every tramp steamer, gave each one the benefit of the doubt, more would survive.

Campbell returned to Devonport. There he waited for his new command. After some days, she sailed into Plymouth Sound from Cardiff. SS *Loderer*, a dirty, scruffy creature of some 3,000 tons, filled with coal, was a long way from a smart destroyer or a hulking battlecruiser.

The civilian crew took their discharge. A casual order came from the Admiral Commanding the Devonport dockyard to 'fit her out'. Instructions seemed non-existent, although three 12-pounder guns and a machine gun arrived with the injunction that he was to ask for no more weaponry. The demands of war elsewhere took priority.

In his own account, Campbell claimed that his only instructions from the Admiralty were to go to Devonport to await his ship. He added that nobody ever told him he was to hunt U-boats. Either Campbell could not resist a joke or his trip to London was an elaborate waste of time.

Beswick had shared the inglorious episode on board *Bittern*. His prewar merchant experience with the Ocean Steamship Company, more familiarly known as the Blue Funnel Line, proved valuable as *Loderer* assumed her disguise.

Before any work started, Campbell fumigated the ship. He professed that she was incredibly dirty if not verminous. After that essential task, dockyard workers fitted the guns. The heaviest of the 12-pounders sat on the centreline of the ship, arranged to swivel to either side. A dummy steering engine-house that collapsed when the ship went into action concealed it from curious eyes. The other two went one to each side. A broadside would thus be of two guns.

The sides of the ship where the guns bore were cut and hinged. When *Loderer* went into action, the flaps collapsed. The machine gun lived in an apparent hen-coop on the boat deck, close to the funnel. This, too, fell away when needed.

Campbell was nobody's fool. He took on board a large supply of paint to alter funnel markings overnight. He ensured that all the deck stanchions could be moved. He built some dummy boats, which similarly changed position during the hours of darkness. Spare cowls and ventilators appeared and reappeared. Other fittings, including a telescopic main mast, added to *Loderer*'s ability to transform herself into a totally different beast.

Despite an apparent air of secrecy, *Loderer*'s conversion attracted common dockyard gossip. The changes were hard to explain away. *Loderer* was not, in any event, the only ship under modification. At least seven other vessels changed from innocent steamers to armed decoys at about the same time.

For some reason, the Admiralty became agitated if the ships' identities became known. As decoys changed their name and appearance at sea, the peremptory order for *Loderer* to change her identity as her purpose was known appears superfluous. Campbell complied. As *Farnborough*, she duly entered the hall of fame.

The arrival of a batch of decoys in the waters around the British Isles in the autumn of 1915 hardly registered with the Kaiserliche Marine. The U-boat arm had problems of its own.

The policy of warning liners and sinking them only if the passengers were in no danger severely inhibited the campaign against Britain's trade. Under it, U-boats sank an average of 100,000 tons of British shipping every month. This formed a tiny bite into a mercantile register of some 20 million tons but it destroyed ships at twice the current rate of replacements.

Admiral von Pohl believed that the Kaiser's less than iron resolution hamstrung the underwater arm. Even without a deliberate slackening of the offensive, the shortage of U-boats forced the campaign to dwindle.

The euphoria that accompanied great successes obscured another problem. Men like Valentiner, who racked up some 75,000 tons of destruction in his 25-day patrol in August, were an exception. Of thirty U-boats that took part in the 1915 onslaught, just ten sank ten or more ships, if tiddlers are ignored. Of the ten, only *U 20* (Schwieger), *U 28* (von Forstner), *U 38* (Valentiner), *U 39* (Forstmann) and *U 41* (Hansen) destroyed twenty or more. Thirteen commanders managed a mere five or less kills. The Kaiserliche Marine could only hope that the less successful improved as time passed.

The cost of sending nearly 750,000 tons of British and Allied shipping to the ocean floor was the loss of twelve deep-water boats. Four of the prefabricated UB and UC boats also failed to return to harbour. The UB were coastal craft; the UC were minelayers that carried no torpedoes. They formed the backbone of the Flanders Flotilla that operated from Ostend and Zeebrugge.

Nine new boats came from the shipyards. Together with the survivors of the campaign, nineteen boats were available to bring Britain to surrender. More joined as each month passed.

The U-boats caused considerable difficulties to the Royal Navy and its allies. They operated with little hindrance in the Channel and the Western Approaches. The number of vessels in the Dover Patrol and on guard elsewhere rose steadily. Many had the sole task of hunting U-boats. They enjoyed limited success. Further support came from more than 2,000 vessels of the Auxiliary Patrol. The waters around Britain were patrolled by 691 armed trawlers and drifters, 270 minesweepers, 156 motorboats, 786 net drifters, and a further 198 trawlers and drifters with the sole task of boom defence.

The U-boat men held most of the cards in a deadly game. Their hunters, the destroyers, the armed trawlers and, indeed, the Q-ships suffered in bad weather. U-boats simply vanished beneath the surface for a while if the weather became too rowdy.

The Admiralty took many months to learn that U-boats operated independently over long distances. They were positive that U-boats used secret bases in remote spots around the coastline. Stolid country constables solemnly checked sales of petrol at rural garages close to the sea, even though U-boats used diesel oil. Similar reasoning suggested that, if no bases existed, U-boats replenished fuel and ammunition through a Teutonically efficient network of heavily disguised merchant ships. These fantasies were ably accelerated by sighting reports from warships, merchant vessels, enthusiastic coast watchers, imaginative boy scouts and practical jokers. Whales, dolphins, floating bottles, bits of wood and seals all became U-boats for the happily credulous.

The cessation of the all-out campaign around the British Isles sent the U-boats to the Mediterranean. There they wreaked havoc. Pickings were easy. Kapitänleutnant Otto Hersing and *U 21* had shown how to do it in the waters around the Gallipoli peninsula. Far fewer neutrals sailed in the Mediterranean, a factor that reduced the risk of further offending a touchy America.

Not only German actions upset the United States and other uncommitted countries. Washington knew too well that a considerable proportion of its population came from German stock. In November 1915, America complained that Royal Navy ships, enforcing the blockade, repeatedly broke international law. They followed up this criticism with a further observation, in January 1916, that arming merchant ships simply demonstrated the Law of Unintended Consequences. U-boat commanders did not trouble to surface, stop, visit and search their targets. They torpedoed them without warning.

Britain ignored the suggestion. Merchant ships had been armed in time of war as long as anybody could remember. Clear proof existed that armed merchantmen dissuaded U-boat attack.

In a neat attempt to regain the initiative, and to put Q-ships in the wrong, Germany promptly and publicly issued instructions that all armed merchant ships should be treated as warships and sunk without warning as long as the guns were visible.

Even at the end of 1915, neither side believed the war would drag on without respite. On both sides, Army commanders convinced themselves that one more offensive, one more effort, one more plan that corrected earlier mistakes, would bring victory. Both sides had absorbed the lessons of the 1915 campaigns. They knew how to win the war on land.

The German army prepared to strike the final blow in the west, against the French at Verdun in early 1916. The German Chief of the General Staff, Erich von Falkenhayn, anticipated a sweeping success that would destabilise and dishearten the Allies. If French armies disintegrated, Britain's growing strength would be dissipated in a desperate attempt to hold the line.

At sea, the strategic situation had not changed. The Hochseeflotte remained numerically inferior to the Grand Fleet. But German naval officers believed, even more firmly, that she still possessed the weapon that could win the war. Das Unterseeboot.

The Royal Navy still had no means of finding U-boats in the wide seas. New weapons, new technology, though, offered a glimmer of hope. The first depth charges, primitive efforts simply tossed overboard, were on their way. They came into service in January 1916. One, issued to the larger and faster ships, contained 300lb of explosive. Smaller ships used a version with 120lb. Both varieties employed a hydrostatic pistol to explode them at either 40 or 80ft.

The other weapon in the armoury was the hydrophone, intended to detect the sound of U-boats under the waves. Crude, unrefined, lowered into the water from a stationary ship with stopped engines, it achieved little. Even if the operator heard a submarine, he had no idea where it was. Nonetheless, it was an advance.

As 1915 faded towards the history books, three men met in Berlin. Grossadmiral von Tirpitz, the War Minister, General von Falkenhayn and Admiral Henning von Holtzendorff, the newly appointed Chief of the Naval Staff. They agreed that a new U-boat campaign was necessary. The USA might be hostile but that was a matter for the civilians to resolve. Militarily, nothing stood in the way. Destroy the French at Verdun. Roll back any attempt by the British to help. Starve England to death.

Holtzendorff believed that Britain could be beaten inside six months. Twice as many boats were in service than a year earlier. The newest were much better. They went faster, dived more quickly, had greater reliability, a longer range and, most important of all, carried more torpedoes. Boats ordered early in the war were coming into service. An average month commissioned ten new boats, more than enough to compensate and expand the striking force. In 1915, the Unterseeboote had fought a reasonably successful campaign, even though their numbers went down. Larger flotillas would drive Allied shipping from the oceans. If, as was eminently possible, the U-boats destroyed over 600,000 tons a month, British resistance would collapse.

On 4 March 1916, a decisive meeting in Berlin reviewed the course of the war. On land, everything looked good. Russia was a spent force. Serbia was crushed. On the Western Front, the Verdun attacks showed signs of success. The British had made no gains in 1915. There was every expectation that they would fail again in 1916, despite their new commander, the dour, deliberate and highly competent Haig. On the other hand, they would defend their lines with a fierce pugnacity in the face of German attacks.

All in all, the military situation was most satisfactory, even if outright victory remained tantalisingly out of reach. The economic scene presented a far gloomier picture. The British blockade against the Fatherland clamped like a vice. Few quarrelled with the assessment that the Allies could hold out longer than Germany and her supporters. The mainstay of Allied endurance was England, damnable England. She had to be brought to her knees. The conclusion was clear, as von Holtzendorff summarised. 'We are not wrong in assuming that an injury inflicted upon England that persuades her to regard peace as preferable could force the others to peace as well. England can be hurt only by war on her trade.'

Neutrals would have to like it or lump it. If the United States joined the war, so be it. The generals and the admirals agreed. American entry could be contained. The politicians felt otherwise but reluctantly acceded to the decision. A campaign that observed the Prize Regulations would begin on 15 March 1916. This would melt into unrestricted warfare by the U-boat arm on 1 April 1916.

Bethmann-Hollweg remained sceptical. He continued to argue against the military conclusions. He doubted if the U-boats, dedicated as they were, could really destroy 4 million tons of Allied shipping inside six months. Even if they could, he doubted that that alone would force the British to negotiate. Further, the results of the 1915 offensive did not necessarily validate a new campaign. England, fighting for her life, would undoubtedly resist 'to the last man and the last penny'. She would surely produce new methods of combating U-boats, increase her shipbuilding, perhaps seize German ships in neutral ports. And, he argued, it was no simple matter to dismiss the United States. Apart from any other consideration, she would give fresh heart to the enemy if she joined the conflict on their side. Conversely, American involvement would depress German morale.

The Kaiser agreed. The campaign was postponed while German diplomats tried to persuade Washington to use its influence to relax the British blockade.

While the German High Command pondered, a handful of boats from the North Sea and Flanders Flotilla went to war. Among them were *U 68*, on her maiden war patrol, under the command of Kapitänleutnant Ludwig Güntzel of the Hochseeflotte Flottille IV, and Oberleutnant zur See Herbert Pustkuchen with his *UB 29* from Zeebrugge.

In the Irish Sea, a shabby merchantman tramped along the sea lanes. His Majesty's Ship *Farnborough* was ready for action.

NINE

TARGETS FOR THE PLUCKING

Lieutenant Commander Gordon Campbell spent the months after October 1915 in bringing HMS *Farnborough* up to standard. She was, after all, a properly commissioned warship in the Navy of His Majesty King George V. An enquiring mind at the Admiralty had realised that *Baralong* and the others, pressed into service without such formality, were, in legal terms, nothing less than privateers, even pirates.

Fighting under the Red Ensign, as opposed to the white, was a slightly dubious procedure. Enemy reactions suggested that francs-tireurs might be the most polite term bandied around by a German court-martial board. No rule existed, however, that forbade grubby tramp steamers from service under the White Ensign. 'HMS' replaced 'SS' to solve any niggling legal doubts. Later in the war, the defensive arming of merchant ships quietly ignored the problem.

One side-effect of commissioning decoys into the Royal Navy was that the mixed service and civilian crew disappeared. Every man either joined the Royal Naval Reserve or left the ship. This draconian approach had a financial benefit. Decoys often had living conditions to depress the brightest. The ship carried, in essence, twice its typical complement. Under normal conditions, many sailors thought their living space improved on the slums of their boyhood. With doubled-up crews, even this consolation vanished.

The Admiralty had the answer. 'Hard-lying money' compensated sailors whose conditions were below the minimum provided in normal service. As this inducement often doubled the wages of an ordinary seaman, decoy crews pocketed the cash, grinned and got on with the job.

The virtual cessation of offensive U-boat operations resulted in weeks of fruitless cruising for *Farnborough*. Campbell, though, was no Godfrey Herbert. His world-weary freighter hid a tightly regulated crew who practised their roles time and time again. Campbell believed in discipline and training. He took extraordinary care to present his ship as harmless.

He transmitted wireless signals to fictitious owners, claimed faulty engines or broken steering in the hope that a listening U-boat would investigate.

Each day, Campbell plotted every report of U-boat activity to help him guess where the enemy might go. On 20 March 1916, Campbell read a report of a U-boat west of Ireland. He gambled that she would probably try to sight one of the lights at the south-west corner before setting off for her patrol area. He set *Farnborough* on an interception course.

When morning came, on 22 March 1916, Campbell was off the west coast. *Farnborough* flew no colours while she pounded northwards toward the Arctic Ocean at a steady 8 knots. The Outer Hebrides lay some 120 miles to the east.

At 0640hr, when the grey dawn had not yet turned to daylight, the port lookout glimpsed something on the horizon, 5 miles distant. Campbell's binoculars showed a U-boat, barely surfaced. He sounded action stations and signalled Queenstown: 'From *Farnborough*. 6.40. Hull of submarine seen. Position, latitude 57° 56' 30" N, longitude 10° 53' 45" W.'

Minutes passed. The U-boat submerged.

Farnborough held her course, a neutral on her way north. The few men on deck puffed idle cigarettes, lounged, chatted.

Twenty minutes slid past. From the starboard side, a torpedo wake bubbled towards the *Farnborough*. Every man tensed. Every man relaxed fractionally as the track slithered under the forecastle. The first torpedo fired in anger from *U 68* failed.

Campbell sailed serenely onwards. A neutral tramp, he reasoned, would not keep a sharp eye open at the end of a long night. Every man waited for another torpedo strike. Kapitänleutnant Ludwig Güntzel had other ideas. Water seethed to *Farnborough*'s port side as *U 68* surfaced. Her gun crew sprinted forward. A shot banged across the water to splash ahead of the tramp. The cautious U-boat promptly submerged in case her prey tried to ram her.

Farnborough's Morse sputtered across the ether to Sir Lewis Bayly. '7.5 Ship being fired at by submarine.'

Campbell's carefully rehearsed crew immediately went into action with a sparkling performance. Steam billowed. Engines idled. The panic party scrambled across the deck to lower the lifeboats, pushing, jostling, in well-simulated alarm.

U 68 surfaced, ahead, on the port side. She closed towards *Farnborough*'s bow, showing her full length, 800yd distant. Her deck gun barked again. The shot fell mere feet from *Farnborough*'s magazine. *U 68* came on, conning tower and deck gun manned, ready to deal a death blow.

Campbell reacted smartly. The next shot might blow him, the ship, and the remaining crew to eternity. He blasted a whistle, the prearranged signal for action. The White Ensign broke at the masthead. Wheelhouse and side-ports clattered down. Three 12-pounders, the Maxim and a selection of rifles stormed into action.

Campbell's deck guns pushed out twenty-one rounds as *U 68* crash-dived. One gun alone managed twelve shots. The machine gun and supporting rifles fired about 200 rounds at the gun crew and conning tower. *Farnborough* thrashed towards the spot where the U-boat went down. Deck crew rolled two primitive depth charges into the water.

Even as they spiralled into the depths, *U 68* appeared, almost vertical in the water, as *Farnborough* steamed forward. The after-deck gun crew saw the torn bows, slammed two further shots into the stricken boat. Two more converted mines plopped into the water. Debris boiled to the surface. Shards of wood. Oil. Wreckage. No bodies. Güntzel went to the bottom with the thirty-seven men of his crew.

Campbell's wireless buzzed another message to the Commander-in-Chief. '7.45 Have sunk enemy submarine.'

Twenty-five minutes dragged by. *Farnborough*'s signals interrupted the Admiral's breakfast. Sir Lewis did not hurry. Another signal came to his table. '8.10 Shall I return to report or look for another?'

Bayly's answer was short and specific. 'Very well done. Please return to Queenstown.'

The Admiral might not have relished the stream of messages that disturbed his attack on his eggs and bacon and intruded into the toast and marmalade if they reported dismal failure instead of success. As it was, Sir Lewis declared jovially that *Farnborough*'s signals were as good as a morning paper. When Campbell docked the next morning at 0700, the Admiral's barge arrived with a letter of congratulations and some fresh-laid eggs. Two hours later, Bayly arrived in person to congratulate the crew. Campbell's tight discipline and strict observance of procedure had proved that decoys could deal with U-boats.

Farnborough went back on patrol. She returned after one week. The Admiral came on board again with a letter of commendation from the Admiralty. He promulgated Campbell's accelerated promotion to commander. He announced the award of £1,000 for division among every man on board, regular Royal Navy officers aside. There was only one of them on the decoy. Commander Gordon Campbell.

Bayly also brought news of immediate medal awards. Campbell received the Distinguished Service Order. Beswick, the first lieutenant, collected a Distinguished Service Cross, as did the engineer lieutenant. Three Distinguished Service Medals went to crew members.

Oberleutnant zur See Herbert Pustkuchen and *UB 29* had already added a new twist to the maritime war. To sink passenger ships without warning was, as every U-boat captain knew, strictly forbidden. The Flanders Flotilla found a loophole. In that hard-fighting organisation, orders stated clearly that surface ships heading for Channel ports during the hours of darkness were deemed military transports. In short, legitimate targets.

On the night of 19 March 1916, Pustkuchen followed his orders. He torpedoed three anchored ships in succession. One French, one Norwegian, one Danish. Four days later, in daylight, he set an angry cat among some pigeons.

The French-registered cross-Channel ferry SS *Sussex* took a torpedo strike. She did not sink, but some fifty men, women and children on her crowded decks died in the explosion. Others were injured, among them American citizens. On the return journey to Zeebrugge, 4 miles off Dungeness, Pustkuchen used his final torpedo on the 3,352-ton SS *Salybia*.

The case for a renewed offensive gained momentum when von Pohl died suddenly in April 1916. The redoubtable Admiral von Scheer took over the High Seas Fleet. Aggressive, determined, vigorous, he had no doubts that the U-boat would triumph.

Unfortunately for the exponents of unrestricted U-boat attacks, political and diplomatic pressures were stronger. After news of the *Sussex* attack crossed the Atlantic, that part of the American press that was pro-Ally screeched in banner headlines. The President, Woodrow Wilson, a man who cherished the notion that he saw, with unerring clarity, all sides of an argument at the same time, declared it 'a truly terrible example of the inhumanity of submarine warfare as the commanders of German vessels for the last twelve months have been conducting it'. His convoluted sentence was replaced by the measured tones of the US note of 19 April 1916 to Berlin. This stopped just short of being an ultimatum but nobody could mistake its meaning. 'Unless the Imperial German Government shall now immediately declare and carry into effect its abandonment of the present method of warfare against passenger and freight carrying vessels, the Government have no choice but to sever diplomatic relations with the German Government altogether.'

Deliberately irritating the United States to the point of war was not part of Germany's war agenda as far as the politicians, and a weather-cock Kaiser, were concerned. On 20 April, all U-boats received emphatic instructions to adhere strictly to international law. In other words, stop, visit, search. Destroy only if they were bound for an Allied port.

Scheer did not tolerate such specious nonsense. Rather than hazard the High Seas boats, he recalled them from the Western Approaches. Only the Flanders Flotilla very occasionally continued to operate in British waters. They had few boats with any offensive capacity. Their efforts hardly rippled the water.

Every U-boat man knew that the British used decoys. Not only the *Baralong* affair alerted them to the ruse. Campbell, the careful, determined victor, gave away the information through no fault of his own because of an incident on 15 April 1916.

A thick mist that reduced visibility to 2 miles covered the swelling Atlantic waters off the south-west coast of Ireland. As dusk approached, at 1830hr, a U-boat surfaced to challenge the Rotterdam-Lloyd Company's 7,000-ton steamer SS *Soerakarta*, bound from Java to the Netherlands. In the distance, another steamer approached. *Farnborough*, steaming northward, flying the Swedish ensign, saw the Dutch ship on her starboard bow. The U-boat floated between the two ships. She hoisted a signal. 'T A F', the commercial flag code for 'Bring me your papers'.

Soerakarta acknowledged, stopped. She began to lower a boat. Campbell in *Farnborough* also replied. 'Signal seen, but not understood.' The decoy slowed, blew off some steam to give the impression that she was losing way, but continued to sidle ahead. The deck crew prepared to lower a boat.

The U-boat fired a warning shot across *Farnborough*'s bows. A Dutch eye-witness, Second Officer R.R.F. Jeneson on the Dutch ship, claimed that *Farnborough* opened fire when approaching the scene. He stated clearly that *Farnborough* was already in action before 'a Navy flag' broke out at her foremasthead.

Campbell's report does not mention the matter. He merely states that the U-boat fired first, at which one of his gun crews assumed the order had been given to engage the enemy. *Farnborough* thus returned fire only after she herself had been attacked, a nicety that cleared tardy hoisting of the White Ensign, should anyone query the matter.

The action was short and apparently decisive. Twenty rounds came from the 12-pounder guns, six from the 6-pounders and 250 shots from the small arms on *Farnborough*. The U-boat managed some five shells in reply. Two hits registered near the conning tower before the U-boat went down. Some saw her go down by the stern. Others noted she sank by the bow. For some, she rolled to her left. To others, she revolved to her right. One witness positively saw her turn over, before she plunged under, covering the sea with oil.

From *Soerakarta*, the first mate recorded his own impressions:

At about 6.15 pm . . . a dark shape appeared on the surface. . . . It gradually became clearer and when we got closer, it was obviously a U-boat, marked with a large white 'U'. The conning-tower hatch opened and about ten men appeared on deck. The German war ensign was hoisted on a short mast and underneath were the signal flags: 'T A F' (bring your papers on board). As soon as the U-boat was recognised, the engines of the *Soerakarta* were stopped and, after the signal was acknowledged, the port lifeboat No. 1 was manned and lowered once the ship's deed box with the papers was handed over. The boat had just left the ship, to row across to the waiting U-boat, when the accompanying steamer – which had also slowly stopped and we eventually saw the signal 'I shall send a boat' – suddenly hoisted the English war flag and fired a shot. The shell flew over the U-boat and fell into the water. The engines of the *Soerakarta* were put to slow astern to get out of the way of the line of fire. We were barely 200 metres from the U-boat. They fired back meanwhile as the English steamer approached. Several shots missed, some falling 40 to 50 metres in front of our bows, until the U-boat's conning-tower was hit. Several men on the deck hurriedly tried to go inside while four or five suddenly vanished; probably they were hit or fell into the water. On the *Soerakarta*, we saw the stern of the U-boat rise and then quickly sink away, leaving a large patch of oil on the surface at the spot where it went down.

The steamer responsible was, to outward appearance, an ordinary merchant ship, hull painted black above and brown below, black funnel with a wide, white band. Rear amidships, there were guns, hidden by the bulwarks.

Campbell dropped two depth charges. They exploded. *Farnborough's* crew saw no oil. No wreckage bobbed to the surface. Campbell doubted he had scored a kill.

The U-boat indeed survived. She was *U 67*. Her commander, Kapitänleutnant Hans Nieland, had been in charge of the boat for less than a month. As soon as Campbell opened fire, Nieland bellowed the order to crash-dive. Her war diary gives a slightly different scenario from that of *Farnborough*:

Black Rock Light abeam to port, distance 19 nm.

Surfaced and sighted two steamships, one to port, the other to starboard, on converging courses. Closed with steamers and signalled them to stop. Order carried out. Ship to starboard is flying the Dutch flag and painted in Dutch colours. The name *Soerakarta* is painted on her side in large letters – according to Lloyd's Register she is a steamship of the Rotterdam Lloyd line. She is empty. The vessel to port is flying the Swedish flag but displaying no national colours, has one funnel with a white ring, seems to have a yellow bridge, 2 masts, with lowered derricks fore and aft. Size around 4,000–4,500 tons.

Both ships have stopped and are about 5,000–6,000 metres apart. I signal 'Send papers' and stand off the Swede at about 3,000 metres. After a while with no response, I fire a shot across the Swede's bows. At the same moment she opens fire on me with a gun mounted broadside below the funnel (7–10 cm). Shots initially fell very short, but with a rapid rate of fire. Alarm, crash-dive. The last observed shot fell about 100 [metres] short, aft of the boat. Impact could be heard very clearly aft in the boat. At 20 metres [depth], violent detonation close to the boat, at 25 metres another detonation, presumably from charges dropped by the steamer on the presumed position of the boat. I had ordered an immediate and sudden change of course. Descended to 35 m. The steamer flew the Swedish flag while she fired and it was not hauled down as long as we observed her. It is likely that, in addition to the broadside gun, she had another gun aft. It seems she is a trapship, like the *Baralong*. I think it unlikely that she was working with the Dutchman.

Safely away, *U 67* surfaced to inspect for damage. 'We find that no. 3 port diving tank has been hit at the waterline. The longitudinal seam is leaking badly and the tank cannot be blown.'

Kapitänleutnant Nieland was convinced that *Farnborough* still flew the Swedish flag when *U 67* crash-dived. The Kriegstagebuch, the war diary of *U 67*, contains a drawing of *Farnborough* in her neutral disguise. *U 67* returned home safely to spread the story of the English decoy.

When *Soerakarta* reached Rotterdam, the crew told their tale to anybody who cared to listen. The Dutch press spread the news. Nobody could doubt that the British used disguised ships to patrol the sea lanes.

Despite the uncertainty of *U 67*'s fate, Bayly at Queenstown was swift to declare that the U-boat's demise was 90 per cent probable. The Admiralty duly coughed up a further £1,000 for the crew. Bayly further gave them all six days' leave, starting when *Farnborough* arrived at Plymouth. In a sudden reversion to tight-lipped secrecy, he advised that it was 'undesirable to allow Special Service vessels to give shore leave in the ports near which they operate, as it is not possible to prevent the men's conversations giving away the nature of their employment.' It was a precaution without purpose. Q-ships were no longer a secret.

British observers comforted themselves that Campbell saved *Soerakarta* from a watery end. As she was an empty neutral on her way to her home port, she was probably in no danger under the Prize Regulations. Nieland might, though, have decided that a neutral that unloaded her cargo of tin and rubber at Falmouth was better off at the bottom of the sea.

The US note effectively brought the U-boat campaign in British waters to a halt. Operations in the less dangerous Mediterranean continued. Five German boats of the 30s Class operated from Austrian ports. The tactics of Flottille Pola pioneered by Kapitänleutnant Lothar von Arnauld de la Perière in *U 35* cut a swathe through Allied shipping. In the Mediterranean, 'stop and search' tactics were hardly necessary. Most heavy merchant shipping belonged to belligerents. As Allied defences against U-boats were all but non-existent, von Arnauld's methods paid handsome dividends. On the surface, some 5,000 or 6,000m from his quarry, he would fire a warning shot. Once the crew abandoned ship, he would cautiously edge forward to within 2,000m, usually in the vicinity of the abandoned vessel's lifeboats. This move alone inhibited possible resistance from his target. A few well-aimed shots from the deck gun, commanded by a first rate gunlayer, settled the matter.

Arming merchant ships helped stem the depredations. Q-ships, British, French and Italian, had little success. In the last six months of 1916, German and Austrian U-boats sank 256 ships, a total of 662,131 tons.

But success in the Mediterranean would not win the war.

Scheer continued to demand unrestricted U-boat warfare. He considered it absurd not to employ a weapon to the utmost of its ability, and he carried his ideas into practice. The full-strength sortie that he planned for May employed airships as well as U-boats. The latter came both from the Hochseeflotte and Flottille Flandern. His aim was to draw out the Grand Fleet to a position where its superior strength was neutralised.

The weather intervened. Scheer's plan did not fully develop. The sortie became the Battle of Jutland.

Captain Charles Fryatt, master of SS *Brussels*, met the Kaiserliche Marine once more on 23 June 1916. En route from the Hook of Holland to Tilbury, this time he had no chance to ram or escape. A squadron of torpedo boats from Zeebrugge intercepted him in the North Sea. They escorted *Brussels*, with its cargo of food and some unfortunate Belgian refugees to the home of the Flanders Flotilla. Fryatt found himself at the business end of a court martial. The day after his execution, an official statement, with echoes of the *Baralong* affair, came from the German authorities on 28 July 1916:

> The accused was condemned to death because, although he was not a member of a combatant force, he made an attempt on the afternoon of March 20, 1915, to ram the German submarine *U 33* near the Maas lightship.
>
> The accused, as well as the first officer and the chief engineer of the steamer, received at the time from the British Admiralty a gold watch as a reward of his brave conduct on that occasion, and his action was mentioned with praise in the House of Commons.
>
> On the occasion in question, disregarding the U-boat's signal to stop and show his national flag, he turned at a critical moment at high speed on the submarine, which escaped the steamer by a few metres only by immediately diving. He confessed that in so doing he had acted in accordance with the instructions of the Admiralty.
>
> One of the many nefarious franc-tireur proceedings of the British merchant marine against our war vessels has thus found a belated but merited expiation.

A high-quality spat followed. Arthur Balfour, formerly a prime minister, now First Lord of the Admiralty, took up the cudgels. In a cold analysis, he drew attention to U-boat 'pirates', stating that it was not illegal to try to stop an aggressor. He added, with a touch of mystery, that 'there was a suspicious character on board the *Brussels*, who spoke German fluently, and was afterwards treated with the utmost consideration by the Germans'.

Balfour played the patriotic card. Fryatt's 'British courage', he stated, 'revolted at the thought of surrender.' The captain had the 'undoubted right under international law' to disregard the U-boat's commands and to resist.

A German reply wasted no words. After a swift reference to the Admiralty bounty, the statement continued that it 'was not an act of self-defence, but a cunning attack by hired assassins'. He received the death sentence 'because he had performed an act of war against the German sea forces, although he did not belong to the armed forces of his country'.

Q-ship sailors wondered how they would fare if captured. Wearing a GER jersey offered a short cut to the cemetery. Claims to be servicemen rang hollow without proof. Those who had acquired poison capsules fingered them thoughtfully. Nearly all accepted the Admiralty's offer of a silver-coloured lapel badge that told the world they were on war service. Whether this would impress a court of hard-nosed German naval officers was, luckily, never put to the test.

After *Farnborough*'s encounter with *U 67*, more decoys entered service. Most people in the know believed that they were the only possible countermeasure to the U-boat. Evidence that clearly armed merchant ships inhibited U-boat attack was ignored.

Q-ships enjoyed success only if a U-boat operated the 'surface, stop and search' policy. Once the secret was out, once every target was regarded with suspicion, the decoy's effectiveness fell away.

In April 1916, Rear Admiral Henry Oliver noted that fourteen regular decoys and two decoy transports were in use. Six decoys worked the Mediterranean. The others served in home waters.

Efforts were made to make the decoys almost unsinkable. Although wood was in short supply, timber replaced cargoes of coal. That had the unenviable habit of spontaneously combusting if undisturbed in airtight holds for weeks on end. Buoyant cargoes would, it was hoped, allow the Q-ship to stay afloat long enough, if hit, to destroy her attacker.

In the days after Jutland, one of the more elaborate, ingenious and, to some, half-witted ideas in the decoy ship and U-boat war came from the fertile imagination of Commander Reginald Henderson, serving with the

Grand Fleet's 2nd Battle Squadron. His ship, the 22,000-ton dreadnought HMS *Erin*, was originally built for the Turkish navy as the *Reshadieh*. Requisitioned on the personal instructions of Winston Churchill when war began in 1914, her seizure pushed Turkey closer to life as a German ally.

Henderson's idea, sublime in its simplicity, was to disguise an armed trawler as a downed airship, complete with crew dressed in German uniforms. The trawler would sail immediately after a Zeppelin raid. No U-boat captain would ignore fellow countrymen in need of rescue. A British submarine would accompany the trawler. When the U-boat surfaced, the British vessel would despatch her with a well-aimed torpedo if the trawler failed to sink the enemy.

The outlandish scheme received the wholehearted support of Sir John Jellicoe himself. Scapa Air Defences constructed the fake, using kite balloon envelopes and fabric. Henderson would command the trawler, the *Oyama*, on the venture.

The scheme ignored some pertinent questions. Not least was the legality of British sailors, masquerading as German aviators on board an airship with German markings, opening fire on a German vessel engaged on a rescue attempt. Even if that were discounted, the distinct possibility remained that the U-boat might win. The trawler crew would be fortunate not to be shot out of hand.

The bizarre contraption began its patrol on 27 August 1916. The next morning, *Oyama* turned and made for home. In anything other than a flat calm, she was almost impossible to manage. Henderson reported to Jellicoe, who noted that the experiment would not be repeated.

Among the new decoy vessels were a number of sailing ships, equipped with an auxiliary engine to help if they met a U-boat. Their proponents believed that their innocent appearance would lull suspicion. More practical were specially adapted Flower Class convoy sloops and the P Class patrol boats. One of the early Flower vessels, the *Begonia*, survived a torpedo attack from Kapitänleutnant Paul Wagenführ and *U 44* in the Atlantic on 29 March 1916. She stayed afloat and was towed to Queenstown, where the dockyard rebuilt her to resemble a cargo vessel. She duly reappeared in August as *Q10* with all her weapons hidden from view.

Subsequent convoy sloops under construction took on the look of small merchant steamers, a reasonable disguise for the 1,250-ton ships. All had guns hidden behind false plating, a major disadvantage.

It prevented training the guns on the target before they revealed themselves. Convoy sloop commanders demanded rangefinders to compensate, a military item that would immediately alert a U-boat commander. Even so, several of the class served as Q-ships or Special Service vessels.

The first forty-four, 660-ton P Class patrol boats were precisely that. Twenty others received modifications to resemble coastal steamers during building. Unofficially, they became known as 'PQ boats'. Their official designation was PC Class patrol boats.

For the German staffs, both Army and Navy, unrestricted U-boat warfare remained a vital issue. Scheer was firmly in favour. So, too, was von Holtzendorff, the Chief of the Naval Staff. The politicians and some of the Naval Staff itself were firmly opposed. They doubted the sweeping claims made for unfettered use of the U-boat arm. More importantly, they had the ear of the Kaiser.

By the end of July 1916, astute observers concluded that the German army, that fearsome fighting machine, needed some help. Falkenhayn's great scheme at Verdun had failed. No breakthrough happened. The German army had suffered enormous casualties. It had indeed drawn the British into battle – not at Verdun but on the Somme, further north. The fighting there dragged Germany into a battle it did not want. German reserves dwindled.

On 30 August 1916, a conference at Schloss Pless emphasised the divide between the two points of view. Falkenhayn was not present. He lost his job as overall commander in the west as a consequence of Verdun and the Somme. In his place, in the very act of picking up the reins, were the awesome pair Feldmarschall Paul von Hindenburg and General Erich Ludendorff. They had conquered on the Eastern Front. Now they had come to work their genius in the west. They joined Admiral Eduard von Capelle, Admiral von Holtzendorff, the Chancellor Bethmann-Hollweg, the Minister for War, Adolf Wild von Hohenborn, the Minister for Foreign Affairs, Gottlieb von Jagow and the Minister of the Interior, Karl Helfferich.

The familiar arguments trotted out. To remove England from the war was essential. The way to achieve this was to cut her lifelines. Without supplies, England would wither.

Holtzendorff dismissed the threat of the United States entering the war. If she did, it made little short-term difference. The Americans would take a long time to influence the fighting on the Western Front. In any event, America did not supply Germany because of the British blockade.

Germany had to cripple English trade. The U-boat was Germany's ace card.

The politicians did not agree. If the United States entered the conflict, the inevitable result was eventual catastrophe for Germany and her supporters. Unrestricted U-boat warfare made that a real possibility. Further, to give the U-boats free rein might lead to other neutrals joining the Allied cause. The Netherlands and Denmark might intervene.

Holtzendorff scoffed. Two weeks of torpedoes would keep them in line. With some scorn, Holtzendorff enquired icily of the Chancellor if he had any alternative to an unrestricted U-boat onslaught. Bethmann-Hollweg had: a negotiated peace. And the best man to approach was Woodrow Wilson, the twenty-eighth President of the United States. Britain was not popular with many nations. In America, many businessmen believed that her blockade was designed to cripple American business, to grab the customers for American exports for herself. Diplomacy, Bethmann-Hollweg argued, was a better weapon than the 21cm torpedo or the 10.5cm deck gun.

Caution came from the Army. Hindenburg, never one to reach a hasty decision, believed that too many uncertainties existed. No firm decision could be taken until the situation was clearer. Neither the field marshal nor the general had even seen the Western Front. Neither had any moral scruples about the conduct of the war. American intervention, if it came, could be dealt with. But Romania was a problem. It was another burden on the Army. If Dutch and Danish troops also took the field, it might be the final burden that broke the German army.

Bizarre as this thought seems, nine decades later, the two men had a valid point. Indeed, within days, at a conference at Cambrai on 7 September, they learned the frightening truth. The western armies must go on the defensive. Morale had fallen. The slaughter at Verdun, the pressure of Haig's armies on the Somme, suggested to the German soldier that the war could not be won.

Bethmann-Hollweg quickly proposed a compromise. The decision would be postponed until the Romanian campaign was settled. In the interim, the U-boats would follow the Prize Regulations.

Everyone agreed. Meanwhile, preparations for a more ruthless approach, including the building of more U-boats, could go ahead.

Only days elapsed before Army minds changed. Ludendorff knew that victory did not come from crouching behind defences. But the land war needed help. As he later recalled, 'the enemy's great superiority in men and matériel would be even more painfully felt in 1917 than in 1916. They had to face the danger that "Somme fighting" would soon break out at various points on our fronts, and that even our troops would not be able to withstand such attacks indefinitely, especially if the enemy gave us no time to rest and for the accumulation of matériel.'

With the Army on board, the unrestricted warfare wagon gained speed. Bethmann-Hollweg faced increasing pressure as months passed. Fears about Romania swiftly vanished. The German offensive flattened her. By December, the streets of Bucharest were under German martial law.

Public opinion in Germany fully supported unleashing the U-boats against the hated English. The blockade hurt badly.

Bethmann-Hollweg's idea had one major drawback. Any peace settlement must reward Germany for its enormous sacrifice of both blood and money. No treaty that failed to give the Kaiser's Reich control of Belgium and other conquered territory would be acceptable. It took no great effort to realise that Britain and France would find those proposals outrageous. Moreover, as it was, Woodrow Wilson was too concerned with fighting the coming November election to consider European matters.

Germany's only hope was victory, even if it were not outright. Her lifeblood was soaking into the mud of Flanders and of France. At home, the Allied blockade created continual problems in munitions production as well as forcing rationing on a country unused to shortages.

Scheer agreed to let the High Seas boats practise restricted warfare. Sent out on patrols to find warships, they received permission to attack merchant ships in the North Sea. The Flanders boats both sowed mines and attacked ships. A steady stream of Allied merchantmen went to the bottom.

The Naval Staff, basking in the approval of the Kaiser, ordered Scheer to unleash all of his boats, except for a few to defend the Heligoland Bight. Even though they were to observe the 'stop and search' rules, every effort was to be made to destroy England's trade.

The U-boats were to act against merchant ships, even if these were armed, in accordance with the Prize Regulations. 'Incidents', the Naval Staff emphasised, 'that may lead to well-founded claims by neutrals are to be avoided at all costs. Commanding officers are thus to act with the utmost caution and exactness. In cases of doubt, the ship is to be allowed to pass.'

Even with restrictions on U-boat attacks, British and neutral losses in October 1916 reached 353,600 tons.

The Germans would have been immensely heartened if they had been privy to Jellicoe's concerns. Writing from Scapa to the Admiralty on 26 October 1916, he stated that the 'very serious and ever-increasing menace of the enemy's submarine attack on trade is by far the most pressing question of the present time.' He went on with the gloomy prophecy that the losses could eventually force Britain to accept peace terms 'which the military position on the Continent would not justify and which would fall far short of our desires'.

Jellicoe continued to pile on the gloom. Current methods of combating U-boats no longer met with success. New weapons and new methods 'must be provided with great rapidity'. He wanted to form a committee of younger officers who had shown inventiveness and originality to work under an energetic senior to explore every possible means of beating the looming menace of the U-boat. There should also be a reorganised system of shipping routes, a diversion of labour to the shipyards and the possible use of the Grand Fleet's own destroyers to patrol the seaways. This would mean dismantling one battle squadron but it was a price that must be paid. Four days later Jellicoe was in London, summoned to a meeting of the War Committee of the Cabinet.

Arthur Balfour, First Lord of the Admiralty, summed up the naval position: 'Of all the problems which the Admiralty have to consider, no doubt the most formidable and most embarrassing is that raised by submarine attack on merchant vessels. No conclusive answer has yet been discovered to this mode of warfare; perhaps no conclusive answer will ever be found. For the present we must be content with palliation.' This cheerful assessment was made while forty-seven decoy ships that ranged in size from drifters and trawlers to medium-sized steamships roamed the seas in search of any one of the 119 U-boats in the service of the Imperial German Navy.

The First Sea Lord, Admiral Sir Henry Jackson, and the choleric Admiral Sir Henry Oliver, Chief of the War Staff, curtly dismissed the suggestion from David Lloyd George and Andrew Bonar Law that the Royal Navy introduce a convoy system. With the not too gentle implication that politicians did not understand the practical complexities of warfare, the admirals explained that merchant ships could not keep together; that a convoy presented one extremely large target instead of a myriad of small ones; not enough fighting ships existed to serve as convoy escorts, for each merchantman would need its own. The best solution, they added, was to arm each merchantman and let them fend for themselves.

The Royal Navy had successfully convoyed ships in time of war since the time of Napoleon and before. The principle was already proven. The battle fleet itself, troopships and transports and other vessels of high importance, went in convoy. One escort per ship was plainly ludicrous but neither Lloyd George nor Bonar Law felt able to argue the point.

Interestingly, Admiral Henning von Holtzendorff would have supported the Admiralty's policy. The English, he declared, would not adopt convoys. Heavy weather, inexperienced merchant captains, the need to travel at the speed of the slowest vessel, allied with congestion in ports, would prevent its adoption. More than anything, convoys 'would be a most welcome sight' for U-boat commanders. Plentiful targets for the plucking.

At Queenstown, Sir Lewis Bayly fiercely supported his Q-ships. He wanted the best for them. He had already successfully campaigned for extra pay for men on Special Service. Now, certain that the secret of decoys was well known to the Germans, he suggested to the Admiralty that the crews should be volunteers. He had already crossed swords with Whitehall about officers and men chosen for Q-ship work. 'At present,' he had written, 'officers and men appear to be drafted without any selection for the special duty.' A further grumble about the appearance of officers who reported for decoy service drew the smart retort from Whitehall that they always sent the best officers available, adding that 'officers appearing in a cheap ready-made suit may not always give an impression of smartness. RNR officers do not carry plain clothes with them, and when detailed for Q-ships, have very often to get a suit at a moment's notice.'

Cheap suits notwithstanding, Bayly had a point. The Admiralty would never send the best officers to grubby steamers in the hope that they might find a U-boat. The cream of the crop went to the Grand Fleet. Special Service work came well down the list of desirable and career-enhancing postings.

The Admiralty agreed to call for volunteers. On 26 December 1916, the call went out. To discourage first lieutenants from emptying their ships of troublemakers, commanders-in-chief were requested to select suitable men and ask them to volunteer. Vacancies existed for 320 seamen, 350 stokers, 40 engine-room artificers and numerous 2nd and 3rd class gunlayers. The candidates learned that the proposed duty was 'special service against enemy submarines; that it is dangerous, at periods monotonous, and not free from discomfort'.

First lieutenants, delegated the task by harassed seniors, duly responded. Calls for applicants for a mysterious 'special service' gave them a heaven-sent opportunity. Ridding a ship of a few King's hard bargains was sensible and practical. Ratings with less than perfect records were encouraged to step forward. To offset them, applications came from many excellent men who were bored with watching clouds and seagulls in the Orkneys.

One brief success for decoy operations lit up the darkness. On 30 November 1916, the Q-ship *Penshurst*, commanded, remarkably, by a retired officer, Commander Francis Grenfell, sank the Zeebrugge-based *UB 19*.

Her captain, Oberleutnant zur See Erich Noodt, seemingly made a basic error on his first patrol as a U-boat commander. *Penshurst*'s panic party left the ship in the approved manner. Noodt closed on the boats to seize his quarry's papers from her master. The Marineamt wanted proof of sinkings rather than the claims of U-boat crews. Noodt strayed too close to *Penshurst*. He apparently intended first to read her name. It was a fatal mistake for eight of his crew. The Q-ship opened fire from a range of just 250yd. Noodt's cry to crash-dive came too late. *Penshurst*'s second round hit the engine room and crippled the U-boat. No fewer than eighty-three rounds smashed into the 40m length of *UB 19*.

Just two U-boats had succumbed to Q-ships during the whole of 1916. The paucity of results was disguised by the number of actions decoys had fought. Nearly every one resulted in a claim for a boat sunk or badly damaged. Both medals and rewards accompanied actions when higher authority decided a U-boat had been destroyed or badly damaged. Wishful thinking, the excitement of combat, led to an often unconscious embellishment of combat reports. Shells splashing short of a U-boat hull could easily be mistaken for direct hits. Men in a conning tower who had vanished when the spray cleared must have been killed.

The four winter months from October 1916, riddled with bad weather, saw the loss of nearly 1¼ million tons of British and Allied shipping.

The holiday had ended. The Unterseeboote had opened shop once more. And, soon, they would have unrepeatable offers.

TEN

VERY GOOD PIECE OF WORK.
WELL DONE

As midnight approached on 31 December 1916, a single British artillery piece near Ypres fired a single round into enemy lines. A pause. Nine more erratically timed shells. Another silence, followed by seven more. A welcome to the New Year from the Royal Artillery. The German guns did not reply. The war went on. On land. In the air. At sea.

In Berlin, the admirals had won the struggle against the politicians. The Chancellor's peace initiative had foundered. A boastful overture to a peace proposal, delivered in the Reichstag on 12 December 1916, trumpeted that Germany and its partners 'had given proof of their indestructible strength'. A written version was duly delivered to the Allies six days later. It gave no indication of the terms that Germany might accept.

Woodrow Wilson made his own appeal. He asked all belligerents to state their aims and the terms on which they were prepared to end the fighting.

In the House of Commons, on 19 December 1916, Lloyd George ensured that any political hopes died. He declared: 'There has been some talk about proposals of peace. What are the proposals? There are none. To enter at the invitation of Germany, proclaiming herself victorious, without any knowledge of the proposals she proposes to make, into a conference, is to put our heads into a noose with the rope end in the hands of Germany.'

Britain's response pleased the militant faction in Berlin. Another conference took place at Pless. This time, the Kaiser listened to the men in uniform. One of those present recalled:

Everyone stood around a large table, on which the Kaiser, pale and excited, leaned his hand. Holtzendorff spoke first, and, from the standpoint of the navy, both well and, above all, confidently, of victory. England will lie on the ground in at most six months, before a single American has set foot on the continent; the American danger does not disturb him at all. Hindenburg spoke very briefly, observing only that from the measure a reduction in American munitions exports had to be expected. Bethmann-Hollweg finally, with a visible inner excitement, set forth once again the reasons that had led him in the past to cast an opposing vote against a U-boat war beyond the limits of cruiser warfare, namely concern about the prompt entry of America into the ranks of our enemies, with all the ensuing consequences, but he closed by saying that in view of the recently altered stand of the Supreme Command and the categorical declarations of the admirals as to the success of the measure, he wished to withdraw his opposition. The Kaiser followed his statements with every sign of impatience and opposition and declared that unrestricted U-boat warfare was therefore decided.

Hindenburg's assessment sobered Wilhelm and several others. The war, the field marshal declared, 'must be brought to an end rapidly'. Although Germany could hold out, her Allies were crumbling.

The conference agreed. The U-boats came off the leash on 1 February 1917. Neutrals would receive some concessions during the first days of the new policy. From 13 February, however, every ship in the blockade zones around Britain and in the Mediterranean would be considered an enemy vessel to be attacked without warning.

The Royal Navy was already cock-a-hoop when Germany announced the new policy. U-boats were no match for Q-ships. On 14 January 1917, in the late afternoon, *Penshurst* made another kill. Again, the victim came from the unfortunate Flanders Flotilla.

Oberleutnant zur See Paul Günther and the crew of *UB 37* were cautious men. They watched the 'panic party' leave. And held back. Unlike Noodt in *UB 19*, Günther resisted temptation. He stood off at a range of some 750yd. The U-boat fired fourteen shots at the decoy. Two shells found the target. They killed two men and wounded two others.

Penshurst had to reply as enemy shells splashed around her. At 1624hr, she fought back. With some luck and a great deal of skill, the Q-ship's first round from her 12-pounder gun demolished the base of the conning tower. An explosion, possibly of stored ammunition, blew away part of the tower. Black smoke rose into the air. The 12-pounder's second shot crashed into the hull just aft of the bridge. *Penshurst's* starboard 3-pounder gun also scored direct hits. *UB 37* reared like a dying horse and sank into the water.

Bayly's decoys, operating out of Ireland, managed several encounters. Each one, seemingly, met with success. The admiral himself believed that his ships destroyed four U-boats in the first four weeks of January. Among the faulty claims came one from HMS *Aubretia*, a Flower Class convoy sloop. To her commander's chagrin, details of his exploit appeared in German propaganda. Not only did the U-boat escape unharmed but her commander stoutly maintained that the Danish flag was flown throughout the fight. Once again, Berlin declared, it was 'one of those shameless cases in which English steamers misuse the neutral flag in the most ruthless manner as U-boat traps'.

Despite the reasonable conclusion that the U-boat returned safely home, the Admiralty merely reduced *Aubretia*'s claim of 'definite' destruction to 'possible'. The £1,000 award reduced to £200.

The U-boat men knew how to tackle trapships. Commanders of the big deep-water boats often adopted von Arnauld's tactics. With their larger guns, they usually outranged Q-ship weapons. The decoys needed bigger and better guns – which were more difficult to disguise or hide.

In Germany, Scheer issued orders that considerably altered the tasks of the Hochseeflotte. Every part of his command was to support the U-boat offensive. He wrote:

We now enter a new stage of the war in which the U-boat arm is to resolve the situation by strangling British economic life and maritime connections. Every means of naval warfare must be put into the service of our U-boat operations. This will, obviously, principally apply to the light forces and auxiliary units charged with escort and minesweeping duties. However, the situation created by opening unrestricted U-boat warfare will have to be taken into consideration for the employment of the Battle Fleet as well.

The new tactics did not become immediately evident. Most of the deep-sea boats on patrol during the bitterly cold month of February 1917 continued to follow the Prize Regulations. When the campaign began, eleven boats from the High Seas Fleet roamed the seas of the South West Approaches and the Bay of Biscay. Seventeen smaller boats of the UB I and UB II Classes spread across the waters of the English

Channel, the Irish Sea and the North Sea. The Flanders Flotilla sent five minelayers on patrol. Between them all, they destroyed thirty Allied merchant ships in the Western Approaches and the English Channel alone during the first week of February.

With so many boats out, Q-ship chances of an encounter rose. It was a haphazard business. With no means of detection, the decoys relied on guesswork, wireless messages and the captain's instinct. Sailing the merchant sea lanes brought either exciting results or excruciating monotony. The decoys enjoyed one small advantage. Although knowledge of the trapships had spread through the U-boat fleet, many commanders believed that they could sort maritime sheep from goats.

On 31 January 1917, Commander Gordon Campbell and *Farnborough*, with a full crew and the ship's lucky black cat, steamed out of Plymouth after a refit. The previous Number One, Beswick, stressed out by decoy work and, possibly, a demanding captain, had left. The new man was another RNR officer, Lieutenant Ronald Neil Stuart.

Stuart's war, since he left the Allan Line to volunteer, had been one of boredom. Like his skipper, he spent long, grinding days, weeks, months on patrol duties in an ancient destroyer. His, at least, was the name-ship of the Opossum Class. A Victorian relic, she spent almost as much time under repair as on local flotilla duties. For Stuart, operating out of Devonport just as Campbell had done, the war was no more than a grinding routine of reporting 'stray logs and boarding Dutchmen'.

His efforts to transfer to any job that even hinted at action and excitement got nowhere. Even the Royal Naval Division, fighting in the trenches of Flanders, had no vacancies for an RNR deck officer. Then his luck changed. Soon after the *Soerakarta* incident and Beswick's departure for hospital, he met Campbell. And Campbell needed an efficient Number One.

German intentions to fight a ruthless U-boat war filled the papers for days. Kaiser Wilhelm, with his usual excited exuberance, wanted great results. 'We will frighten the British flag off the face of the waters,' the All-Highest threatened, 'and starve the British people until they, who have refused peace, will kneel and plead for it.'

The Unterseeboote prepared to oblige their Emperor.

Decoy tactics, Campbell believed, must change. The new German policy of an all-out campaign demanded a different approach. Campbell concluded that the only way to convince a U-boat commander to surface was deliberately to take a torpedo strike. If a wake was sighted that looked as if it would go across the bow, *Farnborough* would increase speed. The trick was to manoeuvre the ship so that she was hit. With luck, the deck guns would still be able to fight on. In the face of the threat, every risk was acceptable.

Farnborough headed for her favourite hunting ground, south-west of Ireland. Campbell calmly disregarded standing instructions to dock after ten days at sea. He conveniently ignored three signals that ordered his return to port. *Farnborough* would stay out until empty coal bunkers forced her return. Fresh food and nerve-straining duty came second to a chance to engage the enemy. For chance there was. Staccato Morse chattered into the wireless room with depressing regularity. Calls for help from sinking ships. It was a matter only of time before *Farnborough*, now officially Q5, attracted a prowling U-boat. So Campbell hoped.

On 17 February, still with coal in her bunkers for four more days, at 0945 on a clear, fine day, *Farnborough* steamed eastward towards the Irish Sea, impersonating a cargo tramp homeward bound from North America. A weary Red Ensign flapped from her stern. Campbell wanted to be torpedoed. To the north-east, some 40 miles distant, County Cork enjoyed the winter sunshine. Nothing disturbed the calm sea. Even sharp eyes missed the slender line of a distant periscope. Kapitänleutnant Bruno Hoppe and *U 83* were on the prowl.

The torpedo came in from the right, at long range. Campbell made no attempt to avoid it. At the last possible moment, however, he swung the helm hard over so that it missed the engine room. The torpedo smacked into number 3 hold instead. Water poured into the ship.

Campbell's cool response saved the lives of men down below in the engine room. With the exception of the engineer sub-lieutenant who suffered a slight injury, everyone else on board escaped unharmed. The blast did knock over the captain and several men and blew the cat into the water.

Campbell's crew was almost too well disciplined. As Campbell stood up, he saw a group of his panic party, lazily looking over the side, smoking, laughing, doing nothing. Rehearsed only to go into their charade when the order came, they still waited for the instruction.

Campbell gave it.

The boat party went into frantic pantomime. One boat, partially lowered, was allowed to hang. The deck crew rushed to another one. Eventually, two lifeboats and a dinghy made it to the water. The periscope that poked up some 200yd away saw the remarkably fat chief steward pushed over the side in the mêlée. Unable to support himself on the rope, he crashed down into the waiting boat, landing on top of the men already there. Any watcher could see that it was unrehearsed. Finally, the 'master', distinguished by his gold-banded hat, left the ship.

Farnborough was badly hurt. She possessed only two bulkheads. The torpedo strike had smashed the one aft. The sea snarled in, filling the ship from the boiler room to the stern. Steadily, inexorably, with increasing speed, she began to settle by the stern. An extremely annoyed black cat paddled round the side to the stern to clamber back on board. It shook sodden paws and body, disgusted at the terrible turn life had taken. On board the Q-ship, nothing moved, except the bedraggled cat.

Still submerged, Hoppe closed on *Farnborough*. The dark hull approached the boats. The periscope swivelled as he took in details of the shipwrecked crew. 'Don't talk so loud,' one sailor muttered. 'He'll hear you!'

U 83 did not surface. Closer, closer still, to *Farnborough*. Campbell, hidden on the right-hand side of the bridge saw the whole length of dark steel hull under the water, mere yards away. He resisted the temptation to open fire. Shells lose momentum in water, even at close range. *U 83* stayed safely under the waves.

Farnborough's stern sank lower into the sea. The crew at the after gun felt the water lap at their feet. The ship was going down. Nobody stirred. Campbell had trained them well.

The U-boat moved along the starboard side towards the bow, crossed over to the left-hand side of the ship. Slowly she shifted away. Campbell crawled across the bridge to change places with the signalman.

Twenty minutes after the torpedo crippled *Farnborough*, Hoppe surfaced. 300yd away. None of *Farnborough*'s guns could bear. Campbell ordered his wireless operator, alone in his cabin, to signal Queenstown that *Q5* was torpedoed.

The panic party's boats floated on the port side between *Farnborough* and *U 83*. Hoppe moved towards them. Time to identify the master, take the ship's papers for the deskbound warriors at the Marineamt, and possibly a chance to acquire English foodstuffs. With luck, the abandoned freighter would yield fresh meat, real coffee, butter, eggs, marmalade, sugar. Anything was a change from issue macaroni and bacon, canned pea soup and hard biscuits. There might even be fat hams to take home when they docked. It was one of the perks for a U-boat man. That, and dying for the Fatherland.

U 83 opened her conning tower. Water streamed down her hull as she rose, 100yd distant from her victim. Broadside on at 1010hr.

Campbell crisped the fire command. The wheelhouse collapsed. The ship's sides fell down. The hen-coop vanished. The White Ensign broke out at the masthead to flutter in the breeze.

At close range, at 100yd, the human brain does not react quickly enough when a 6-pounder gun fires directly at it. *Farnborough's* first round was a direct hit on the unfortunate Hoppe. His head vanished in a flurry of blood and bone. The body dropped into the control well before the crew reacted. After which, three 12-pounder guns and one 6-pounder pumped forty-five shells at *U 83*. Nearly all found the target. Small-arms rounds peppered the hull and tower. After eight months of service with the Imperial German Navy, *U 83* went down. She took all but eight of her crew with her. Only two were dragged alive from the icy, oil-heavy water. One officer and one rating. The panic party returned to a wounded ship.

Farnborough had destroyed her target but she was in no great shape herself. The engine room and boiler room had flooded. Water rose steadily in the two aft holds. Only the cargo of wood stopped the ship from sliding, stern first, to join *U 83*.

The wireless room chattered busily as Campbell called Queenstown for help. One reply came from Bayly himself: 'Splendidly done; your magnificent perseverance and ability are well rewarded.'

With his panic party back on board, Campbell called for twelve volunteers to stay on board. The rest of the crew would take to the boats for real.

Every man volunteered.

Campbell picked twelve men to join him. Nobody commented that an unlucky thirteen now manned the ship.

Time ticked past. 1100hr. *Farnborough* sat sluggishly in the water. No rescue ships appeared. Campbell calmly followed procedures. The crew burned the secret charts and confidential papers. A last coded message stammered across the ether to Queenstown: '*Q5* slowly sinking respectfully wishes you good-bye.' After which, the ship's safe, the code books securely inside, went over the side with a satisfying splash.

Nothing further could be done except to wait.

The destroyer HMS *Narwhal*, arrived in a hurry at noon. Most of Campbell's crew transferred to her. Close behind scurried HMS *Buttercup*, a Flower Class sloop. After some discussion, *Buttercup* took *Farnborough* in tow. Still down by the stern, she had not settled deeper in the water.

The chances of saving Q5 were slender but better than simply letting her founder. Campbell recalled the scene.

'No sooner were we in tow than the cable parted, owing to our helm being jammed hard over and immovable. Luckily, our donkey-boiler, or auxiliary boiler, was high up in the ship, and we were able to raise steam in this, which gave power to steer and assistance in working the cable, and we eventually got in tow about 5 p.m.'

As dusk stole across the ocean, another destroyer, HMS *Laburnum*, arrived to relieve *Narwhal*, who then left for Queenstown with most of *Farnborough*'s crew and the two prisoners.

Buttercup and *Farnborough* plodded slowly homewards with their anxious destroyer escort. With no warning, at 0200hr in the cold morning night, the Q-ship started to heel over. The water rose enough to quench the auxiliary boiler and cut all power. Campbell just had time enough to centralise the rudder before the steam died.

Campbell and his chief engineer, Lieutenant Leonard Loveless, RNR, tried to find the cause. Armed with guttering candles, they toured the unlit ship. The candles went out with disturbing ease. Finally, they discovered that one starboard bunker had lost its coal. The sea took its place. Q5 lurched once more. Their last candle expired. Nearby they heard the cat meowing. Campbell and Loveless spent some minutes crawling around in complete darkness to find a coal-black cat. They failed.

At 0330hr, Campbell ordered the last of the crew into the remaining lifeboat. It was time to go. As he checked one last time that all was clear, one of the depth charges in the stern exploded. As it was located just above the ship's ammunition store, Campbell moved towards the boat at a smart pace. Lieutenant Ronald Stuart waited at the rail. He had ignored the order to leave. He argued that it was part of his job to ensure the captain was 'all right'.

The motor-boat's engine decided not to work. Campbell and his men drifted around in the black morning until *Laburnum* rescued them. *Buttercup* had left after the depth-charge exploded. Her captain thought another torpedo had hit *Farnborough*. Aware that the sinking ship could drag under his own command, he swiftly slipped the tow. The sloop hurried back to Queenstown to report that the decoy was probably lost, along with Campbell and his men.

Dawn came. *Farnborough* floated. Campbell and five others rejoined one black cat on board the ship. *Laburnum* took up the tow. The unlikely duo edged towards safety.

Campbell ignored an order from Sir Lewis Bayly to sink the ship. The admiral believed that she would become a half-submerged derelict, a danger to any vessel in the area. Campbell simply carried on. Most of his command was above water, the tow held, and land was not far distant. Berehaven, County Cork. They reached harbour. *Farnborough's* list had reached 20 degrees and her stern wallowed under 8ft of water. *Laburnum* dropped the tow. A tug, *Flying Sportsman*, assisted by the trawler *Luneta* pushed the old lady on to the beach at Mill Cove. It was 2130hr.

Another message came from Queenstown, direct from Sir Lewis. 'Very good piece of work. Well done.'

Campbell and his twelve loyal disciples worked on for seven days. They salvaged the guns, for *Farnborough* was mostly clear of the sea at low water. When the tide came in, they retreated to the foredeck, played records on a wind-up gramophone, fed the cat, and waited for the sea to retreat.

Finally, with as much salvaged as possible, Campbell and the remaining crew returned to Devonport. In accordance with the custom of the Service, the ship's company were paid off at their vessel's home port.

The Admiralty rewarded the destruction of *U 83* in the normal way, with a bounty of £1,000 for the crew. Their Lordships also sent a telegram to express their 'keen appreciation of the skill nerve and gallantry they recently displayed'. Then came the decorations.

A few days later, Campbell reported to Buckingham Palace. The sovereign, himself a naval man, informed the commander that he was to receive the Victoria Cross. Lieutenants Ronald Stuart and Leonard Loveless were awarded the Distinguished Service Order. More decorations went to other officers and ratings. Indeed, it was the King's personal wish that every man who remained on board after *U 83's* torpedo struck should receive recognition.

They did. The Distinguished Service Cross went to three more officers. Nine men received the Distinguished Service Medal; a tenth received a bar to the medal he already held. The list of awards ended with twenty-four Mentions in Despatches.

On 19 February 1917, Oberleutnant zur See Wilhelm Kiel and the crew of *UC 18* of the Flanders Flotilla paid the price for a moment of carelessness. In six patrols, Kiel and his men despatched thirty-four merchant ships, albeit with a total tonnage of a mere 33,616 tons.

Steam coasters were *UC 18*'s speciality. The 702-ton *Lady Olive* that he met 8 miles to the west of Jersey neatly fitted his requirements. One torpedo found the mark.

The crew, showing the final stages of panic, left. Kiel surfaced. *UC 18* motored serenely closer to read the name of her victim for the war diary. The diminutive *Lady Olive* carried, by coincidence, another identity with the number 18. *Q18*. Four 12-pounder guns and one 4in gun exploded into action. Flottille Flandern lost one more boat and a further twenty-eight men.

The decoy's triumph was not entirely a success. A Q-ship for a mere two months, *Lady Olive* sank soon afterwards as a result of her own damage. The two Numbers 18 had fought a tie, although the Admiralty felt that the Royal Navy had the better of the exchange.

Five days after Campbell's epic fight, on 22 February 1917, Commander Grenfell and *Penshurst* struck once more. He was attacked at 1250hr by *U 84*, a sister boat of Campbell's victim. Having missed with a torpedo, the U-boat surfaced to open fire with her deck gun. The panic party took to the boats. Kapitänleutnant Walter Roehr took no chances. He dived to spend some twenty minutes in a close assessment of his quarry. *Penshurst* lay still, silent. Finally, one hour after the attack was launched, Roehr nodded, satisfied. His boat was in no danger.

'Auftauchen! Ausblasen!'

The Kriegstagebuch of *U 84* tells the story. The diary times are one hour ahead of British time:

2.49 PM Steamer opens fire from four guns. Crash dive. Conning tower hit five times: one shot through the bridge, one above the aerials, the third goes through the conning tower, explodes inside, nearly all equipment destroyed. Second Watch Officer slightly wounded. Fourth shot smashed circulating water tubes. Fifth shot hit a mine deflector. Evacuated conning tower. Central hatch and speaking tube closed. As the conning tower abandoned, had to work the boat from the central area below the tower.

Grenfell, a remarkable officer who had left the Navy to market a physical training regime, had trained his gunners well. Once again, they found the target fast with a fusillade of shells. Under water, Roehr struggled to control the boat. Depth charges exploded close by. A shiver ran through the hull.

Switch and main switchboard held in place by hand. Electric lamp over magnetic compass goes out. Boat is top-heavy. Swings crossways. Several connections between the tower and the hull no longer watertight. Because of short circuits, lose in quick succession gyro-compass, lighting circuit, main rudder, voice links forward and aft. Forward horizontal rudder jams.

Roehr managed to get the boat under some control. He blew the tanks. The boat rose, still at an angle. Flooding the forward tanks failed to cure the slant completely. At an angle of 8 degrees, with water spurting in through the damaged conning tower, with no steering under water, the starboard electric motor ceased to work. Roehr decided to fight it out on the surface.

3.10 PM The steamer is 3,500 metres distant and immediately opens fire. Shots all round the boat. One 7,5 cm and one 4,7 cm shell hit the deck forward of the boat's 8.8 cm gun. Second officer receives other slight wounds. Replied to fire, unfortunately without telescopic sight as conning tower is still full of water. Distance rapidly increases to 5,000 metres. Then the steamer follows slowly. To starboard, a destroyer opens fire at us at 8,000 metres. Shots fall short. Life jackets on! Intend to continue firing until the boat can be scuttled close to a sailing ship 8 nautical miles distant, to save the crew from a *Baralong* fate.
3.17 PM The destroyer is a Foxglove, [Flower Class sloop *Alyssum*] . . . cannot steam faster than the boat. At about 7,500 metres returned fire. The Foxglove quickly starts to try and avoid our shots. She is hit twice and increases the range. Her guns only carry about 7,500 metres.
3.20 PM Conning-tower can be made watertight. Boat cleared, ammunition for gun cleared. Except for conning tower all damage can be repaired gradually.
Course 165 degrees. The Foxglove follows in our wake. Have lost sight of steamer. If essential, the boat can dive but leaves a heavy oil track. If no destroyer appears before nightfall, boat can be saved.
6.50 PM The Foxglove has approached to 7,000 metres. Again opens fire. Return fire. A hit! Enemy sheers off and falls back to over 10,000 metres.
8.00 PM Twilight. Pursuer out of sight. Because of oil track, set zigzag course. Reach another oil track, turn to port and ease on to course of 240 degrees.

Roehr and his men made their home port. The Germania dockyard at Kiel built well. *U 84* was only one of many boats to return to Germany after receiving fearsome damage. Von Scheer inspected her when she reached safety.

> It was little short of a miracle that, in spite of such heavy damage, she reached home. It was chiefly due to the assurance with which the commander handled his boat, the perfect co-operation of the whole crew in these trying circumstances, and the excellent practice made by the gunners, in connection with which it must be remembered that the height of the platform of a U-boat on which the gun is mounted, is only 2 metres above the water-level and that aiming is thereby rendered far more difficult.

Roehr subsequently evened his account with the trapships. On 13 August 1917, he swiftly despatched the decoy sloop *Bergamot*.

The U-boat's ability to absorb damage regularly fooled opponents into false claims. The Royal Navy, in the latter part of the war, emphasised the ease of jumping to conclusions.

> These vessels are all built with two hulls – a partial outer hull, which is given a ship form, and an inner cylindrical pressure hull. Damage to the outer hull alone will not appreciably impair the diving qualities of the submarine, and certainly will not disable her. Should the fuel tanks, which are situated between the inner and outer hull, be penetrated, oil will, of course, appear on the surface. In addition, an arrangement is fitted for ejecting oil in case of accident, to mark the position of the submarine. German submarines are instructed to use this arrangement if it appears advisable, in order to mislead and delay the enemy. Oil seen on the surface must, therefore, never be accepted as proof of a submarine having been sunk, or even damaged.

Further, commanders such as Kapitänleutnant Kurt Tebbenjohanns developed the trick of releasing carefully selected waste to the surface when under attack. Worn pieces of uniform, old cabbage stalks and other clutter sent more than one hunter away, rejoicing but unsuccessful.

Sinkings in January were worrying. February threatened to be far worse. Even night-time did not deter the more thrusting commanders.

The aristocratic commander of *UC 26*, Oberleutnant zur See Matthias, Graf von Schmetow, used bright moonlight to attack *Mona's Queen*, a well-used paddle steamer impressed into service from the Isle of Man Steam Packet Company. On the approach to Le Havre, with 925 soldiers on board, Captain William Cain of *Mona's Queen* saw a torpedo wake cross his bow. Already travelling at 15 knots, Cain called for even more speed.

Von Schmetow surfaced. *UC 26* emerged, water cascading down her sides, so close to her target that the *Queen's* port wheel smashed into her. Steel paddle blades chewed their way through the U-boat's outer hull as 1,559 tons of Victorian craftsmanship from Barrow-in-Furness crunched along the casing of 500-odd tons of Hamburg-constructed U-boat. Thirty tons of paddle wheel buried itself forward of *UC 26's* conning tower.

The submarine promptly went back under the surface. Water gushed into her even as hatches slammed shut. *UC 26* limped back to Zeebrugge and the repair pens of the Flanders Flotilla. Cain and his crew claimed a victory. One U-boat destroyed. Six months later, the captain and crew received a £300 reward from the Isle of Man government.

In Downing Street, Lloyd George decided to involve himself more closely with the battle against the U-boats. Ultimately, responsibility for winning the war remained with the politicians collectively, and with the Prime Minister personally.

He had cause for concern. On 9 February 1917, Lloyd George lunched in the House of Commons with Colonel Charles Repington, the Military Correspondent of *The Times*. The Prime Minister knew that, on the streets of London, Edinburgh, Exeter and the smallest village, anxiety bubbled about escalating food shortages. Repington recorded that Lloyd George believed the Admiralty to be apathetic and incompetent, with no idea of how to protect merchant shipping.

He was not alone. Lord Derby, Secretary of State for War, noted in a letter to Sir Douglas Haig that the Navy 'are really at their wit's end as how to deal with these submarines'.

The Admiralty had tried. The Navy laid more mines and steel nets. Air and sea patrols increased. Deck guns appeared on merchant steamers. Patrol craft guarded the approach routes to British ports – a two-edged system, for the canny U-boat commander discovered route changes simply by watching. Safely submerged until the guardians passed by, they patiently waited for the merchantman.

Lloyd George rarely spared the men in uniform. In his *War Memoirs*, serial selective parading of facts that supported his views, allied with a serious disregard of contrary ones, gave him a reputation as the most mendacious Prime Minister in British history. Only recently have some questioned that ranking.

Lloyd George particularly detested Haig – and Jellicoe. He excused his approach by stating firmly that it was the duty of politicians to take advice from wherever they found it. If that conflicted with the considered opinions of generals and admirals, the politicians finally took the decisions, not the military.

On 17 February 1917, Lloyd George called a breakfast meeting at Downing Street. The First Lord of the Admiralty, Sir Edward Carson, the First Sea Lord, Sir John Jellicoe and Rear Admiral Alexander Duff, director of the recently formed Anti-Submarine Division, joined him. It was no social occasion. Presented to them was a document prepared by Sir Maurice Hankey, the Secretary of the Committee of Imperial Defence.

Hankey's paper was calm in approach, moderate in tone and devastating in its conclusions. The Admiralty needed to reorganise its approach to anti-submarine warfare completely. In particular, the convoy system should become an integral part of Admiralty policy. Hankey pointed out that

> The enemy can never know the day nor the hour when the convoy will come, nor the route it will take. The most dangerous and contracted passages can be passed at night. The most valuable vessels can be placed in the safest part of the convoy. . . . The enemy submarines, instead of attacking a defenceless prey, will know that a fight is inevitable in which he may be worsted. All hope of a successful surface attack would have to be dismissed at once.

In a few short sentences, Hankey had rejected the role of the decoy. Their whole technique was based on the U-boat coming to the surface. And, in case the Admiralty did not realise that the answer to the U-boat stared them in the face, Hankey's memorandum concluded, 'Perhaps the best commentary on the convoy system is that it is invariably adopted for our main fleet, and for our transports.'

Sir Maurice was right. He need only point to the constant cross-Channel traffic to the Western Front. The ships of the Dover Patrol, under Admiral Sir Reginald Bacon, protected the transports back and forth without loss.

Jellicoe did not agree. Even after the war, he continued to emphasise the difficulty of the U-boat problem.

The desire of the Anti-Submarine Division to obtain destroyers for offensive use in hunting flotillas in the North Sea and English Channel led to continual requests being made to me to provide vessels for the purpose. I was, of course, anxious to institute offensive operations, but in the early days of 1917 we could not rely much on depth-charge attack, owing to our small stock of these charges, and my experience in the Grand Fleet had convinced me that for success in the alternative of hunting submarines for a period which would exhaust their batteries and so force them to come to the surface, a large number of destroyers was required, unless the destroyers were provided with some apparatus which would, by sound or otherwise, locate the submarine. This will be realized when the fact is recalled that a German submarine could remain submerged at slow speed for a period which would enable her to travel a distance of some 80 miles. As this distance could be covered in any direction in open waters such as the North Sea, it is obvious that only a very numerous force of destroyers steaming at high speed could cover the great area in which the submarine might come to the surface. She would, naturally, select the dark hours for emergence, as being the period of very limited range of vision for those searching for her. In confined waters such as those in the eastern portion of the English Channel the problem became simpler. Requests for destroyers constantly came from every quarter, such as the Commanders-in-Chief at Portsmouth and Devonport, the Senior Naval Officer at Gibraltar, the Vice-Admiral, Dover, the Rear-Admiral Commanding East Coast, and the Admiral at Queenstown. The vessels they wanted did not, however, exist.

In simple language, neither ships nor equipment existed in sufficient numbers to provide hunting packs. Diversion of the available destroyers to convoy duties simply reduced numbers elsewhere.

At the end of February 1917, the U-boats put down a monthly haul of 464,599 tons of Allied shipping. Add in some 50,000 tons damaged, and simple arithmetic ruled. The total tonnage that Britain could use was about 11 million tons, 3 million of it neutral hulls. If U-boats sank

600,000 tons per month, and frightened off neutral shipping into the bargain, they would drive Britain out of the war before the Americans joined the conflict.

By 23 February, forty-four Scandinavian ships in British harbours refused to leave. Outside Britain, 250 neutral vessels stayed in port, refusing to leave for England.

Nearly half a million tons destroyed. And this was just the start.

The U-boats had the upper hand.

ELEVEN

LIKE RATS IN A TRAP

If February was bad, March underlined the grim truth of the unrestricted U-boat campaign. Sinkings increased. In the Admiralty, the doctrine reigned that only if large numbers of escorts sailed with the merchantmen were convoys effective. A rule of thumb suggested they should outnumber the merchantmen by two to one. Optimists suggested that one escort per steamer would suffice. Only the madly hopeful reckoned that 8 destroyers could shepherd 26 ships, that 7 escorts could cope with between 16 and 22 vessels, and that gaggles of less than 16 were well protected with 6 escorts. While arguments raged in Whitehall, the slaughter continued. And the Q-ships sailed in hope.

The call for volunteers brought forward many men. With little else to combat the U-boats, more and more decoys came into use. Although shreds of secrecy still clung to the decoys, it seemed easily penetrated, as the preparations for the *Result*, officially *Q23*, indicate. Lieutenant G.H.P. Muhlhauser, RNVR recalled: 'Fitting out, which by the way was done alongside an open quay so that everyone in Lowestoft knew about us, was a long affair, and it was not before the 3rd February, '17 that we were ready for some of the trials.'

Some U-boat captains, still clinging to Prize Regulations, occasionally lacked caution. Even so, *Privet*'s encounter with a U-boat clearly showed that Q-ships now had to run incredible risks to destroy an opponent.

On 12 March, on a chilly afternoon, the 800-ton coastal steamer *Privet* meandered warily from Land's End to Alderney. At about 1500hr, a torpedo tracked across her course, zipping under the engine room, to disappear in the distance. The panic party duly milled around on deck. Ten minutes ticked by. The U-boat surfaced. From around 2,000m range, she shelled *Privet*. One shot burst among the panic party; it destroyed both boats and caused severe casualties. After ten minutes, *Privet* had lost her engines. Her port battery was hit. She was in a bad way.

Her captain, Lieutenant Commander Charles George Matheson, RNR, went for broke, despite the range. An SOS buzzed across the ether. *Privet's* remaining gun opened at the U-boat, 2,000yd distant. Four hits. The U-boat managed only a single round in reply before she appeared to dive. Witnesses on the decoy thought she tried to surface before sinking once more, stern first.

Privet had suffered. The shell that took out the engines had left a nasty hole in the hull that busily admitted water. Slowly, remorselessly, the sea crept higher and higher in the engine room. The first lieutenant tried to plug the hole with the time-tested remedy of bundled-up hammocks and timber. To no avail.

Creaks and groans told Matheson that his ship strained to stay in one piece. If a bulkhead collapsed, it would all be over. He ordered the crew to abandon ship in the one remaining lifeboat and a skiff.

Two destroyers hustled into position. HMS *Christopher* and HMS *Orestes* arrived minutes before the rear bulkhead gave way. Water rushed in. The code books went overboard; the depth charges made safe. Matheson joined *Orestes*, then returned in a futile attempt to arrange a tow before his command vanished under the water.

The Admiralty, working from wireless intercepts and more craftily garnered information, decided that the U-boat was *U 85*, under the command of Kapitänleutnant Wilhelm Petz. It was certain that Petz had not returned from his third operational patrol in command.

U 85 left port in company with *U 81*, commanded by Kapitänleutnant Raimund Weisbach, on 6 March 1917. Both boats soon encountered extremely heavy seas, so bad that Weisbach reported his boat was taking in water. She also developed an oil leak. *U 81* carried extra oil in her ballast tanks to increase her range. Consequently, she sat low in the water with a considerable loss of sea-keeping qualities. Weisbach, intending to go through the Straits of Dover, decided against it. He turned back to head north around Scotland.

U 81 returned home on 27 March 1917. Petz was overdue. Weisbach wrote: 'From the report of *U 85* that she had a larger oil leak and the detail from *U 81*, that *U 85* took a northerly course from Terschelling, it is inferred that *U 85* took the Northern Route. This would be in accordance with Flotilla instructions.'

It also ties in with Petz's own opinions. He was no enthusiast of the Dover route. He said as much in his patrol summary from his previous trip. The two factors effectively rule out *U 85* as *Privet's* victim. If she took the long route, she would have been nowhere near the scene by the time of the action. With a severe oil leak and bad weather, it is possible that Willy Petz and his men perished on the long haul around Scotland. As there are no unexplained sinkings in *U 85*'s patrol area, it is possible she foundered or met a mine on her way to war.

The Q-ship undoubtedly engaged a U-boat. A prime contender for the role of victim is *UC 68*. She sailed from Zeebrugge two days before the fight to lay mines in the Plymouth area. En route, she probably torpedoed the 2,897-ton SS *Tandil*. Four men died.

Minelayers usually cleared their cargo within the first couple of days, on their way out rather than on the return journey. On 14 March 1917, the 12,036-ton SS *Orsova*, a P&O liner, in service as a troopship, struck one less than 10 miles from where *Privet* sank her U-boat. *UC 68* was under orders to lay mines in the exact area where *Orsova* was hit. It would have taken *UC 68* two days to get there.

Eight people died on *Orsova*. She survived to sail again, eighteen months later.

The coincidence of date casts *UC 68* neatly as *Privet*'s victim.

The Royal Navy subsequently claimed that the British submarine *C7* sank *UC 68* on 5 April 1917 in the North Sea. For this to be valid, the U-boat needed to be on an exceptionally long patrol. The claim arose from intelligence that *UC 68* did not return to base. As *C7* had reported destroying a U-boat it followed, with dubious logic, that she must have met *UC 68*.

There is a chance that *UC 68* sank on one of her own mines. On 13 March 1917, a fierce underwater explosion occurred in the English Channel, some 25 miles south of Torquay, east of Start Point. After the detonation no débris, apart from dead fish, floated to the surface. Some German mines were found but random mine explosions happened. Similarly, mines sometimes did deploy prematurely and blow up their own boat.

No wreckage. No remains. All that can be said firmly is that *UC 68* failed to return from patrol.

Decoys had a busy month. Some had good fortune, others bad. On 13 March 1917, *U 61*, under Kapitänleutnant Victor Dieckmann, torpedoed *Warner*, otherwise known as *Q27*. Dieckmann suspected that he faced a trapship. Her 'high bridge and high deck erections', combined with 'meaningless deviations from her route and her wild zigzag course', persuaded him that a torpedo was safer than a deck gun. When the crew managed to lower only one boat in a clumsy manner, suspicions hardened into certainty.

A survivor from the Q-ship, Lieutenant Frederick Yuile of the RNR, later claimed that the U-boat captain told him that *Warner* was a victim of *U 38*. This was the command of Kapitänleutnant Max Valentiner. Both he and his boat were with Flottille Pola in the Adriatic. Yuile suffered either a ponderous Teutonic joke or subtle propaganda to show that Valentiner had torpedoes with an extremely long range.

At Lowestoft, the sailing ship *Result* finally completed her trials. She had a new auxiliary motor to help her manoeuvre in action. On 15 March 1917, sailing as the *Capulet*, she met her first U-boat, *UC 45* under the command of Oberleutnant zur See Hubert Aust. Muhlhauser recalled:

> The wind was freshening at the time, and we were just lowering and stowing the topsails when a submarine was sighted coming up astern, and immediately afterwards the report of a gun was heard. In a few seconds the men were at their stations, but only five showed on deck. The CO ordered the helm to be put down, to bring the ship into the wind, and the headsails to be hauled down. While this was happening shells were dropping around, and bursting. One of them grazed the flying jib stay, and went on making a most curious whistling noise. The submarine commander refused to accept our apparent surrender, and continued firing steadily from a distance of 2,000 yds.

Aust's tactics, like those of many other U-boat men, had changed. Shell from long range. The action continued.

> The CO then ordered the panic party to abandon ship . . . they made a gallant attempt to capsize the boat when lowering it. We thought that this would give a realistic touch to the affair, but the boat refused to capsize and righted itself when it reached the water and they had to get into it as it was. Reid and four hands were then in the boat, and they were supposed to represent the whole of the crew, while the ship was lying head to wind with the sails flapping, and apparently deserted.
>
> No one showed on deck, but below the bulwarks were the three guns' crews lying alongside their guns, the LTO alongside his torpedo tubes, the engineers standing by the motor ready to start it when required, while the CO perambulated the deck on his hands and knees

watching the course of events through holes in the bulwarks, and I sat on deck at the wheel trying to keep the ship in the wind so as not to get too far away from the boat. As soon as the latter left the ship the submarine ventured to approach to 1,000 yds, but would not come any closer. They went on firing from that distance for some time without hitting the hull or a spar. The sails and gear were cut about by shells and splinters, but as long as nothing vital was hit we would continue to lie low in the hope that it would come nearer. But that was just what it had not the slightest intention of doing unless it could first get hold of the boat. That, on the other hand we could not allow, as with the boat alongside them we should not be able to fire should an opportunity occur. Things therefore remained at a sort of deadlock.

Lifeboats that stayed close to their ship alerted U-boat crews. Either the men in the boat planned to return on board if the U-boat went away or they were proof of a U-Boot-Falle.

Reid rowed about first in one direction, and then in another, as if he did not know what to do for the best, but he took care to keep within 200 yds of the ship. He said afterwards that he felt very lonely with a large and hostile submarine in his immediate neighbourhood, and the ship tending to work away from him. Never had the latter seemed to him so desirable. He even found time to admire the beauty of her lines. Then the submarine turned its gun on the boat, possibly with the idea of inducing it to approach, but it had the opposite result, and Reid rowed away. After firing three shells, the first of which went short, the second over, while the third nearly hit it, the submarine commander seemed to come to the conclusion that the men in the boat were too much upset to understand what was required, and turned his attention to the ship once more.

Staying at relatively long range was often enough to tempt the Q-ship captain into action. As seconds became minutes, the temptation to open fire on the seemingly unsuspecting enemy increased.

Our ordeal had started again. The CO on hands and knees, with his eye to a hole in the bulwarks, watched the firing in an impersonal and critical spirit. He considered that it was bad. The submarine was only 1,000 yards distant, and, though there was a nasty short sea which caused it to roll a good deal, he thought that it should have done better. It was firing about one shell short to three over. 'Ah,' he said once, 'that was better. That very nearly hit the counter.' As I was sitting at the counter, it did not strike me at all as an admirable effort on their part. On the contrary; . . . added to the feeling of personal insecurity caused by shells and fragments of shells hurtling past one's ears, was a distinct feeling of humiliation. It was true that was what we were there for, and it was all part of the game, but somehow it did not seem right to be sitting in water at an idle wheel, doing nothing, while a submarine plugged shells at the ship for what seemed an interminable time.

Lieutenant Philip Mack, the *Result*'s captain, broke the impasse.

At length after the firing had gone on for 45 minutes, and the submarine commander seemed as determined as ever not to come any nearer, the CO decided to try and wing him as he was within easy range, and accordingly gave the word to open fire. The White Ensign shot aloft, the engine was started, down crashed the bulwarks, and round came the guns.

The submarine had taken alarm at the first movement, and was doing a crash dive, but the aft twelve-pounder, Gunlayer W. Wreford, AB, hit him at the base of the conning tower at its junction with the deck, and the 6-pdr, Gunlayer H.G. Wells, AB, also hit the conning tower higher up. The second shot from the 12 pdr missed. In 30 seconds the submarine had disappeared. Had we sunk it? We knew that the 12 pdr had hit it, and that in a good spot, but beyond that it was impossible to say anything.

Shells hitting the conning tower regularly feature in Q-ship combat accounts. They apparently did remarkably little damage. Hubert Aust and *UC 45* escaped with nothing more than a shaking.

During the cold, bitter March of 1917 that blustered across the North Sea and the Western Approaches, eighteen Hochseeflotte deep-sea boats and fourteen coastal minelayers from Flottille Flandern sank 211 ships for a total of 507,000 tons with a loss in cargo capacity by damaged ships of a further 60,000 tons.

Only four U-boats were lost during the month: *U 85*, *UC 68*, *U 43* and *UB 6*. The British submarine *G13* torpedoed Kapitänleutnant Erwin

Sebelin and *U 43* as she passed the Shetland Islands, north of the finely named Muckle Flugga. Nobody survived from the crew of twenty-six. Oberleutnant zur See Oskar Steckelberg in *UB 6*, of the hard-worked Flanders Flotilla, ran aground on the Dutch coast in thick fog. He and his men were politely interned, then repatriated as shipwrecked mariners.

Four boats lost. To replace them, nine new boats entered service.

April 1917 saw no remission in sinkings. The Admiralty worried at ways to stop the slaughter. Thoughts about convoys met the same, apparently insuperable, argument. The Royal Navy did not have enough escort vessels. Signs that the convoy system was the answer were, nonetheless, there for the looking. France had lost nearly all of its coalfields to German occupation. In consequence, she imported about 1½ million tons of coal from Britain every month. The coal came from the mines of Wales and the pits of Northumberland and Durham: coal to make gas for light and heating, coal for the railways, coal for power stations, coal for industry, coal for French ships. Colliers from Cardiff, colliers from Newcastle made some 800 trips every single month, in good weather and bad. They were easy prey for the U-boats. They gobbled up the vital colliers by the dozen. In the face of anxious demands from France, the Admiralty agreed to 'controlled sailings' for the New Year. Convoys by any other name.

The first, scarcely organised, had an escort of a few armed trawlers. Not a single collier went down. Other 'controlled sailings' followed, with the same result. Over the next weeks, hardly an escorted ship was lost. The convoys avoided known danger areas but that alone was not the full solution. That came because U-boats preferred to attack unescorted ships. Even a couple of trawlers, each with a 4-pounder deck gun, shaded the odds against the U-boats. In March, 1,200 coal ships plodded between England and France. Three fell to the U-boats. Similar figures marked the 'Beef Route' between Britain and the Netherlands. The Admiralty failed to appreciate their significance.

At last, on 6 April 1917, the United States joined the fray. As the German High Command predicted, their entry did little to improve the Allied situation. Nonetheless, the US Admiral William Sims arrived in England on 9 April 1917. He travelled incognito as Mr W.S. Davidson. As President of the US Naval War College, he saw all the information sent to Washington by US naval attachés throughout the world. Their despatches came nowhere near reflecting the gravity of the situation.

What Sims learned in a few short days in Britain about the effects of the U-boats appalled him.

The Allies, he reported to Washington, had 'not been able to, and are not now, effectively meeting the situation presented'. The Royal Navy's policy, he explained, relied essentially on three factors – patrolled routes, dispersion and arming merchant steamers.

Sims immediately offered help to the Admiralty. This was not much. The US Navy could provide six destroyers immediately, with the promise of more to follow.

Jellicoe was, by nature, no optimist. As the daily toll of sinkings rose, his confidence slumped into his shoe leather. Unwilling to delegate, he spent long hours of each day writing minutes, reading memoranda, and doing tasks that the other Sea Lords should have handled. Each day he reported to the War Cabinet with gloomy figures that showed that the war at sea was Germany's to win.

The British offensive in Flanders, at Arras and Vimy, would be in vain if the flow of supplies to the fighting soldiers collapsed. The First Sea Lord decided that it was a race against time. He believed that Britain was losing it.

On 23 April 1917, St George's Day, Jellicoe penned a particularly gloomy forecast for the War Cabinet. With the ponderous title of 'The Submarine Menace and the Food Supply', he revealed that sinkings for the first two weeks alone in April came to 419,621 tons. Even the most innumerate Cabinet member could double the number to make an estimate for the whole month.

Jellicoe's paper, with no apparent irony, observed that 'it appears evident that the situation calls for immediate action'. Sadly, Sir John had nothing new to suggest, other than the proposal that enormous unsinkable ships could solve the problem. As none existed, this did not impress his readers. To build them would take eighteen months. Otherwise, the admiral proffered the same panacea of more destroyers and patrol vessels, more merchant ships, more depth charges and mines, more armed cargo vessels.

The War Cabinet, led by a ferocious Lloyd George, discussed the paper with Jellicoe on 25 April. The Prime Minister, like a terrier with a rat, dragged convoys into the middle of the arena. They were not mentioned in Jellicoe's paper. He wished to know why.

Jellicoe did not duck the question. He replied that the convoy system was under consideration. He added that trial convoys to Scandinavia had not been a great success. He then reiterated his eternal objection. The Navy did not have enough ships. He personally was not prepared to withdraw patrol vessels from the trade routes to employ them as escorts.

He could have added that both the French Ministry of Marine and the US Navy Department supported the Admiralty. They also believed that merchant ships, especially the more aged tramp steamers, had neither the engines nor the crews to operate in a disciplined convoy. Some steamers did not even have a voicepipe to connect the bridge and engine room, so they could not possibly maintain station.

Lloyd George issued what might be thought a threat. He would visit the Admiralty himself. He would chair a meeting of the whole Board to take, in his words, 'peremptory action on the question of convoys'.

In fact, the ground had already shifted beneath Jellicoe's pessimistic black leather shoes. Admiral Alexander Duff and his Anti-Submarine Division had studied the convoy question for some while. One of Duff's officers, Commander Reginald Henderson, analysed the statistics. The weekly statement of ships entering and leaving British ports stood at a staggering 2,500 each way every week. These would make many enormous convoys. The figures, though, held a significant flaw. They included every ship over 300 tons, be it a cross-Channel ferry, a coaster edging along the Suffolk shoreline or a collier sneaking across the Irish Sea from Liverpool to Belfast.

A different picture emerged when only deep-water, long-distance hulls came into the calculation. The ships that needed protection numbered between 120 and 140 per week. Henderson, who organised the 'controlled sailings' of the colliers, had demolished one of Jellicoe's main arguments.

The commander, very properly, supplied the statistics to his superior, the tall and handsome Admiral Alexander Duff. More clandestinely, he also gave them to Sir Maurice Hankey. He passed them on to Lloyd George.

Duff lost no time in presenting proposals to Jellicoe, in a memorandum in which he stated that a comprehensive convoy scheme should be introduced. He outlined a selection of prospective schemes. Jellicoe, if not convinced, agreed. By the time that Lloyd George swept into the Admiralty on 30 April 1917, ready to slice admirals into thin salami with his sharp tongue, the question was already settled.

Lloyd George, in later years, unhesitatingly claimed full credit for introducing the convoy system. As he constantly reminded readers of his memoirs, the Admiralty was 'palsied and muddle-headed'. Without his personal intervention, Lloyd George modestly implied, the war would have been lost. His interest may well have spurred Jellicoe and Duff into action. Henderson, thoughtfully passing his researches to Number Ten, gave impetus to the Prime Minister's intervention.

Sir Maurice Hankey set straight the record in his diary entry for 29 April 1917. The Admiralty, he stated specifically, moved to the convoy scheme on its own initiative. As for Lloyd George's fierce descent upon the Admiralty, Hankey laconically recorded that he and the Prime Minister spent a pleasant day, lunching with Jellicoe and his wife and four little girls. The Prime Minister, Hankey added, enjoyed flirting with a 3-year-old.

Lloyd George's venom in his *War Memoirs* is understandable. Admiralty inaction could have cost the war. To convoy merchant ships was no new strategy. It was employed in previous wars. The Prime Minister, anxious to claim the credit, signally failed to mention his own lethargic progress on the matter. Hankey's original memorandum was on his desk on 1 February 1917. The Admiralty may have been less than lightning-fast. The War Cabinet, chaired by Lloyd George, themselves showed no outstanding pace either.

On the high seas, men continued to die. As 30 April dawned, the Q-ship *Prize*, a three-masted schooner of 227 tons, sighed her way in a light wind some 150 miles south-west of Ireland. Her captain was Lieutenant Willie Sanders, RNR, the same lad who had gone to sea at the age of 16 in New Zealand.

He spent the early months of the war as first officer of the Union Steamship Company's *Moeraki* of 4,392 tons. He took the opportunity to gain his Extra Master's qualification in November 1914, as well as a compass adjuster's certificate. *Moeraki* became a troopship. Willie volunteered for the Navy, only to find he had to wait.

In December 1914, Willie moved to another transport, SS *Willochra*, as third officer, sailing from New Zealand to Egypt. In June 1915, with the Gallipoli campaign well under way, an impatient Willie passed a letter to a friendly officer on his way to England. It was addressed to the Admiralty. He wanted to join the Royal Navy.

Willie Sanders went to SS *Tofua*, another transport. Like *Willochra*, she took soldiers to war; like *Willochra*, she brought back the maimed and injured.

At the end of 1915, Willie Sanders learned that if he presented himself to the Royal Navy in Britain, he would receive his commission.

He promptly signed on as second mate of the *Hebburn Jan.* He reached Glasgow on 7 April 1916. Twelve days later, he became a sub-lieutenant in the Royal Naval Reserve.

After a gunnery course, Sanders first joined HMS *Sabrina*, then moved on to HMS *Idaho*. Neither went to sea, for both were depot ships. *Sabrina*, some forty years old, was a Medway Class gunboat. *Idaho* was a requisitioned steam yacht moored at Milford Haven, where she gave her name to an Auxiliary Patrol base.

By 6 September 1916, Sanders had finished his training and familiarisation with the ways of the regular Navy. As an officer with sailing ship experience, he was an excellent choice to join a twin-masted brigantine, the 182-ton *Helgoland*. Dutch-built and newly commissioned, *Helgoland* was an ideal decoy. Borne on the Admiralty list as *Q17*, she roamed the waters south-west of the Lizard under the names of *Hoogezand II*, *Horley* and *Brig 10*.

Sanders went as second in command and gunnery officer. His first two months of sea service attracted the attention of three U-boats in succession during *Helgoland*'s first cruise. She lay becalmed after the first attack; a torpedo skimmed close to her in the third. Sanders drew approval for his cool behaviour under fire, although the brigantine failed to destroy a submarine. Perhaps more importantly, three U-boats went back to base with the news that the 'beefeaters' now used sailing ships as decoys.

Promoted to lieutenant on 5 February 1917, Sanders took over his own decoy ship: *Q21*, or *Prize*. Built in 1901, the three-masted schooner carried three 12-pounder guns. Originally German-owned with the name *Else*, she had the misfortune to be en route from Germany to England when the war began. The first enemy ship to fall into British hands, her name chose itself. Sold to the Marine Navigation Company, she became *First Prize*. Requisitioned in November 1916, her name changed a fraction to, simply, *Prize*.

Sanders and his second in command, Lieutenant William Beaton, took special gunnery training while Falmouth fitted out their ship. On 26 April 1917, *Prize* set out to patrol the seas to the south of Ireland.

For four days they saw nothing. By 30 April, they neared the limit of their patrol area. Sanders decided that they would turn north at midnight. Frustration and inaction was the daily diet of Q-ship crews.

At 2030, the alarm sounded. In good visibility, on a calm sea, the lookouts sighted an unmistakable shape. A U-boat. She proved to be *U 93*, on her maiden war patrol, under the command of Kapitänleutnant

Adolf Karl Georg Edgar, Freiherr von Spiegel und Peckelsheim. The boat had left Emden on a Friday, an omen that was bad enough. That it was also the 13th of the month made it ten times worse. Even now, on the homeward leg, many of the crew muttered that some terrible catastrophe lay in store. As sunset sneaked closer, *Prize* waited for action. It came quickly.

Already on the surface, *U 93* did not dive. All but two torpedoes had gone, for von Spiegel was a remarkable U-boat captain. In the seventeen days since he had left Emden in his new boat, he sank twelve ships in twelve encounters. Five he could easily prove. Their masters sat as prisoners on board *U 93*. So much for superstition.

The tiny schooner, half the length of the U-boat's 80m and a quarter of her tonnage, was hardly a worthwhile thirteenth victim. Von Spiegel, eating his evening meal in his cabin, was ready to let the windjammer go. His 'Heinrich', Oberleutnant zur See Wilhelm Ziegner, urged that they should sink her. Every vessel that went down was a blow against England.

She was not worth one of the two remaining torpedoes. *U 93* surfaced. At 4,000m, von Spiegel fired a warning shot. It splashed some distance ahead of the target. A second shot dropped astern. The sailing ship was bracketed, a sure sign that the gunners had the range. *Prize* lowered her topsails. Seven men launched a lifeboat in full view of the U-boat.

Baron von Spiegel did not rush to battle. He knew about decoy ships. Sometimes they acted in concert with a submarine. Approach too closely, too carelessly, and the reward was a British torpedo.

'Beide Maschinen halb Kraft voraus!' The U-boat nudged forward.

The forward gun crew leisurely dropped more shells onto the schooner's deck. One a minute. Every sixty seconds. The baron nodded approval. 'Good shooting,' he remarked to his two watch officers, Ziegner and Leutnant zur See Hans Leo von Usedom, beside him on the bridge.

Prize suffered. Sanders wrote later:

The ship's head fell slowly away to the eastward and the enemy slowly followed us round, all the while approaching closer. He continued to fire at the ship in a deliberate manner until satisfied that she had been abandoned. Up to this time a total of sixteen rounds had been fired, two of which struck the water-line, exploded inside, and caused considerable damage. The motor was put out of action, the wireless room wrecked, the mainmast shot through in two places, and all the living rooms shattered. The lubricating oil tank was holed and the contents filtered on to the deck. The ship also began to make water at a fairly rapid rate.

U 93 closed. She circled the burning hulk. All three officers gazed through binoculars. Nothing moved on board. No sign of a British submarine. No danger of a crafty torpedo as they moved in. Satisfied, Spiegel ordered *U 93* to approach her victim, dead astern. A final close look before the gun crews despatched her.

On *Prize*, tension nagged at every man. Sanders held his fire:

> The enemy continued to approach from dead astern until she was within 150 yards. My anxiety was great, as the after gun would not bear right astern owing to the position of the wheel. Fortunately at this moment she altered course several points to clear our stern, and when about three points abaft the beam and distant 80 yards I considered that the critical moment had arrived. It was then 21.05, and the order was given to 'down screens and open fire' at point blank range. I may add that, from the moment of going to 'stations' until fire was opened on the submarine, sights had been carefully adjusted by the estimated range of the approaching enemy. Almost as soon as our screens were downed the enemy opened fire with both her guns. One shell struck the water-line, passed through the side, and was deflected upwards through the deck. The other, as far as I could tell, hit the superstructure. As a result, three hands were wounded.

As the shell from *U 93* smashed into *Prize*, the schooner fought back. Von Spiegel recalled:

> There was a loud whistle aboard the schooner. The white war ensign of Great Britain ran up the mast. A movable gun platform slid into view. A roar and a rattling, and 7.5 cm guns opened at us, and machine guns, too. We offered a fair broadside target. One shell put our fore gun out of commission and wounded several of the gun crew. Another crashed into our hull.

'Beide Maschinen äusserste voraus! U-boot-Falle! Voll nach Backbord!'

U 93 made a quarter-circle, showing her stern to *Prize*. More rounds crashed into her hull as she turned, but her aft gun now had a chance to even the score. Both engines stopped. The U-boat slowed, helpless, less than 500m from the schooner.

Spiegel swore, shouted orders. He joined the three gunners. They had hardly got a single shot away when a shellburst took off the head of the petty officer gunlayer. The body smacked into von Spiegel, who went into the water precisely as *U 93* fell away beneath his feet. 'I could', he recalled, 'see her black shadow vanish into the depths of the ocean. A pang of anguish shot through me at the thought of my fine new boat and my crew going down to their last port on the cold silent bottom of the sea.'

Luckily for the baron, the panic party rowed as fast as they could towards him and two other crewmen who struggled in the water. Spiegel remembered little as he went under, dragged down by the weight of his leather jacket and thick clothing. His U-boat-crew-issue boots of leather with wooden soles behaved like concrete blocks.

On board the badly damaged *Prize*, Sanders knew he had sunk the U-boat:

> The submarine finally came to a standstill at about 500 to 600 yards away, slewed broadside on, heading in an opposite direction to mine. The after gun continued to find the target. Time after time a hit was registered, and out of a total of 14 rounds fired from this gun 12 appeared to find a billet. The forward gun was not so successful, and only scored an occasional hit which did not materially affect the result of the action. Altogether 36 rounds were fired before the submarine disappeared from sight. She settled down stern first, ablaze internally, the fire being distinctly visible through the wreckage. As she sank the jagged end of the conning-tower came into view for a moment and was lost to sight. Previous to sinking a white vapour was emitted from the hull.

Spiegel spluttered back to life on a deck 'knocked into kindling wood'. *Prize* had lost her auxiliary engines. Water raced in through shot holes. Despite frantic efforts to stuff the leaks with hammocks, mattresses, even hatch covers, the sea gained steadily.

Pulled from a watery end, Spiegel and his crew were well treated. In dry clothes provided by one of the officers, the baron drank cocoa and smoked a contemplative cigarette. Aware that *Prize* herself was close to sinking, Spiegel decided that Friday the 13th had been a bad omen after all:

> I couldn't forget my crew, my friends going down out there, drowned like rats in a trap, with some perhaps left to die of slow suffocation . . . some might even now be alive in the strong torpedo compartments, lying in the darkness, hopeless, waiting for the air to thicken and finally smother them. No, they were not rapping on the iron hull. They knew no help could ever reach them.

Sanders, well experienced with sailing ships, decided to list the ship so that the holes made by *U 93* rose clear of the water. To do this, he explained, 'the small boat which was swung out on the davits was filled with water . . . coal shifted from port to starboard side and port fresh water tanks emptied. The vessel was also put on port tack. These measures were instrumental in relieving the pressure, and the shot holes were left almost clear of the water.'

Prize was fortunate. The sea was flat. Almost any swell would take her under within minutes. Even with the holes plugged, the schooner was in a bad way. No wireless meant that she could not cry for help. Without engines, she could not move, for the evening calm did not fill the sails. Neither Sanders nor his engineer could fix the damage. So Willie Sanders asked Kapitänleutnant Adolf Karl Georg Edgar, Freiherr von Spiegel und Peckelsheim for help. He got it.

Obermachinistenmaat Deppe came to the rescue. *Prize* was a German ship with German engines. Deppe knew diesels 'as a parson knows his Bible'. He swiftly coaxed the surviving engine into action.

Sanders, indefatigable, and *Prize* began the long journey home. With shot-holes fractions above the waterline, the crew bailed steadily for the next forty-eight hours until *Prize* reached Kinsale.

April 1917 was a bloody month on the sea lanes. U-boats and mines destroyed 834,549 tons of British, Allied and neutral shipping – 354 ships in all. The Kaiserliche Marine bore the loss of two boats. One went down in a minefield; the other apparently failed to reach her patrol area.

The Royal Navy made no sinking claims for the whole month. Not a single boat apparently fell to the hunters – except for *U 93*, claimed by *Prize*.

Disaster beckoned.

TWELVE

FORTITUDE. VALOUR. DUTY. DETERMINATION

U93 WAS NOT an iron coffin at the bottom of the Atlantic. An enemy shell burst in front of Ziegner's face as he stood in the conning tower. After brief, dazed moments, he picked himself up to find *U 93* apparently out of control. Usedom had fallen down the tower. Ziegner, unable to see the captain, took command. The boat's war diary elaborated:

> Boat takes on a heavy 14 degree list to starboard because of hit forward on the starboard side in compressor set 5, bursting of no. 2 starboard bunker, and one hit that penetrated starboard dive tanks 5–3. We turn away hard to port at full speed. Coxswain seems to be trying to man the after gun, which stopped firing under No. 3 after two shots. Apparently due to an airburst shell, Captain, coxswain and petty officer engineer Deppe thrown overboard between the tower and the after gun. Captain and pilot were slightly wounded in the legs earlier by machine-gun fire on the bridge. Forward gun [crew?] overboard due to explosion of compressed air cylinders forward on the starboard side and hit on the mounting of the sighting mechanism. Gun can no longer fire due to turning of the boat. As the boat turns too far, I become aware that no-one is in command, so I take command and head away from the sailing ship on a zigzag course.

Prize continued the fight. Her shots smashed into *U 93*. As Ziegner tried to escape, a shell exploded in the conning tower. Another blew up in the hatch that led to the captain's quarters. It caused savage damage to number 4 port dive tank. Ziegner carried on his zigzag course, a trail of oil like a snail's track behind him. Dusk and smoke finally helped hide the wounded boat from the schooner.

Engineer and wireless petty officers both badly wounded. . . . As a result of this hit, the boat is not fit to dive. In control area, a hit on the periscope housing produces hazardous smoke, which is cleared with extractors. Starboard trim tanks are blown and port trim tanks partly flooded. Control area reports 'All compartments clear'. Boat is now under cover of darkness and no longer under fire. Boat is drawing about 5 metres of water, listing to starboard and losing much oil. As we are likely to be pursued by the sailing ship or a destroyer, I decide to head west all night and the next day until noon . . . assess damage and oil loss and then contrive another plan. If possible, we must make the boat fit to dive. During the night we look for internal damage: several rivets are leaking in the bow compartment, control area, diesel engine compartment and engine room and none of the starboard bunkers deliver fuel. Badly wounded men bandaged and given morphine.

No. 3 . . . Bay dies in the night.

As dawn broke the next morning, the cook boosted morale. He produced hot coffee. As the light grew stronger, *U 93* delicately changed course to avoid a three-masted sailing ship in the distance. Ziegner took stock. Externally, *U 93* was a disaster. Damage on the outside showed eight shell-holes in the deck. The bridge superstructure was all but destroyed. A hit on the base of the conning tower on the port side had wrecked valves and piping. On the starboard side of the tower, a shell had taken out both periscopes, although as *U 93* could not dive, this was of minor importance. Another round from *Prize* had shattered the instruments inside the tower. Some 10m of the deck itself were nothing but gashed and mangled metal. Both fore and aft guns were damaged.

Hopes of returning the boat to diving trim vanished as Ziegner and Usedom considered the destruction. Starboard dive tank number 5 had an enormous hole and was full of water. The shell that caused it passed through and exploded in dive tank number 4, smacking against the pressure hull and rupturing dive tank 3.

Like Sanders, busy with his own problems on *Prize*, Ziegner was not a man who gave in. Strained rivets throughout *U 93* were a minor problem; that the starboard fuel lines failed to work, no more than an irritation. Worse was the damage to the command compartment. The pressure hatch was buckled and stove in. The wireless was out of commission. Venting pipes to the port and starboard number 6 dive tanks were damaged.

One shot had hit number 5 compressed air cylinder set. The cylinders exploded. That, in turn, holed number 2 starboard fuel tank. The pressure hull had a few dents in it. If *U 93* ever managed to submerge, she had every chance of permanently going to the bottom of the sea.

Ziegner decided. A brief service and the body of Bootsmannsmaat Bay, dignified by the Imperial German Navy Ensign, slipped overboard into the chill water. Then the Oberleutnant spoke to the crew. He would take them home to Germany.

While the crew deafened themselves with the sounds of hammering, cutting, riveting and metal-bending, Ziegner and the senior engineer calculated how they could manage on the remaining fuel. The war diary entry was terse:

Worked out that 27.425 tonnes of fuel had been lost and 24.166 t remained. Calculated this was sufficient, at 7.5 knots on the diesel electric motors, burning 2.2–2.3 tonnes per day and allowing a reserve for emergency high-speed evasive action, if needed, to get the boat home round the Shetlands, providing a torpedo boat escort could be arranged from the Skagerrak by wireless. Boat rigged with explosives in case of need to scuttle and kept primed throughout return voyage. As the watertight hatch could not be sealed for diving, I decide to remain on the surface and blow torpedo tubes, torpedo tanks and forward trim tanks to lighten the boat, make it ride higher in the water and thus make better headway. List to starboard corrected by blowing the relevant tanks every 1–3 hours, depending on sea state.

Two thousand sea miles to run at less than 8 miles an hour. The boat needed every drop of fuel. The mechanics drained 400 litres from the starboard supply tank to drip-feed the engines directly through a funnel. An attempt to recover oil from the port side failed. It had already leaked through a shell-hole in dive tank number 5. The crew managed to make a large patch to bolt over the hole. Once that was secure, they managed to blow the starboard dive tanks to reduce the list.

With a final flourish of wood and canvas to patch the damage to the bridge, *U 93* dug her way through the waves. The weather worsened. With the stern already under water and a rising wind, Ziegner ordered everything possible overboard. The holes, patched with anything to hand, continually let in the sea. Every thirty minutes, the starboard tanks filled. Every thirty minutes, the engineers blew it back out. The pumps worked frantically, day in, day out.

Short water rations hardly helped. The sea had contaminated some fresh water tanks. The U-boat carried on. Day after day. A fleet of armed trawlers failed to see *U 93*, low in the water, grey as the waves surrounding her, as they scoured the ocean for U-boats.

Wilhelmshaven, once a dream, came nearer. After a close encounter with a hungry destroyer that lost *U 93* in a rain squall, Ziegner reached the Danish coast. He ignored the 3-mile limit, creeping along so close to the beach that his men heard the tinkling bells on the wether sheep among the flocks grazing in the meadows.

Nine days after *Prize* met *U 93*, two German fishing steamers responded to Ziegner's signal. They accompanied the boat to Sylt. At 0500 the next morning, her oil tanks empty, *U 93* returned to Wilhelmshaven under tow.

Prize. U 93. Lieutenant William Sanders. Oberleutnant zur See Wilhelm Ziegner. Neither knew when he was beaten. Fortitude. Valour. Duty. Determination. The two lieutenants had much in common.

On Friday 22 June 1917, the Second Supplement to the *London Gazette* carried a brief notice at the very beginning of the first of its six pages. It stated simply that the King had approved the award of the Victoria Cross to William Edward Sanders 'in recognition of his conspicuous gallantry, consummate coolness, and skill in command of one of HM ships in action'. The remainder of his crew were not ignored. Every one received a decoration.

Recognition came as well to Wilhelm Ziegner. Not, perhaps, as much as he deserved. The Iron Cross First Class, a normal perquisite of the first watch officer on a U-boat, arrived earlier than normal.

May offered some faint hope to the Allied cause. Convoys were still few and far between. The Scandinavian routes benefited from the new system in April but Atlantic routes were another matter. It was not simply a question of organising convoys, although that was complicated enough. In practice, the Admiralty remained unconvinced that they worked. Many admirals continued to believe that the older methods countered the U-boat more effectively.

One change did occur without any prompting. Aware that the concept of the Q-ship was known to the enemy, the designation changed. The men and the vessels were allocated to 'Special Service', a bland term that implied much but revealed little.

Lloyd George clenched the bit firmly between his Welsh teeth when it came to convoys. Prudence alone at the Admiralty suggested that the system should be tried as soon as practicable. On 10 May 1917, sixteen merchantmen left Gibraltar for Britain. Two decoys and three armed yachts escorted them.

At a speed a shade under 7 knots, they chugged across the Bay of Biscay without incident. After eight days, they came within 100 miles of the Irish coast. Six destroyers from Devonport met them. An RNAS flying boat from the Scilly Isles searched the ocean ahead. The convoy arrived safely at the Smalls, one of two tiny clusters of rock lying close together in the Irish Sea, 21 miles due west of Milford Haven. There it split, each ship making its way to its individual destination, each one accompanied by an armed drifter.

No ship was lost. The motley collection of vessels had kept station reasonably well. Dog-leg manoeuvres caused no great problems. Ships' engines had managed without breaking down.

While the Gibraltar convoy was on its way, a 'protected sailing' of ten ships left Virginia on 24 May. A U-boat picked off the one straggler as the group reached the Western Approaches. Otherwise, every ship made port safely.

Casual analysis of the figures apparently shows that the tide had turned. A total of 596,629 tons of shipping went to the sea floor. The Allies claimed to have sunk six boats. None fell to decoys.

The truth was less encouraging. The reduction in ship losses resulted from a drop in the number of boats on patrol. In April, U-boats were at sea for 660 days. In May, this dropped to 535 cruise days.

The Gibraltar convoy did not meet a U-boat for most of its journey. A protective guard of eleven ships surrounded the sixteen merchant steamers when they reached the most dangerous part of the route, enough to deter most U-boat captains. The true sign of things to come was the air patrol. Attacks from the air did not concern U-boat commanders especially. The small bombs used by the airmen were lethal only if they went directly into the conning tower. What worried them was that a sighting from the air could bring speeding destroyers hurrying to the spot. At 2,000ft, in clear air, pilots and observers could scan the oceans for 40 miles in every direction. To loiter on the surface could bring harm to a U-boat.

The RNAS flew both aeroplanes and airships on patrol. By April 1917, regular flights spied on the ocean all the way from the north of Britain to the Channel and the southern entrance to the Irish Sea.

Only the south coast of Ireland, where so many U-boats sank so many ships, had no air cover. Sir Lewis Bayly did not believe in aeroplanes. He felt that his ships were better employed hunting U-boats than rescuing naval aviators from the sea when their machines crashed. He did not grasp the simple fact that eyes in the sky made life more difficult for the U-boats. Further, they could warn shipping of lurking danger.

Like many admirals, Bayly thought hunting U-boats was akin to chasing the fox. Killing the fox saved the chickens from attack. The real answer to the U-boat problem, and the one that the convoy eventually provided, was to protect the chickens. The Kaiserliche Marine could send as many boats to sea as it wished. They were of little use if they could not find victims.

This philosophy directly contradicted the traditions of the Royal Navy. Training emphasised the importance of seeking the enemy and bringing him to battle. Nelson's final signal at Trafalgar, 'Engage the enemy more closely', was dear to British naval hearts. The U-boat, with its ability to vanish from sight, caused bitterness and chagrin. All anti-submarine warfare until April 1917 was rooted in the belief that the U-boat must be hunted to destruction. Every suggestion, every weapon, every measure, was judged by its ability to do that.

The statistics for the war up until the end of March 1917, available to the Admiralty, pointed up the truth. The Official History later recorded: 'There had been one hundred and forty-two actions between German submarines and British destroyers, and the destroyers had only sunk their opponent in six of them.' In simple terms, the odds against the hunters were 24 to 1, even when they found their quarry.

In May, as the convoy from Gibraltar steamed towards Britain, Jellicoe formed a committee to consider convoy operations in detail. A Royal Navy captain chaired the group of five serving officers and a civilian adviser from the Ministry of Shipping.

They worked quickly. In less than one month, on 6 June 1917, they produced their report. They proposed a system of eight outward and eight inward convoys, every eight days. They chose four ports as collection points for British-bound vessels. Gibraltar would be the rendezvous for Mediterranean traffic. Vessels from North American ports would congregate at New York. On their way to Britain, ships from Canada would join them. Hampton Roads would be the starting point for ships from southern American ports, the Caribbean, the Gulf of Mexico and Panama. Dakar, on the west African coast, would cover the South Atlantic trade as well as act as the marshalling port for ships travelling round the Cape of Good Hope to the Far East and Australasia. Each port would provide a convoy for Britain every eight days.

In the opposite direction, vessels from Britain gathered at Lamlash on the Isle of Arran, Queenstown and Plymouth for the Atlantic run. Milford Haven and Falmouth were the assembly points for Gibraltar and Dakar.

The Admiralty agreed. A formidable organisation quickly came about. In June 1917, four convoys, a total of sixty ships, crossed from Virginia to Britain. Only one was sunk. The incoming Atlantic convoys enjoyed the company of an aged battleship or cruiser until just outside the U-boat danger zone. There, destroyers took over. They shepherded the convoy until it reached a dispersal point, where the ships went their separate ways under the watchful eyes of coastal escorts.

Despite the introduction of convoys, the Admiralty still believed in the tactics of the fox hunt. During June, no less than thirty-one destroyers, supported by ten submarines, patrolled the North Sea and Atlantic either side of Fair Isle, where the U-boats made their way out and back from patrol. Twelve attacks yielded not a single kill.

The Kaiserliche Marine replaced its losses in May with new vessels. They had 150 U-boats in commission. About fifty stalked the waters around the British Isles. A mere dozen or so patrolled the Mediterranean, Adriatic and Aegean together with Austro-Hungarian boats.

On 7 June, Commander Gordon Campbell, VC, DSO, entered the war once more. *Farnborough* was replaced by a new decoy, the 2,817-gross-tonnage *Vittoria*. Campbell found her at Cardiff Docks in March 1917. She acquired a new name: HMS *Pargust*. Rapidly requisitioned, she steamed to Devonport for fitting out as a decoy. Despite an ongoing shortage of weaponry, she emerged with one 4in gun mounted aft, fitted inside a hatch with collapsible sides. Two 12-pounder guns, suitably disguised, took position each side of the ship's deck cabins. Two more sat amidships so that they could fire to either side. Two 14in torpedoes and four depth charges completed the hidden armament.

To enhance the impression that *Pargust* was a genuine tramp steamer, a conspicuous dummy gun dominated the after deck. Armed merchant-men were no longer a rarity. A highly visible gun would do much to convince a sceptical U-boat commander that the genuine article sat in his cross-hairs. As a final flourish, Campbell had two uniformed bluejackets to man the dummy. Their task was to point it at the enemy with much bravado but to scamper away without attempting to fire.

Most of *Farnborough*'s old crew joined him in his new command. Lieutenant Ronald Stuart remained as Number One. Extra guns meant more gun crews. More volunteers joined Campbell, among them Lieutenant Walter Henry Frame. He wore the ribbon of the Military Medal he won with the Anzacs. To show it was no fluke, he added a bar before he received his commission in the Royal Naval Reserve.

Campbell had kept himself informed of U-boat behaviour. He realised that torpedoes were far more likely than leisurely shellfire. He introduced two ideas to fool a suspicious U-boat commander. One was an electric bell to recall the panic party after an hour or so. If the apparent crew returned, the U-boat might surface to finish off the attack. His second idea was to have a second panic party. He thought that once the torpedo had struck and the panic party abandoned ship, the U-boat might realise it had attacked a decoy. As Campbell explained in *My Mystery Ships*:

> . . . our disguise might be disclosed, possibly through the torpedo having caused the guns to be unmasked or through some other mishap. In the event of this happening, the idea was to have a second, or as we called it '"Q" abandon ship.' For this purpose, we were to pretend the game was up, and leaving the White Ensign up and our guns disclosed, the remainder of the men who had been left on board were to abandon ship! The boats were to be called back to collect more men, any spare boats were to be lowered, and we carried a Carley float (or raft) which was to be launched specially for this purpose, being things normally only carried by men-of-war. This we hoped would convince the enemy that we were really all out of it – in fact, two guns' crews only were to remain on board, together with the necessary people on the bridge and a couple of men at the tubes.

After working up, *Pargust* sailed to Queenstown. By 31 May 1917, she was in Campbell's favourite territory, off the south-west of Ireland. Each night, *Pargust* cruised west, heading for America. Each day, she steered east, a British-bound cargo ship.

On 7 June 1917, *Pargust* ploughed through a choppy sea. Raindrops bounced off the deck, tarpaulins, hatch covers, driven by a stiff southerly breeze in an ill-tempered display of early summer weather. Well after dawn, at 0800hr on a gloomy morning, 50 miles from Ireland, a torpedo slammed into *Pargust*, plumb on the waterline. The decoy shivered with the impact. The torpedo struck precisely at the engine room, ripping a 40ft hole in the ship's side. The after bulkhead collapsed. Water avalanched into the engine room, the boiler room and number 5 hold. The starboard lifeboat disintegrated into splinters. Blast rattled every loose fitting as well as freeing the weights that held the starboard gun port in place. Seaman William Williams, the man from Amlwch, moved quickly. He took the whole weight of the port on himself so it could not fall to reveal the gun that lurked behind it.

Pargust's helm slammed over to provide a lee for the remaining lifeboat and the two dinghies. The panic party went over the side, finally joined by Lieutenant Francis Hereford, with a gold-brimmed cap, as the master. He clutched a cage with a stuffed parrot inside. The dummy gun crew ran from sight. At the last moment, pretend stokers crawled out to join the escapers.

Petty Officer Isaac Radford died when the torpedo hit. One engineer, Sub-Lieutenant John Smith, soaked through, his body peppered with bits of coal, shards of steel and other fragments, apparently went through the engine-room hatch with the blast wave. Less than a minute later, he staggered towards his boat station. He was quickly hidden but remembered nothing other than that he 'was swimming in the water for hours'.

At 0815, the last boat cleared the *Pargust*. Four hundred yards distant on the port side, the slender stalk of a periscope gazed at the scene. Minutes later, it moved closer. By 0825, it was 50yd distant. Then it retracted.

On board the decoy, nobody moved. Even breathing seemed too noisy. The periscope reappeared, this time close astern, passing to *Pargust*'s right. Round the decoy to the port side once more, close to the lifeboat and dinghies. Back to the starboard side. Finally, the U-boat surfaced, this time back on the left of the ship, a mere 50yd away.

The conning tower hatch stayed firmly shut. On *Pargust*, Campbell fought the temptation to open fire. Unless the first shot hit true, the U-boat would simply dive to freedom. She lay almost parallel to the ship, her bow pointing at the stern. The wind and waves had caused the boats to drift there. Hereford, in his captain's masquerade, stood upright. He realised that the 4in gun could not depress sufficiently if *Pargust* did open fire at such close range. The lifeboat carefully pulled towards the right of the decoy. The U-boat followed in a wide circle.

The lifeboat reached the starboard side, clear of the decoy's stern. Hereford moved the boat towards clear water. The U-boat went after it. It passed close to *Pargust*'s stern before it pulled clear, far enough away for the 4in gun to bear. An officer with a megaphone stood on top of the now-open hatch. He shouted orders to the boat. Hereford ordered his men to row back towards *Pargust*. This apparently annoyed the man with the megaphone, who began to signal at the recalcitrant lifeboat. An armed crewman joined him.

The U-boat sidled along *Pargust*'s right flank. Thirty-six minutes had passed since the torpedo struck. Seaman William Williams had been holding the starboard gun port closed for all but a few seconds of them.

At 0836, Campbell opened fire. The U-boat was sideways on at less than 50yd range. The first shot hit the conning tower. Several more followed. Almost at once, the U-boat listed to port. Oil leaked into the sea. *Pargust* fired a torpedo. It raced away into the distance, never to be seen again. The U-boat's after hatch flew open. Several crew climbed out. More came through the conning tower. Some raised their hands. Others waved. *Pargust* ceased firing.

The U-boat, her stern under water, surged ahead. The men on the after deck splashed into the sea. Campbell, thinking that her captain was making a desperate escape bid into the mist that hung over the ocean, resumed the action.

Pargust's forecastle gun barked. For some thirty seconds, it was the only gun that could see the target. With no engine power, Campbell could not turn his ship. Only when the U-boat herself cleared the decoy's bow could the other guns join the fight. After a few shots, the submarine's front end exploded. She rolled over onto her side, bow a few feet above the waves, then vanished from sight.

The panic party rescued two men. One officer, Leutnant zur See Hans Bruhn and one rating, Obermachinistenmaat Stelan. Kapitänleutnant Ernst Rosenow and twenty-two of the crew of *UC 29*, a minelayer from I Flottille, joined the lengthening list of the Imperial German Navy's casualties in the U-boat arm. Four days earlier, *UC 29* had despatched the Q-ship *Mavis*, south of Wolf Rock, killing four men.

Unable to move, *Pargust* wirelessed for help. Sir Lewis Bayly, confirmed once more in his belief that the best way to protect civilian ships was to hunt down U-boats, sent congratulations. At 1230, almost four hours later, the sloop HMS *Crocus* arrived to take *Pargust* in tow. Shortly afterwards, USS *Cushing*, one of the first six destroyers from America, bustled up in company with HMS *Zinnia* to escort the conqueror to port.

The Admiralty coughed up another £1,000 in bounty. More problematic was the question of awards and decorations. To soldiers on the Western Front, the haul would have seemed lavish indeed for an action that lasted only a little over thirty minutes. Campbell himself received a bar to his Distinguished Service Order and advancement to the rank of captain, a promotion that leapfrogged him over 500 others. Hereford, the fake master, received a DSO to add to his DSC. Two other DSCs and eight Distinguished Service Medals received royal approval. Eleven members of Campbell's crew received a Mention in Despatches.

Pargust, though, was to make history. The action, cool, well-disciplined, successful, deserved more than a hatful of lesser decorations. The Victoria Cross was the only appropriate award for such a display of determined gallantry. In the thirty-six minutes that *Pargust* waited after the torpedo strike, any one man could have betrayed her true purpose. One injudicious movement would send *UC 29* diving to safety.

King George V personally settled the matter of who should receive the nation's highest award for valour. He activated Clause 13 of the Statutes of the Victoria Cross. This allowed an officer or rating to be selected by a secret vote by his comrades. It was rarely used; this was the first time it was authorised for a ship's crew.

Pargust was to ballot two awards, one for an officer, one for a rating. Campbell's officers initially suggested that he should again receive the decoration. Campbell felt that this was not the purpose of the election and declined, explaining later 'that the Victoria Cross I wore was on behalf of my crew and through no special act of my own'.

The vote proved decisive. Lieutenant Ronald Neil Stuart, who already held the DSO, was chosen to receive the Victoria Cross. The other went to William Williams, DSM, who held the starboard gun port in place for half an hour. Without his action, *Pargust* might not have survived. Both men won their previous decorations for the fight with *U 83*.

Only one other U-boat went down in June 1917. Oberleutnant zur See Herbert Pustkuchen and *UC 66* failed to return to Zeebrugge. British records suggest that she was the victim of the armed trawler *Sea King*. Pustkuchen was the man who sank *Sussex* to incur American displeasure. *Sea King* was under the command of a certain Commander

Godfrey Herbert who once captained *Baralong*. The world of hunter and hunted was not large.

Whether Pustkuchen believed that the trawler was an easy kill or he simply did not see it before he surfaced only a mile away is a matter only for idle debate. *UC 66* dived as *Sea King* hurried towards her. The trawler dropped a depth charge. It sank and exploded. Six heavy detonations followed, probably on-board mines. Later intelligence confirmed that a boat of the Flanders Flotilla was missing. With an apparently valid claim, *Sea King* and her crew duly collected their bounty.

Some doubt exists about the claim's validity. The encounter happened off the Lizard, virtually in the U-boat's assigned patrol area, three weeks after she sailed. This gives her an extraordinarily long period at sea for her class.

Whether she sank by accident or design matters little. Only two U-boats were destroyed in June 1917, while in the same period 631,895 tons of shipping went to the bottom.

That month, the Kaiserliche Marine ordered more U-boats. Sinkings averaged over 600,000 tons per month but the English were peculiarly stubborn. Five out of the six months that the Naval Staff believed would bring a cowering enemy to the conference table had slipped by. Great Britain continued to fight on, apparently undeterred by the U-boats' depredations. To ratchet up the campaign a few more notches, orders went out for a further ninety-five boats. Of these, thirty-seven were the coastal UB II Class, thirty-nine were UC II minelayers, eight were deep-water boats and ten were monsters of 2,000 tons each, with the ability to stay on patrol for three months at a time.

The chief of the U-boat arm, Hermann Bauer, handed over his job to Käpitan zur See Andreas Michelsen. He took over a fleet of 132 boats. Sixty-one of them were on patrol, forty in the seas around the United Kingdom.

In Britain, officialdom realised that the U-boat campaign was succeeding only too well. In April, the month when losses soared, the chance of an ocean-going merchantman leaving the United Kingdom and returning safely was one in four. Jellicoe, pessimistic as ever, told a War Cabinet Policy Committee meeting on 20 June that shipping losses made it impossible to continue the war into 1918.

This miserable prophecy enraged Lloyd George. It was also a naval sideswipe at the Army. Haig and the BEF should have captured Zeebrugge and Ostend. This would end the activities of the Flanders

Flotilla. Eventually, the desire to stamp out that particular wasps' nest led to the abortive raids on the two ports in April and May 1918. Full of heroism, they became legendary. Properly planned, they would have succeeded with fewer casualties. Glorious failure redeemed by outstanding gallantry attracts more publicity and plaudits than a successful operation, meticulously organised, that avoids unnecessary sacrifice. The former is rewarded by medals, the latter by a footnote in history books.

More immediately, Jellicoe's gloom-laden opinion gave Haig the chance to proceed with the Third Battle of Ypres, soon emotionally known as Passchendaele. It would not only break the German army in France. It would liberate the Belgian North Sea ports from the German Imperial Navy. The almost mythical status of the two harbours as U-boat lairs had grown steadily since the start of the war. In November 1916, when Asquith was still Prime Minister, the War Committee made it clear that there was 'no operation of war to which the War Committee would attach greater importance than the successful occupation, or at least the deprivation to the enemy, of Ostend, and especially Zeebrugge'. For neither the first nor last time in history, intelligence got it wrong. The blue-water boats were the ones that mainly threatened British trade. They came from Kiel, from Emden, from Heligoland, not from occupied Belgium.

Lloyd George was not pleased. Already convinced that most generals and admirals were dullards, he planned to push Jellicoe out of office. Criticism already appeared in the press, particularly in Lord Northcliffe's papers, *The Times* and *Daily Mail*. 'You kill him,' allegedly remarked the Prime Minister to the newspaper peer, 'and I'll bury him.' But even he could not deny that the apparent need to neutralise the Flanders Flotilla outweighed any other matter.

Although the convoy system gradually gained ground, the lack of escorts hampered its growth. The Admiralty, still wedded to hunting patrols as well as a belief that the Grand Fleet needed two destroyers to every capital ship, emphasised its lack of escorts. Not only British admirals believed that this was still the better way to fight the U-boat. Admiral William Sims, temporarily in command at Queenstown while Sir Lewis Bayly took much-needed leave, pressed the US Ambassador in London, Walter Page, to lobby Woodrow Wilson to send more anti-submarine vessels across the Atlantic. The United States had been in the war for three months. Of sixty destroyers available, though, only twenty-eight operated in European waters.

The need for numbers received no help from the Convoy Committee, who believed the average convoy of twenty ships needed six destroyers as escorts. That meant fourteen flotillas, eighty-four ships in all, as well as fifty-two cruisers to supply the escorts across the ocean where the U-boats did not venture. It proved to be an overgenerous allowance.

Two facts stared every knowledgeable observer in the face. Germany sank merchant ships faster than the world's shipyards built them. German dockyards built U-boats faster than the Allies sank them. Given time, Germany would win the war. All Germany had to do was to keep going.

In July 1917, U-boats sank 492,320 tons of shipping. Seven boats failed to return. *UC 61* ran aground near Boulogne. *UB 20* fell foul of a mine while on a diving trial off Zeebrugge. Two boats, *UC 1* and *U 69*, simply disappeared. *U 99* was claimed by the British submarine *J2*, while *UB 27* is linked to a dubious claim by HMS *Halcyon*. Oberleutnant zur See Hans Niemer, captain of the seventh boat, *UB 23*, took his badly damaged boat to Spain rather than try to reach Zeebrugge through the Dover Straits. Depth-charged by the Royal Navy's *PC 60* on 26 July 1917, Niemer reached Corunna three days later.

Seven boats down from a variety of causes. The Kaiserliche Marine commissioned eleven new boats to take their places.

In Wilhelm's Second Reich, discontent on the home front marred this rosy prospect. Three years of war, marked by the British blockade, caused great privations. If the successes on the Eastern Front had turned into real benefits, there would be a different tale. For all her efficiency, though, for all her reputation, Germany could not seemingly bring grain, food, comforts from the conquered lands to home.

Worse, the U-boat campaign had not delivered. Admiral von Holtzendorff rashly claimed that it would bring peace before the summer harvest was gathered. Germany went to war in 1914 immediately after harvesting on 1 August. By the same date in 1917, the enemy showed few signs of crumbling.

Germany's allies showed the strain. Austro-Hungary neared total collapse. Despair, civil unrest, came from hunger, enormous casualties, and a growing belief that the war was lost.

The complaints echoed in Germany. Many no longer believed the Navy's claims of tonnage sunk and U-boat successes. Even Ludendorff apparently considered the Kaiserliche Marine's claims overblown. The First Quartermaster-General concentrated on planning a new offensive to win the war.

In the Reichstag, more deputies demanded an end to the war. Gustav Hoch, a member of the newly formed Independent Socialist Party, summed up their mood: 'U-boat warfare was to have been the solution, but it has failed. The Government is constantly urging us to hold out. Can we do that? We have exhausted our strength. We are in the midst of revolution. Working men already think of revolution. Trust in the Government has gone. Hope has ended and it cannot be restored.'

On 19 July 1917, the first crack appeared in the smooth façade of the Imperial Navy. The crew of a battleship, *Prinzregent Luitpold* complained about their rations. To make the point, they refused duty. Discontent swiftly surged through the Kaiser's pride and joy, the Hochseeflotte. The next day, many of the crew of the light cruiser *Pillau* walked off the ship. On 1 August, fifty of the more-disgruntled from *Prinzregent Luitpold* joined them. By 4 August, the men of *Kaiserin* and *Friedrich der Grosse* refused orders. A few days later, the men of *Westfalen* and *Rheinland* joined in. If not mutiny, it was close to it.

Matters were resolved, although an investigation revealed a startling truth. The protest originated from links between some ratings and discontented deputies in the Reichstag, deputies who wanted a negotiated peace. The politicians judged that Germany had reached the end. They sensed that revolution was close.

The war had become a race against time. Both for Britain and Germany.

THIRTEEN

GLORY IN DARK WATERS

On 4 August 1917, three years to the day since Great Britain entered the war against Germany, Captain Gordon Campbell, VC, DSO, left Devonport with his new command, HMS *Dunraven*. Just over 3,000 tons, built in 1910 at Newcastle upon Tyne, she was slightly larger than either of Campbell's previous decoys. She carried the essential 4in gun, together with four 12-pounders. She also had two 14in torpedo tubes and two depth charges.

Conspicuously displayed on her aft deck was a genuine defensive gun, a 2½-pounder, the sort carried by many armed merchant steamers. Campbell took meticulous care to make his decoy look like any ordinary tramp. Among his happier ideas were four carefully made railway trucks to act as deck cargo, produced entirely from wood and canvas.

As with *Farnborough*, as with *Pargust*, a masterly system of wires and hinges collapsed railings, hatches, cabins and derricks on command. When Campbell heard that an errant shell splinter killed an old friend on the bridge of his Q-ship, he installed armour plate behind the wooden sides of *Dunraven*'s bridge. A perforated steam-pipe was another refinement to confuse an attacker. Liberally punched with holes, it snaked round the decoy's upper works. A valve on the bridge allowed steam to enter the pipe on demand. When it did, an impressive cloud of vapour escaped amidships to simulate a hit on the engine room.

Most of *Pargust*'s crew joined the new ship. Stuart, the previous Number One, left to command his own ship. Anecdotal evidence suggests that he felt unhappy with Campbell's methods of command.

Whether or not this was true, his place was taken by the previous Number Two , Lieutenant Charles George Bonner, the former *Conway* cadet, in Antwerp the week German troops marched across the border. Bonner left his ship, *Incemore*, on 17 August, one day before it sneaked from harbour and returned to Britain. Determined to join the war, Bonner enlisted in the Royal Naval Volunteer Reserve in London on 8 September

1914. The enlistment papers show his trade as Second Officer in the Merchant Service and noted that he held a Master's Certificate. Bonner duly reported to London's Crystal Palace for basic training. One of his early instructors, Arthur Egerton Watts, later wrote that Bonner enlisted as an ordinary seaman because he thought the Admiralty would not employ him to run a ship during the war. Indeed, his entry into the RNVR nearly turned him into an infantry soldier. Most of the eager enthusiasts were earmarked for the Royal Naval Division, which proudly kept naval ranks and terminology but trained its recruits as infantry soldiers. For those volunteers, their future sea experience would be confined to sitting on troop transports taking them to fight overseas. Arthur Watts himself later served with the RND at Gallipoli. He wrote of Bonner that the authorities discovered 'he was a fully-qualified man and took him away. Bonner was a nice chap. I liked him.'

The Admiralty had realised that it needed officers of experience after all. The war was going to be bigger and more exhausting than anybody initially realised. Bonner was accordingly commissioned into the Royal Naval Reserve in December 1914. He eventually joined the Trawler Section at Larne in Northern Ireland to work on drifters. These one-time fishing vessels towed special types of nets which would, it was devoutly hoped, entangle any evil-intentioned U-boat.

In due course, he met Campbell and boarded *Pargust* as her Second Officer. Bonner subsequently collected a Distinguished Service Cross for the fight with *UC29*.

Campbell originally intended to sail *Dunraven* to Queenstown. A stream of reports from the Biscay area persuaded him to detour. He sailed eastward for three days, the dummy railway wagons clearly visible. *Dunraven* impersonated a Blue Funnel Line steamer on her way to Salonika or elsewhere in the Middle East.

No U-boat snapped at the tempting bait. On the night of 7 August 1917, Campbell turned back. The railway trucks became flat piles of timber and canvas. *Dunraven* took on the guise of a Blighty-bound tramp.

At 1050 on 8 August 1917, *Dunraven* was almost clear of the Bay of Biscay. She followed a zigzag course, like any prudent merchantman, at a steady 8 knots, 150 miles west of the Brittany coast. Eight minutes later, she sighted a U-boat on the horizon, ahead on her starboard beam.

On board *UC 71*, Oberleutnant zur See Reinhold Saltzwedel studied the juicy target. A steamer, roughly 3,000 tons, would add nicely to his tally.

Saltzwedel was a leading light of the Flanders Flotilla. If his hand occasionally strayed to his neck in anticipation of the 'Kaiser's Necktie', the Orden Pour le Mérite, it was hardly surprising. In the two years since he left U-boat school, he had despatched more than 100 vessels to destroy 100,000 tons of Allied shipping. Saltzwedel thoroughly knew his business. *Dunraven* continued on her course.

At 1117, Saltzwedel gave the order.

'Tauchen!'

UC 71 dived.

Dunraven ploughed on.

Twenty-six minutes later, *UC 71* surfaced behind *Dunraven*, 5,000m distant. It was a standard ploy. Surface ships rarely had guns that fired backwards, over the stern.

UC 71's gun crew moved to the 8.8cm deck gun. Their target was at almost maximum range but they did not hurry. If the stranger proved to be a U-Boot-Falle, it would stay in range. If it were not, a few shots would cripple it before it escaped. The Oberleutnant had already met a trapship and knew their behaviour. In June, they had a run-in with a French decoy, SS *Normandie*. Saltzwedel was well aware that appearances could be deceptive.

On board *Dunraven*, the Red Ensign fluttered in the breeze. Campbell reduced speed by 1 knot but ordered the engine room to make smoke. This, he trusted, would give the impression that his ship was trying to get away. The decoy was heading into wind which was not ideal for the U-boat. In real life, a genuine tramp steamer could have given *UC 71* a run for her money.

The 2½-pounder returned fire. Its shells were in the general direction of the U-boat. They fell to the left, then to the right. Always, they were too short. Its crew, Leading Seaman Edward Cooper, Seaman William Williams, VC, and Wireless Operator William Statham gave a fine display of incompetence.

To impress the U-boat with her innocence, *Dunraven* transmitted panic-stricken wireless calls. 'Submarine chasing and shelling me. Help, come quickly.' 'SOS. Submarine overtaking me.' She wirelessed her position.

Dunraven escaped damage from *UC 71*'s deck gun. Most of the rounds splashed into the sea a little way ahead of the decoy's bow. From the U-boat, Saltzwedel believed he was regularly hitting his quarry.

Shortly after noon, Saltzwedel ordered full speed ahead. *UC 71* surged through the water to overhaul *Dunraven*. Unimpressed by his quarry's efforts at gunnery, the Oberleutnant decided to go for the kill. The choppy sea made accurate shooting difficult. Saltzwedel concentrated on catching up with the steamer.

At 1225, broadside on, slightly to *Dunraven*'s port quarter and 1,000yd distant, *UC 71* opened fire once more. Campbell warned his panic party to stand by. With the range reduced, Saltzwedel's gunners splashed their shells nearer and nearer. When one landed a few feet short, close to the engine room, Campbell opened the valve on his steam pipe, stopped engines and swung the helm to fully expose his port side to the watchers on the U-boat's deck. *Dunraven* lost way, wreathed in escaping steam.

'Abandon ship! Abandon ship!'

The panic party rushed into action. As a final touch, *Dunraven* wirelessed the news to a listening world: 'Am abandoning ship!'

Saltzwedel moved in for the death. His forward gun fired three times. The first shell crashed onto the poop deck where the 4in gun hid. Campbell heard a fierce explosion. He at once thought that the magazine had blown up, that the disguised gun was visible to his attacker. Hidden guns on freighters meant only one thing: a decoy. He ordered a distress call to any British naval ships within range. A reply came immediately. HMS *Implacable*, on her way home from the Mediterranean with a destroyer escort, detached one of her guardians, HMS *Attack* to help. Smoke and steam cleared from the poop. The deck was intact. The gun stayed concealed.

The shell exploded a single depth charge. It caused havoc. Statham, of the 2½-pounder gun crew, fell, severely wounded. Seaman A.S. Morrison, 25 years of age, from New Brighton, responsible for the depth charges, was thrown through the poop doors. A member of the panic party found him staggering back to his post despite fearful injuries.

Able Seaman Bennison, of the 4in gun crew, recalled:

. . . the magazine caught fire, and we got a message from the bridge to abandon ship. We thought, if we abandon ship we'll give the game away more so we stuck though the decks were getting red hot where we were laid and kneeling. The decks were quite hot, not red hot, but we couldn't bear it. When you go into action, you more or less throw all your clothes off and went [sic] barefoot – I was in stockinged feet. I always had an idea I wouldn't like to die with boots on; I had seaboots on previous to that and I just threw them off and was knocking around in bare feet. When the decks got hot we had some magazine boxes there and we stood on those and the other people were looking after themselves. We stayed out at the gun; the others weren't in stockinged feet but all kinds of rig, we were disguised to look like any old sailors.

Bonner was in command of the gun; he was in his controls which consisted of a dummy wire reel. His action stations was standing under the poop so that he could look right round the horizon. He did get blown out of that after the explosion. . . . We were alright, not serious wounds, except the man who was in charge of the depth charges. He was very seriously wounded. . . . he eventually died about two days later.

Bonner, the Number One, initially stunned by the explosion, crawled to the hatch in which the 4in gun and crew lay in wait.

The second and third shots from *UC 71* also landed on the poop. Fire raged across the deck. Flame fondled wood and canvas. Smoke, thick, murky, choking, curdled into lungs. One sailor ripped his shirt to pieces to provide gags against the fumes. Others lifted boxes of cordite clear of the hot deck. Nobody showed themselves to the watching U-boat.

Aboard *UC 71*, a mass of orange-red fire and black smoke billowed directly towards them from the steamer's poop. The U-boat moved closer to *Dunraven*'s stern.

Campbell made another signal to any ships that hastened to help. 'Keep away for the present.' He used his three letter Q-ship call sign, three letters in urgent Morse that naval wireless operators recognised. Campbell had decided to fight on.

The poop blazed with flame. The 4in gun crew, above the magazine, remained stoic. Communication between the bridge and the poop was cut. Campbell knew that the magazine would explode. So did the gunners. When it went it would take with it the gun, its crew and anybody nearby, as well as revealing *Dunraven* for what she was: a trap.

It is a measure of Campbell's leadership that every man on board was ready to die if necessary. If the magazine exploded, it might take the whole ship with it. Chances are there to be taken.

The U-boat was hardly visible through swirling smoke. But she came on. Soon, she would pass behind the decoy, out of the smoke into the clear light. Saltzwedel and his gun crew were below, the conning-tower hatch slammed shut. Not ideal for an attack. Campbell waited, prepared to take the chance. Duty decreed that *Dunraven* sink the U-boat.

A handful of lives lost against the saving of ships, supplies and other sailors was no bad bargain.

UC 71 passed the stern. Only seconds remained before the three 12-pounders would have her in their sights. At 400yd distance, at 1258hr on 8 August 1917.

At that precise moment, an explosion rocked the 3,000 tons of freighter. The 4in gun, complete with crew, flew into the air. The ammunition, stacked around, took flight, thumping back to the decks in every direction. The gun smashed into the well deck. One member of the gun crew fell straight into the water. The panic party rowed to his rescue. The others slammed down on top of the wood and canvas of the fake railway trucks. Petty Officer Pitcher, wounded, bleeding, finished up near the engine room. Bonner, head pouring blood, scorched, burned on his hands, found his way to Campbell on the bridge. Still the complete Number One, he apologised for leaving his gun position without orders. Dazed, he enquired what they were fighting. Campbell told him. Bonner expressed surprise. 'Is that all?' he answered. 'I thought it was at least a battle-cruiser.'

Bennison recalled little: 'I don't remember going through the air. There was just the explosion and I did nothing until I was picked up and taken to the wardroom; I don't remember who took me and I don't remember going there.'

The 12-pounder on the boat deck cracked off a couple of rounds. Saltzwedel did not wait for more.

'Alarm! Tauchen! U-Boot-Falle! Zwanzig Meter!' *UC 71* vanished below the surface.

Campbell knew that U-boat captains detested decoys. As long as *Dunraven* stayed afloat, she presented a tempting target. If the U-boat had the ability, she would try to sink the trapship. *Dunraven* waited. The White Ensign drooped at her masthead. Her civilian sister hung in the wreckage of the poop. The guns were clear to see. Campbell realised he still had a chance to win.

He ordered the doctor, Surgeon Probationer Alexander Fowler, to move the wounded into cabins and the saloon. The remaining crew fought the crackling wall of flame on the poop deck. The steel deck glowed cherry-red. The magazine, however, had not exploded. The depth charges had caused the damage, set off by a single shell.

At 1320, Saltzwedel came back to the fight.

From 1,000yd out on the starboard side, Campbell watched, with a sense of detachment, a torpedo head for his ship. It cracked into *Dunraven* between the engine room and the stern. Hatches and the long-suffering railway trucks scattered into the air and across the deck. The bulkhead between the hold and the engine room collapsed. The Atlantic rushed in to claim the space.

Campbell gave the command he introduced on *Pargust*.

'Q Abandon Ship! Q Abandon Ship!' A fresh panic party rushed into its performance. One boat splashed into the water. A makeshift raft of barrels and rigging spars joined it. The original panic party rowed back to take on a few extra men. With luck, it looked like the final curtain.

The crews for two guns remained to work the forecastle 12-pounder gun and either of the cabin pair. Four men occupied the bridge. Two torpedo operators stayed behind. Below, Fowler attended nine wounded men.

Nothing happened.

Twenty minutes passed. Flames continued to lick the poop. Boxes of cordite and shells exploded without warning as the heat reached them. The sea steadily flooded the ship. The boilers lost steam. Slowly, *Dunraven* began to die. Out on the water, the panic party huddled in the lifeboats and dinghy. The raft, abandoned, floated away.

At 1340, *UC 71*'s periscope poked above the waves on the starboard bow. For the next fifty minutes, Saltzwedel inspected his prey. From the starboard, from the port, from the stern, from the bow. All the time carefully submerged.

Campbell was reluctant to try and torpedo her. If he missed, which was probable, the end for him and his crew would be swift, sudden and brutish. *Dunraven*'s torpedoes were strictly a weapon of last resort.

By 1430, Saltzwedel was satisfied. Satisfied but still cautious. *UC 71* came out of the water to finish the business. Dead astern, 500m away. None of Campbell's guns could bear.

The hatch opened. The gun crew emerged. The first shot burst on the bridge. So did the second. Shell splinters buried themselves in the providential armour plate. For twenty minutes, *UC 71* battered the stationary ship in leisurely but determined fashion. To add to the unpleasantness, a Maxim machine gun joined the fray. Bullets rattled off deck fittings into the water. The men in the boats wondered if its evil snout would turn towards them.

No man on *Dunraven* left his post. No man moved. Campbell's crew were ready to follow him to the end.

At 1450, Saltzwedel submerged. Another inspection through the periscope. At 1455, when the U-boat passed a mere 150yd from *Dunraven*, Campbell tried his final card. He personally fired the port torpedo. It passed over *UC 71*, just ahead of the periscope. Saltzwedel did not see it. Seven minutes later, Campbell tried once more. Lieutenant Francis Hereford fired the starboard torpedo. This ran behind the periscope to pass over the conning tower. This time, Saltzwedel knew. The periscope vanished as it slid into its housing.

Dunraven's wireless muttered for help. Campbell, game to the end, arranged yet another panic party. He fully anticipated that the U-boat would make another attack.

He was wrong. With no torpedoes remaining, short on ammunition for his deck gun, the Oberleutnant called it a day. *UC 71* went home.

Vincent Astor's private yacht, *Noma*, arrived. The millionaire loaned her to the US Navy as a patrol vessel in May 1917. As the USS *Noma*, equipped with guns and depth charges, she became the first vessel to reach the crippled decoy. She fired at what might have been a periscope before she arrived at 1600hr. Close on her heels came HMS *Attack*, an Acheron Class destroyer, bone between her teeth, from the 3rd Battle Squadron. She had waited patiently in response to Campbell's earlier requests. HMS *Christopher* from Devonport followed.

Noma and *Christopher* sent their medical officers across to *Dunraven*. The two badly wounded men were transferred to *Noma*, which promptly headed for Brest at full speed. *Christopher* took *Dunraven* in tow once the fire was out and the worst damage patched. At 1845, the long haul began. *Dunraven* took in water faster than the pumps could handle it. Several feet of water sloshed about in the engine and boiler rooms. The rudder failed. No power. No steering. *Dunraven* was a disabled hulk.

The weather worsened. *Christopher* towed on through the night. As grey dawn stole across the Atlantic, hope still triumphed. Although the ill-assorted pair travelled at less than 2 knots, the stern was under water and the sky threatened poorer conditions to come, *Dunraven* showed no immediate signs of going under.

The sea tightened its grip. The swell broke over the stern with increasing anger. Campbell ordered sixty men still on board to transfer to the trawler *Foss* that arrived to give help. Twenty men stayed, including the injured Bonner. Head bandaged, unfit for duty, he persuaded Campbell to let him remain.

By 2100hr, *Dunraven* had little left. Most of the ship was flooded and under water. Two tugs, *Atlanta* and *Sun II*, arrived to take over the tow from a struggling *Christopher*. By 0130 the next morning, nobody doubted that the ship was done for. The remaining men assembled on the well-deck, forward. The tugs cast off the tow. Nothing could save *Dunraven*.

In the black night, in a freshening cold wind, *Christopher* closed on the decoy. Her open whaler prepared to take off *Dunraven*'s men. With the heavy sea, Campbell realised that only four men could make the trip to safety without mishap.

Campbell gave the order. 'Four men only to get into the boat.'

Nobody moved. Not a single man wanted to desert his mates. Campbell rapped out four names. They went. Reluctantly.

Rising water forced the remaining men to the forecastle head. Nobody shouted. Nobody panicked. On board *Christopher*, Lieutenant Commander Frederick Thornton Peters, her captain, took decisive action. The destroyer moved forward to bump her bow against that of *Dunraven* as it slowly rose higher. Each time the destroyer's delicately sharp nose bumped against the decoy, it fell away with the sea. Each time she bumped, one man from *Dunraven* jumped, in the darkness, onto her deck.

No man leapt until Campbell gave the order. No man questioned his discipline and control. Every man knew that Campbell himself would be the last man to go. If time ran out, Campbell would die. Real leaders accept the agony.

Dunraven fought to the last, abandoned as she was. Shells from *Christopher* failed to sink the hulk. Finally, the destroyer dropped a depth charge to deliver the final blow. At 0317, the Tyne-built steamer reluctantly slipped to her grave in 60 fathoms of water. The White Ensign still flew defiantly as her stern disappeared.

The Admiralty produced a rash of honours. Awards went to no fewer than forty-one members of the crew. Campbell himself received a second bar to his DSO, although many thought it should have been a second VC. The bronze cross did, indeed, go to two men. The Number One, Lieutenant Charles George Bonner, received his for exceptional personal bravery.

More controversial was the award of the Victoria Cross to Petty Officer Ernest Pitcher under the rules of Clause 13. To invoke the ballot for a group so tiny as the crew of a single gun caused comment. Nonetheless, their gallantry was an inspiration. Pitcher had commanded the gun. The other members received the Conspicuous Gallantry Medal.

The *London Gazette* of 30 October 1917 carried the news of the awards. The same issue advised that Campbell received the French Croix de Guerre by order of the President. Rear Admiral Sir Henry Oliver at the Admiralty was honoured with the Order of the Sacred Treasure, First Class, by the divine will of the Japanese Emperor.

Saltzwedel and *UC 71* reached Zeebrugge on 11 August 1917. A few days later, news came from Berlin that the Supreme War Lord had approved the award of the blue enamel cross with its gilt eagles to the Oberleutnant.

Glory could still be won in dark waters.

FOURTEEN

THROW THE CONFIDENTIAL BOOKS OVERBOARD AND THROW ME AFTER THEM

Details of trapships circulated throughout the U-boat arm. Commanders became wary. Further, once a vessel was identified as a decoy, it became a point of honour with the men of the underwater arm to put it out of business.

On 13 August 1917, Lieutenant Commander William Sanders, VC, and *Prize* patrolled the seas north-west of Ireland. The schooner had a companion: submarine *D6* under the command of Lieutenant Commander William Reynard Richardson. The two vessels sailed in loose formation, often several thousand yards apart. In theory, when *Prize* met an enemy, the submarine would be an unseen ally. *D6* would work her way round to torpedo the U-boat.

At about 1630hr, with the Swedish flag hoisted at her stern, *Prize* sighted a U-boat on the surface. *D6* was out of contact.

On *UB 48*, the crew came to action stations. The first of the UB III Class, she was on passage from Travemünde to join the Mediterranean Flotilla. Her commander, Oberleutnant zur See Wolfgang Steinbauer, enjoyed a reputation as a pugnacious and aggressive officer. Steinbauer decided to look more closely at the little Swedish schooner. The deck gun pumped out a single warning shot. *Prize* backed, her sails flapping, and heaved to.

Signal flags ran up the U-boat's mast. 'Leave your ship.'

Six men from *Prize*, the panic party, left the ship.

Steinbauer submerged. *UB 48* eased through the water to take a closer look at the schooner. She lay, sails flapping idly, apparently deserted. A slight list showed her empty deck. The U-boat motored round the little ship. Steinbauer saw nothing suspicious. No sign that she was a trapship. He moved some 1,200m away. *UB 48* surfaced. The lifeboat moved towards *Prize*. Steinbauer sent a warning shot over her head. Stay clear. The U-boat advanced a few hundred metres. The gunlayer squinted through the sights of the 8.8cm gun. Steinbauer, like most U-boat captains, maintained that his man was the best gunner in the U-boat arm if not the whole fleet.

Nothing stirred on *Prize*.

At 250m, Steinbauer ordered his gunlayer to open fire. Even as the words left his mouth, the Swedish flag came down. For a split second Steinbauer thought his earlier shot had damaged the jackstaff. *Prize* ran up the White Ensign. A gangway collapsed to reveal a small gun muzzle. The best gunlayer in the German fleet did not react. He suspected more to come. The small gun fired. Fragments hit the wireless mast. A deck side came down. A much larger barrel poked out.

'Alarm! Tauchen!' The helmsman, next to Steinbauer, jabbed the button that sent the alarm bell clanging through the boat. The bows dipped. The gunlayer, water already up to his knees, shot a single round, then ran for the conning tower, the deck falling away beneath his feet. His shell smashed into the 12-pounder as the water lapped over *UB 48* as she sought safety. Two shots from *Prize* followed her. They did no damage.

UB 48 positioned herself for a torpedo attack. Her periscope slid up. *Prize* moved out of her line of fire. Periscope down. Steinbauer tried again. Periscope up. *Prize* changed course. After several attempts, during which the decoy moved as if she read Steinbauer's mind, he gave up. He later recalled:

I decided to try and sink this ship because it was dangerous for all our boats. I went away, under water and stayed submerged until it began to get dark. It was late afternoon and, while on the surface to look around, I didn't see anything. It was too dark. Nothing to see around the horizon.

I went some miles to where I reckoned to find the schooner – but I saw nothing. It was pitch dark. I wondered how to find her.

When he surfaced, Steinbauer discovered how his target had read his mind. A shell had stopped the signal mast, next to the periscope, from fully retracting. Still with its flagged command to leave the ship, it poked up nearly 2m higher than the periscope. Every time Steinbauer looked for his target, the flags signalled his presence. The boat's engineer had to cut it down with an oxygen burner.

Prize and *D6* met in the gathering gloom. Sanders told Richardson about the scrap with the U-boat. Although the schooner had taken minor damage, they agreed to continue the patrol. *D6* would always be within a few miles of *Prize*.

Steinbauer decided to sail in a wide circle. The schooner could not have gone far. A circle would cut across its course. He spent two hours in the search. Nothing to be seen. He could not afford to use up much more fuel. It was a pity but he would have to let the decoy escape. He had to set course for Gibraltar.

At that moment, I saw suddenly a light, a small light. For less than a second. I immediately took course on this light. It was the schooner. I thought someone had lit a pipe or opened a porthole.

It may have been a moment of carelessness or somebody possibly attempted to contact *D6*, some miles away.

Steinbauer would not let her escape again. At 0305hr, with rain squalls sweeping across a phosphorescent sea, Steinbauer tried a bow shot.

Now I made the first attack of my life on the surface during the night. During a dark night.

And I shot a torpedo and missed him. Made all the observation notes . . . one can shoot a torpedo on the surface but it is different – the distance, the speed, of the torpedo, speed of the attacked vessel – all this must be exactly observed by triangulation and one can't see in the dark night. The observation is difficult and I failed.

. . . on a dark night when you approach a sailing ship, the sails are high and big and you have the impression you are very near . . . I thought I fired from about 400 metres – a distance for a sure hit. Impossible for the ship to turn away. Then I . . . went on the same course that he was going. I realised then that he was not sailing – he was using an engine and I suppose he was making 4 or 5 knots.

I began a new attack. We were parallel . . . and fired a bit nearer. I thought about 300 metres . . . I counted when the torpedo left the boat. My observation – about 300 metres, 20 seconds and nothing happened, 30 seconds – nothing. 40 – nothing. At 45 seconds, the torpedo blew up. That was a distance of 700 metres – and I thought 300! My first shot was at least 1,000 metres!

. . . he blew up with a terrible explosion – I suppose we hit his ammunition room because it was like a firework.

Well, it was late at night, just before dawn. I was cautious enough to zig-zag in case there was a submarine in the area. I worried the schooner wirelessed after the events in the afternoon. It was now many hours later, so it was very likely a submarine or other craft had come to help.

We didn't see anything. The sea was calm and when light grew brighter we found wreckage where the ship sank. We went into the debris to search for survivors and we found in a lifebuoy, one sailor. We took him on our boat and tried to revive him. But he was dead. We committed his body overboard.

On the far side of *Prize*, about 3 miles distant, *D6* heard two explosions. A cone of fire spiralled into the sky. When they reached the scene the next morning, they found no survivors, only the débris of destruction.

Steinbauer went on his way. His orders allowed him to sink ships on his journey. He took full advantage of the instructions. *UB 48* sank two sailing vessels and the 3,270-ton collier *Winlaton* before she reached her new base.

Doubts in Germany about the U-boat war intensified. Bethman–Hollweg, the sceptical Chancellor, finally resigned. The German High Command, with a fine disdain for public opinion, planned to prolong the whole war into 1918. This was not something the politicians wanted. They anticipated revolution. Ordinary German citizens, promised that their U-boats were the bringers of victory, had little stomach for another winter of privation.

In Britain, Lloyd George continued his vendetta against the Admiralty. The Prime Minister believed that changes at the top were essential. He wanted Service chiefs who saw things his way. In August, he made his first move. Sir Edward Carson, the First Lord, supported Jellicoe. The Ulsterman had too much influence to be tossed aside, so Lloyd George booted him into the War Cabinet. This counted as a nominal promotion that could later be discarded. To replace him, Lloyd George appointed Sir Eric Geddes. Already a member of the Admiralty Board as Controller of the Navy, Geddes knew that Lloyd George wanted Jellicoe out of office. Lloyd George explained it simply. If Geddes found it impossible to work with the First Sea Lord, the Service chief must depart, not the civilian.

In a democracy, the military power must always subordinate itself to the civilian. Even so, Lloyd George began a process that courts disaster. The Prime Minister was not content simply to overrule Jellicoe, something that was his right. He wanted a more amenable admiral. Unchecked, this process leads to the appointment of generals, admirals and air marshals who agree with ministers at the expense of the men they command. Instead of standing up for their Service, they concur in the destruction of tradition and morale.

It is a sad truth that presidents, prime ministers, politicians and their assorted advisers rarely experience the dirty business of conflict. They never blister their hands to dig the graves of those who pay the price for their decisions.

Geddes had no qualms about wielding a blunt axe. His simple initial move created a new post of Deputy First Sea Lord. Geddes chose Sir Rosslyn Wemyss. When Jellicoe departed, a man stood ready to take post.

In fact, the Admiralty was moving ahead with some speed on convoys. More ships sailed with escorts. Sinkings fell. Not by much, it was true, but the maritime graveyard west of Ireland had less victims in August. For the first time since February, fewer ships fell to the U-boats in the Channel Approaches and the Bay of Biscay. The Mediterranean and the entrance to the English Channel remained highly dangerous. So, only the foolishly optimistic felt that the August total of 489,806 tons destroyed, minutely down from the July figures, showed that events had turned in the Allied favour. Pessimists pointed to a new and worrying development. The huge Deutschland Class U-cruisers, originally built as blockade runners, had become warships. At 2,000 tons displacement, they had phenomenal range and endurance. Able to stay at sea for three months or more, with remarkably good crew quarters, they carried two 105mm deck guns as well as eighteen torpedoes. The first patrol, by U 151, netted nineteen victims totalling 53,000 tons in a patrol of 105 days. With the ability to roam some 15,000 miles, the U-cruisers made the Atlantic around the Azores their fiefdom.

The fishing grounds of the North Sea continued to attract the killers of the Flanders Flotilla. As one RNVR officer explained:

Before the war, Lowestoft had a fine fishing fleet of about 250 smacks, of anything from 25 to 60 tons, besides a number of drifters. The latter were taken over by the Government on the outbreak of war, and nine of them were lost before it ended, but the sailing smacks went on fishing as usual about Smith's Knoll, which is a sandbank 25 miles north-east of Lowestoft. At first all went well with them, but before very long the enemy started sending submarines over to sink them. These submarines used to come up in the middle of the fishing fleet, and order the crews of the nearest smacks to abandon ship. They then went alongside and sank the ships by putting bombs on board, after taking away anything they wanted in the shape of food or gear. The matter became serious. Smacks were being sunk at a great rate – 150 were lost during the war, the bulk being sunk by submarines – nor was it easy to see how they could be protected, as they were obliged to fish spread out over a fairly wide area. It was finally decided to try and discourage submarines from suddenly bobbing up, and sinking the nearest smacks, by arming a few of them, and sending these armed vessels out to fish with the others.

. . . the enemy very soon knew all about the armed smacks and avoided them. Quite a number of men in the submarines had fished out of Lowestoft before the war, and occasionally sent in messages to former acquaintances in the town. They also sent threatening and insulting messages addressed to the armed ships through the crews of the smacks which they had sunk.

. . . The ordinary smack when fishing carried five hands, but the armed smacks, on account of the gun and motor, had to carry nine, or ten if an officer were on board. Smacks without an officer or motor carried eight hands. The difficulty was to keep the extra hands out of sight during daylight.

Tom Crisp lost his sailing smack, *George Borrow*, to Oberleutnant zur See Otto Steinbrinck and *UB 10* of the Flanders Flotilla on 11 August 1915. A determined man, he possessed skill, tenacity and a fierce desire to fight back. He took command of *Nelson*, a 61-ton smack armed with a 3-pounder gun. As the *G&E*, it exchanged fire in August 1915 with another Zeebrugge boat, *UB 6*, under the command of Oberleutnant zur See Erich Haecke.

G&E went through a catalogue of names before she became *Nelson*. *Bird*, *Extirpator*, *Foam Crest* and *I'll Try*. As *I'll Try*, in company with another smack *Boy Alfred*, Tom Crisp, with his son as mate, fought another action against the prowling enemy, on 1 February 1917.

The two smacks sighted a pair of U-boats. One signalled *Boy Alfred* to approach her. As Skipper Wharton complied, a few small-arms rounds spattered his hull. An officer in the conning tower ordered the crew to abandon ship. *Boy Alfred* promptly opened fire at close range with her single 3-pounder. The U-boat hastily submerged.

It was now time for *I'll Try* to fight. For two hours, the U-boat stayed at periscope depth. Each time Crisp sighted the periscope he would head straight for it. Finally, the U-boat disappeared. Tom Crisp decided to head home in the hope that the U-boat would surface. It did – at a mere 150yd on the starboard side of the fishing boat. According to Crisp's son, the U-boat fired a torpedo that missed. In return, *I'll Try* loosed off a shot at a range of 20yd. This hit, as Tom Crisp Junior recalled, 'right between the conning tower and deck. It blew the whole part of the sub to pieces. The sub went down head first with her stern sticking up in the air and the sea now covered with oil.'

The Admiralty rated both U-boats as 'possibly destroyed'. Tom Crisp received the Distinguished Service Cross for a gallant action. The skipper of *Boy Alfred*, Walter Samuel Wharton, received a bar to his DSC.

The two U-boats involved in the action were *UB 6*, commanded by Oberleutnant zur See Oskar Steckelberg, and *UB 16* under Oberleutnant zur See Hans Ewald Niemer. Both boats came from the ageing *UB I* Class. They had no deck gun. They carried no mines. Their armament was limited to two torpedoes and an assortment of rifles, pistols and a machine gun. Laid down in November 1914, only four of the type still served with the Flanders Flotilla. Both captains were inexperienced.

The war diary of *UB 6* basically corroborates the general outline of the fishing skippers' reports. Without guns of their own, they both dived as soon as a shot was fired. Neither boat suffered noticeable damage. They continued their patrol and returned to Zeebrugge as planned, to tell the tale of trawlers with hidden guns.

On Wednesday 15 August 1917, the two smacks joined together again at the Jim Howe Bank fishing grounds, 40 miles north-east of Lowestoft. *Boy Alfred* now displayed the name *Ethel & Millie*. Her skipper, 45-year-old Charles William Manning, universally known as 'Johnsey', took command of his smack only a short while earlier. *Nelson* carried nine all told. *Ethel & Millie* had seven souls on board.

Well aware that U-boat captains inspected fishing boats with extreme care to ensure they were not decoys, the two skippers spent the morning genuinely fishing for herring. In the early afternoon, the smacks presented a picture of innocence. Crisp, with two men, Ross and Hale, both regular Royal Navy ratings who formed the gun crew, worked below deck. The cook, an 18-year-old, was on deck with two other hands, gutting fish.

At about 1430, Crisp took a break in the fresh air. A mere 100yd away, *Ethel & Millie* went about her work. On the horizon, Crisp saw a shape, north-west of the Jim Howe Buoy, some 3 or 4 miles distant. He focused his binoculars. A U-boat. It commanded the water between the two smacks and the English coast.

Crisp alerted his men. Not only did they have to fight. They had to manoeuvre round the U-boat to run for home.

A spout of water marked the U-boat's opening round. It splashed into the sea 100yd from *Nelson*'s bow before the trawler's crew reached their action stations. Oberleutnant zur See Karsten von Heydebreck, commander of the Zeebrugge-based *UC 63*, wasted no time. Heydebreck had, in fact, handed over command of *UB 6* to Steckelberg six months earlier. In the closed world of the Flanders base, he probably heard enough to make him extremely wary of two Lowestoft boats in company, with not another fishing smack in sight. Q-boats or not, two English fishing boats, gobbled up on his way back to Zeebrugge, made a pleasing end to a successful patrol.

The second shot fell short. Crisp ordered the fishing gear cut away to help manoeuvre his smack. The next shell rocketed into *Nelson*, tearing through the bow just below the waterline.

Crisp turned the smack so the deck gun could bear. Ross and Hale did their best but von Heydebreck possessed cunning and skill. Having opened fire at 5,400 metres, he withdrew to between 6,000 and 7,000m. He could hit the trawlers. They fired short of the target. With her seventh shot, *UC 63* cut Crisp, at the tiller, in two, causing damage only too familiar to the men in the trenches. The shell went through his left side, carried on across the deck and through the bulwark without detonating. Blood spurted over the planking. Disembowelled, with both legs roughly amputated at the thighs, Crisp somehow retained consciousness. His son took over the tiller. Crisp ordered the crew to dump the confidential books over the side. Finally, he dictated a message to be sent by pigeon. '*Nelson* being attacked by submarine,' it read. 'Skipper killed. Jim Howe Bank. Send assistance at once.'

All four birds on the smack took off. The first three circled the fishing boat until the final pigeon joined them. At last, they all flew towards land. *Nelson* had little left. The hungry sea started to claim the boat. The time had come to abandon her.

Crisp refused to go. 'No,' he said, 'throw me overboard.' His son refused. The crew left him to go down with his command.

At about 1630hr, *Nelson* sank. On *UC 63*, Heydebreck watched the carrier pigeons wing their way into the air. The crew took to their rowing boat.

UC 63 turned her attention to *Ethel & Millie*. Heydebreck was in no hurry. His boat sat squarely between the trawler and safety. After an interval, *UC 63* continued the action.

Ethel & Millie received a direct hit that swiftly ended her resistance. At about 1820, Manning and his men abandoned the trawler. Her carrier pigeons flapped their way into the sky. *U 63* closed in.

Tom Crisp Junior told the Court of Inquiry, convened at Lowestoft's depot ship, on 18 August 1917, what happened next:

> The submarine left off firing at the *Ethel & Millie* and picked her crew up. We saw the submarine's crew line the *Ethel & Millie*'s crew up on the submarine foredeck. They tied the smack's boat up astern. . . . The wind being from the south-south-east was blowing the *Ethel & Millie* away from us . . . we rowed into the south-east as hard as we could, the opposite direction in which the smack and the submarine were going.

Mist crept over the water. Crisp and his comrades rowed away as hard as they could until both the abandoned *Ethel & Millie* and *U 63* disappeared into the haze. Minutes later, Crisp and his men saw black smoke billow from that direction but heard nothing. They presumed the smack had been sunk.

It had. Before they scuttled the trawler with an explosive charge, Heydebreck's men collected a trophy of war from her. With much effort and some choice curses, they brought the deck gun on board. They also collected letters and lists from the Admiralty and the naval authorities at Lowestoft that made it clear *Ethel & Millie* was a decoy.

Heydebreck's report states that both trawlers fought under the Red Ensign, yet some of their crew were undeniably regular Navy men in civilian clothing. Both boats had carrier pigeons. On the trawler, his men found hand guns and a Very pistol and he had brought back to Zeebrugge the deck gun and some ammunition.

Manning and his six crew never returned to Lowestoft. The war diary of *UC 63* does not mention their fate. In all probability, they were put in their dinghy to row home, a standard procedure among the U-boats of the High Seas Fleet and the Flanders Flotilla.

Heydebreck clearly thought his prisoners had not played by the rules. Trawlers with a hidden gun aroused little affection among the men of the Flanders Flotilla. Yet wilful murder is unlikely. To dump prisoners in their lifeboat with 60 miles to row was another matter. Even in August, the North Sea is a dangerous place for a small craft. It becomes back-breaking to row against the prevailing contrary wind. Exhaustion and exposure would end their efforts.

Concerned that the U-boat might return, Crisp and the crew rowed out to sea rather than towards land. At midnight, in the darkness and cold, they turned about to head for England. By daybreak, a freshening wind blew them further out to sea.

One pigeon delivered its message. At 1120 on 16 August, HMS *Dryad*, a Lowestoft-based Victorian-era gunboat still giving good service wirelessed its base: 'smack *Friendship* picked up pigeon 10pm last night from *Ethel & Millie* with message attacked by submarine Jim Howe 2/10. I have patrolled area since 4.30 am but have not met *Ethel & Millie*.'

Dryad, with a group of minesweepers, continued to patrol the Jim Howe Bank. They narrowly missed sighting the *Nelson* survivors on the afternoon of 16 August, despite the frantic waving of a large piece of oilskin and a pair of trousers tied on two oars.

The fishermen spent another night at sea. A rising wind frustrated their efforts to pull to land. At daybreak, they saw boats in the distance but made no progress. Finally, they spotted the Jim Howe Bank Buoy in the distance. It was 1030. Almost two days of struggle in an open boat had brought them back virtually to where they began. With a last determined effort at the oars, they reached the buoy. Tied to it, they hoped for a quick rescue. At 1300, *Dryad* appeared once more. Crisp scrambled to the top of the buoy and waved his handkerchief frantically.

At 1419 on Friday 17 August, *Dryad* signalled Lowestoft: 'Picked up crew of *Nelson* at Jim Howe. Skipper killed remainder all right. Crew of *Ethel & Millie* reported aboard submarine.'

On 29 October 1917, Lloyd George proposed a vote of thanks in the House of Commons to the nation's armed forces. It took only moments for the lilting voice to reach full flow. A crowded Chamber murmured agreement as the Prime Minister used every oratorical trick at his command. The soldiers, the airmen, the sailors received sweeping praise. Then, Lloyd George turned his attention to the merchant marine. The

House listened, spellbound, as the Welsh Wizard wove his spell with a tale of a humble trawler skipper who fought a U-boat:

> Though armed only with a 3-pounder gun and out-ranged by her opponents, she refused to haul down her flag, even when the skipper had both legs shot off, and most of the crew were killed or injured. 'Throw the confidential books overboard, and throw me after them,' said the skipper, and refusing to leave his ship when the few survivors took to the boat, he went down with his trawler.

The story Lloyd George told bore little relationship to the facts. That did not matter. When it comes to propaganda, to rousing a nation's soul, the mundane truth is usually less than inspiring. Lloyd George, having peopled the trawler's deck with dead and dying, glossed over the details. *Ethel & Millie* did not rate a mention. Their presence would detract from Lloyd George's thrilling tale of derring-do.

Four days later, the Fifth Supplement to the *London Gazette* of 2 November 1917 announced an award to Thomas Crisp, Skipper, Royal Naval Reserve. His name came immediately below those of Charles Bonner and Ernest Pitcher.

In 1917, only two awards could be made posthumously. One was a Mention in Despatches. The other was the Victoria Cross.

FIFTEEN

THE OCEANS BECAME BARE AND EMPTY

September 1917 brought faint glimmers of hope. Allied naval policy had, since the war began, been devoted to two aims. The first was that U-boats should not reach open waters. The second was that, should they succeed, they would be hunted to destruction. Admirable ambitions that met with little success.

It took three years of war for the Royal Navy to produce a reasonably efficient mine. Based almost in its entirety on the German version, it did at least explode when required. The minefields of the Straits of Dover and the Heligoland Bight, did not, however, stop the U-boats of the High Seas Fleet and the Flanders Flotilla.

Swarms of German minesweepers, protected by destroyers, swept the Bight regularly. They kept it clear enough for the big U-boats to journey more or less as they pleased.

The Straits of Dover proved no great obstacle either. A reasonably competent captain could take his boat through their minefields on the surface at night. Admiral Sir Reginald Bacon, in command of the Dover Patrol, considered that his major function was protection of cross-Channel traffic. As long as that remained safe, he believed his deterrents worked.

Bacon, like many highly intelligent men, found it difficult to acknowledge that he was ever wrong. He refused to accept that any U-boats ever found their delicate way through the complex system of mines, 750 miles of nets and myriad of surface craft, including two cruisers and, until the end of 1915, an ancient battleship.

Bacon agreed that smaller U-boats might try to run the gauntlet. Ocean-going boats, however, had to take the longer route around Scotland. The Kaiserliche Marine assiduously fostered this assumption. A directive to commanders stressed, 'Those craft which in exceptional cases pass around Scotland are to let themselves be seen as freely as possible, in order to mislead the English.'

U-boat commanders had strict instructions not to attack shipping in the area between the minefields and the nets. If the British realised that the Straits were regularly breached, they would take more effective measures.

Bacon was, however, substantially correct in respect of the High Seas Fleet boats that sank the majority of the deep-water merchant shipping. The big U-series boats essentially stopped using the Dover passage after *U 37* went down in April 1915. Apart from a few stray incursions and the brief periods of February to early March 1917 and December 1917 to January 1918, the big boats took the long route to their patrol areas. It was the smaller boats, the UC II Class minelayers and others, that sneaked through the Channel.

An event in August 1917 severely challenged Bacon's stance. According to Royal Navy sources, British low cunning sank the minelayer *UC 44* in one of its own minefields in shallow water near Waterford. She entered a field that the British pretended to have cleared. Subsequent research almost certainly proves she went up when laying her ninth mine. The explosion wrecked her stern. Minesweepers subsequently found eight other mines.

Whatever the cause, she yielded a rich intelligence harvest. Papers in her safe proved without doubt that the U-boats considered the Straits of Dover no hazard at all. That the documents referred only to the smaller boats made no difference. To many admirals, to Downing Street, and most of the British public, all U-boats were one and the same.

Apart from better mines, technical advances did not amount to much. Hydrophones were finally in service, although they gave poor results. Hunting flotillas so equipped chased around the ocean, only to learn that to track a submerged U-boat was no simple task. Under water, she altered course and speed at a rate the hydrophones could not detect.

Better depth charges appeared, along with mechanical 'throwers' that spread the charges in a pattern.

Most British submarines now patrolled the areas through which the U-boats passed to the war zones. They saw rather too many U-boats for complacency. They destroyed rather too few for congratulations. Low speed underwater and notoriously unreliable torpedoes handicapped the notion of the hunter-killer submarine.

Air patrols showed promise. Both aeroplanes and airships ranged far out over the sea. Working with direction-finding stations on land, they pinpointed surfaced boats by their wireless messages. Air attacks failed to destroy any U-boats. They did become one more niggle at the morale of U-boat crews.

At an inter-Allied conference in early September 1917, held to review the anti-submarine war, most delegates still believed the outlook was, at best, bleak. At worst, total defeat remained possible.

Jellicoe made two proposals. Both satisfied the Admiralty's yearning for aggressive moves. His first was to mount a colossal blocking operation against all the German harbours in the North Sea and the Baltic. The move envisaged the capture of one or more islands in the Heligoland Bight to act as a base. From there, British ships could sally forth on offensive operations. The possible enemy reaction was glossed over. Not surprisingly, the assembled admirals felt it was impracticable.

As an alternative to this stupendous scheme, they reached agreement on constructing a huge minefield to block the North Sea from Shetland to Norway. An enormous number of minelayers and escorts would drop 100,000 mines as soon as ships and weapons became available. As the British munitions industry, with all its other commitments, had no chance of making so many mines, the scheme required American help. The promise came. Production would, though, take some while.

As Kapitänleutnant Max Valentiner commented about a similar proposal to block the Otranto Straits: 'One day they will realise what every reasonable person knew from the beginning: the attempt to completely block a stretch of water 40 miles across is condemned to failure at the outset.'

Norway to the Shetland Islands is rather more than 40 miles.

Jellicoe's second scheme was to seal the German North Sea bases by sinking block ships at their exits. Destruction of the bases themselves was an alternative which, Jellicoe admitted, 'was an operation involving large military assistance'. A note of desperation sounds in this proposal. It was another step on the path to the 1918 Zeebrugge and Ostend raids that so thrilled the British public.

Only one man among the plethora of gold-braided sleeves realised that the answer to the U-boat had already arrived. Admiral William Sims of the United States pointed out that, contrary to most naval opinion, the convoy system was actually an attacking measure. It forced the U-boats to fight at a disadvantage. Then he sounded a note of prophetic warning. If the Germans decided that the convoy system frustrated the U-boat campaign, they might use surface ships. A determined attempt to attack convoys with heavy powerful ships would force the Allies to use their dreadnoughts as escorts.

If the conference had met four weeks later, the situation would have seemed brighter. In September, shipping losses fell to 351,478 tons from all causes. Further, in October, it became clear that the U-boats had moved to inshore waters from the open ocean where they failed to find targets.

The Atlantic is large. In good weather, a U-boat could spot a merchant ship up to 10 miles distant. A U-boat 15 miles away would not sight a convoy of twenty ships. In contrast, those twenty ships sailing separately could each be seen from anywhere on a 20-mile-diameter circle.

A certain Kapitänleutnant Karl Dönitz, sometime later an admiral in Hitler's navy, expressed the problem clearly:

. . . the oceans at once became bare and empty; for long periods at a time the U-boats, operating individually, would see nothing at all; and then suddenly up would loom a huge concourse of ships, thirty or fifty of them or more of them, surrounded by a strong escort of warships of all types. The solitary U-boat that most probably had sighted the convoy purely by chance, would then attack, thrusting again and again and persisting, if the commander had strong nerves, for perhaps several days and nights, until the physical exhaustion of both commander and crew, forced a halt. The lone U-boat might well sink one or two of the ships, or even several; but that was but a small percentage of the whole. The convoy would steam on. In most cases no other German U-boat would catch sight of it, and it would reach Britain, bringing a rich cargo of foodstuffs and raw materials safely to port.

Dönitz wrote of his time in the Mediterranean. The same applied around Britain. For the U-boats, it seemed as if someone had waved a magic wand. Ships became invisible. Like all predators, the U-boats duly migrated to seek their prey. They moved from the ocean to coastal waters. They still sank ships in large numbers but these were minnows of less than 500 tons that sailed alone.

Inshore, the Kaiserliche Marine also found the convoys – well protected by patrols and aircraft. No longer were the U-boats wolves among sheep. Attacks became a most risky business. Firing a torpedo invited almost instant retribution.

The statistics proved it. Ten per cent of ships sailing alone fell to U-boats. In convoy, the proportion plummeted to one or two in every hundred.

Convoys were not the sole reason for lower lost tonnage. Some redeployment of U-boats caused a drop in patrols. Temporary exhaustion of crews and support services also cut the effort. During September, some sixty U-boats put to sea. Eleven were lost by various means, the first month in which U-boat losses reached double figures. Seven new boats came into service. They entered the fray with inexperienced crews. In the British service, every submariner was a volunteer. In the more disciplined world of the Imperial Navy, ratings did not enjoy that luxury.

Q-ships still roamed hopefully, with little success. Decoys even fooled each other, as Lieutenant Muhlhauser of the *Tay & Tyne* recalled:

. . . a large steamer of about 5,000 tons appeared coming towards us. This was the very sort of ship that Fritz was looking for, a slow, unescorted tramp of comfortable tonnage, and the CO decided to escort her along the coast. The lack of depth charges handicapped us very severely as far as attacking was concerned, but he hoped if the big ship were torpedoed we might manage to get a blow in somewhere. We accordingly closed the approaching steamer and signalled: 'There is an enemy submarine ten miles south-east of you. I will escort you to the Tuskar.' The reply shook us to the core. 'Thank you. There is no need. I can look after myself. I am HMS *Starmount*.' It was another 'Q' ship!

Starmount served as an alias for *Stormount*, a Q-ship of half the tonnage Muhlhauser estimated. Less than three weeks later, on 28 September 1917, an unsympathetic U-boat torpedoed her without warning. She managed to reach Devonport.

In October, shipping losses increased to 458,558 tons, mostly down to the unchecked rampage in the Mediterranean. There, convoys were not yet standard practice. The five Allied powers working the area – Britain, France, Italy, the United States and Japan – squabbled over precedence, prestige, politics and policy at the expense of fighting the enemy. Convoys only began to operate in November, between Port Said and Gibraltar. They were poorly organised, with inadequate escorts both in number and ability and with little air cover. Ships continued to go down at a high rate.

In British waters, individual boats destroyed fewer and smaller ships on each patrol. Despite hopeful British claims that the morale of the U-boat crews had slumped, the volunteers and pressed men of the Kaiserliche Marine showed an unyielding single-mindedness. They fought on, to the best of their considerable ability. Against them, the Royal Navy showed equal resolution to control the sea lanes.

On 1 October 1917, an elaborate ambush operation began in the North Sea. Intercepted wireless messages suggested that a number of U-boats would return to base by the northern passage and down the North Sea. Accordingly, forty-seven destroyers, twenty-four trawlers and forty-two drifters, equipped with mine nets, and four submarines attempted to put a barrier across and along the route. The flotilla had some 300 miles of narrowing funnel to patrol. It needed 10 miles of mined nets to block the narrowest part alone.

Bad weather intervened. Some destroyers returned to harbour three times. Others abandoned their patrols to fight towering seas and howling winds. Only the fishing boats of the Auxiliary Patrol rode out the weather. In spite of ferocious seas, driving rain and gales, the skippers grimly maintained their posts, listening to the odd sounds that came from their primitive hydrophones.

At the end of ten days, the Admiralty believed that they had destroyed three U-boats, identified as *U 50*, *U 66* and *U 106*. These certain identifications came from intelligence reports, interrogations and guesswork. As was often the case, reality was vastly different. All three were destroyed elsewhere on various dates. The body of Kapitänleutnant Gerhard Berger, commander of *U 50*, washed ashore on 23 September 1917, three weeks after his boat succumbed to a mine off Terschelling. Similarly, *U 66* perished on 3 September, again from a mine, with Kapitänleutnant Gerhard Muhle and the entire crew. *U 106* failed to return from her maiden patrol. Kapitänleutnant Hans Hufnagel and forty men were lost in a newly laid minefield near Heligoland.

The forebodings of Admiral William Sims at the September Conference came harshly true in October. The Scandinavian convoys that had operated for nearly five months became the target. The Admiralty listening service warned on 15 October that German warships were about to move. Some eighty Royal Navy vessels flooded into the North Sea to stop them.

SMS *Brummer*, captained by Fregattenkapitän Max Leonhardi, and Fregattenkapitän Siegfried Westerkamp with SMS *Bremse*, both 'baby' cruisers of more than 4,000 tons and a top speed of 28 knots, hammered north from Wilhelmshaven. Designed as minelayers, they also carried four 15cm quick-firing guns. Their mission was simply to aid the U-boat war.

On 17 October, 65 miles east of Lerwick, they found a twelve-vessel convoy escorted by the British destroyers *Strongbow* and *Mary Rose* and two armed trawlers, *Elise* and *P. Fannon*. *Strongbow* was just astern of the convoy, *Mary Rose* some 6 to 8 miles ahead of it. Matters had not gone well for the escorts. What followed was a demonstration that chance in war can sometimes mean death, glory or both.

Mary Rose, under Lieutenant Commander Charles Leonard Fox, and *Strongbow*, commanded by Lieutenant Commander Edward Brooke, left a rain-swept Lerwick on Shetland on 15 October. With the two trawlers, they escorted a convoy bound for Scandinavia. Shortly before noon the next day, *Mary Rose* hurried ahead to meet an incoming convoy off Marsten in Norway. *Strongbow* was to continue westward, to oversee the dispersal of the convoy before rejoining *Mary Rose* at sea.

Darkness had already fallen when Brooke and *Strongbow* overhauled the Marsten convoy of two British, one Belgian, one Danish, five Norwegian and three Swedish merchantmen on the evening of 16 October 1917. A wireless fault prevented *Mary Rose* and *Strongbow* talking to each other. Brooke used his initiative to take up a position on the left of the convoy.

At 0600 British time the next morning, in poor visibility, *Strongbow* saw two ships she assumed to be British cruisers. *Brummer*'s war diary detailed the action:

> . . . vessel in sight . . . is identified as a destroyer with three funnels and two masts. Astern, 11 steamers in a two-column formation are soon discerned. Approximate course West by South. At the end of the north column, stationed somewhat north, is another three-funnelled destroyer of the same type as the first.
>
> The first destroyer sends recognition signals with a small searchlight. It is immediately repeated by *Brummer*, initially with a low-powered lamp, then with a proper signal light. She is apparently fooled by this and maintains her course. She then signals again with a series of characters to which *Brummer* replies with a string of poorly

semaphored letters. In the meantime, *Brummer* turned about one point to starboard. Range about 3,000 metres.

7:06 First salvo at the lead destroyer. Range 2,800; splashes short right. At this, the destroyer turns starboard. Second salvo: hit observed that apparently went into the engines so that she was without power. *Brummer* had by now turned to starboard, so the enemy was about 4 points to port. More straddling salvos and apparently many hits. Substantial smoke and steam engulfed her amidships.

A steamer, apparently a trawler, two points ahead to starboard, fired on *Brummer.* Judging from an impact 50 to 100 metres short, and bright yellow-green in colour, apparently with gas shells.

In the meantime, a larger steamer from the south column brought under fire, about 3 points to starboard. Vessel was armed and definitely fired a shot. Then numerous steamers of the convoy brought under fire in turn.

Brummer chases a steamer that is trying to escape. *Bremse* busy with destruction of the convoy. A destroyer is sighted to the NW, which is promptly flashed recognition signals. The destroyer sends six to eight characters in Morse code. Distance circa 6,000 metres.

Opened fire, which was returned at 7:40. Engagement with varying courses and speeds lasts until 8:06. Opponent fires quick salvos with good ranging on the bridge. Several straddling salvos. *Brummer* takes a hit on the forecastle that causes only minimal splinter damage. The destroyer received in total 15 hits. At 8:03 fire was no longer being returned. The destroyer is by now so badly damaged that she is dead in the water and enveloped in smoke and steam. Approached to circa 500 metres and fired three salvos. The boat was at the point of sinking. *Brummer* chases after a steamer.

Steered for steamer *Stella* from Ejsberg . . . Crew had already abandoned the ship. In passing, fired one torpedo at 500 metres, set for a depth of 5 metres which went under the target. Blinker signal to *Bremse*; sink by gun fire as *Brummer* has used a lot of ammunition.

A steamer, apparently a trawler, escapes. All ships of the convoy are afire or sinking. Entire convoy except for one trawler destroyed. Rescue work left to the ships' boats and the escaped steamer as position probably reported to the enemy via wireless. In addition, *Bremse* had reported a submarine in sight.

Neither Fox nor Brooke hesitated for a single moment to confront two vastly superior ships, each four times their own size. *Mary Rose* had an additional handicap. Neither her range nor deflection transmitters worked. Despite this, both ships sailed into battle to uphold the Royal Navy's long and gallant tradition of fighting no matter how high the odds against them. The Admiralty had issued no orders to destroyer escorts should they be attacked by superior forces. Lacking instructions, the two destroyer captains engaged the enemy. The official historian, Sir Henry Newbolt, observed with some acidity that: 'Little can be done if two destroyers and a number of unarmed merchantmen are attacked by two powerful cruisers; and still less is likely to be done if the contingency has never been considered or discussed. The incident proved, moreover, that if the Germans decided to raid the Scandinavian route with surface ships, it would be very difficult to stop them.' To add certain insult to definite injury, the Royal Navy failed even to glimpse *Brummer* and *Bremse* on their return journey.

The Admiralty were not pleased. Neither were the War Cabinet. Jellicoe, acting the part of a Job's comforter, solemnly assured the Prime Minister that the incident was 'the first occasion on which neutral ships had been sunk by surface craft without taking off the crews, which was a most serious breach of International Law'. Lloyd George was not impressed.

The convoy system continued to show results. Monthly tonnage losses in November reached just over 300,000 tons. Of this total, more than half was lost in the Mediterranean. In December, overall losses rose to about 400,000 tons, 50 per cent in the Mediterranean theatre. As with all tonnage figures, doubt arises. Some losses were quoted in gross tonnage, others in deadweight and some in net weight. As a general rule, totals from various sources can differ by about 50,000 tons per month.

In Britain, despite the improvement, the civilian population felt increased hunger pains. Shipping space remained at a premium. The need to transport and supply the US Army in France was the new priority.

The High Seas Fleet now had five U-boat flotillas. Flottille I was at Brunsbüttelkoog, at the mouth of the Elbe, with Flottille II at Wilhelms-haven. Emden was the base for Flottille III and Flottille IV. A new Flottille V, formed in September 1917, took up residence at Bremerhaven. As 1918 crept closer, U-boat construction slightly outpaced destruction.

With the collapse of Russia on the Eastern Front, Hindenburg and Ludendorff decided that a land victory was, after all, a possibility. The U-boat became even more important. The blow against the Allies in the west must be delivered before the Americans played a real part in the war. In December 1917, a massive programme of new U-boat construction received approval. Twelve U Class, thirty-six UB III, thirty-four UC III minelayers and twenty small UF boats, a new type for coastal defence. The programme brought the total number of boats ordered in 1917 to 273. As the Allies destroyed only sixty-three boats during the year, thirty-two of which were UC Class, the future held a certain bleakness for Allied shipping – provided only that growing unrest, increasing raw material shortages, hostile workers and demands from the Army did not ruin the construction programme.

On 12 December, German surface ships struck again. The eight destroyers of II Torpedobootflottille left their Wilhelmshaven base with damage in mind. *G101*, *G103*, *G104* and *V100* raced north towards Bergen. The others headed for the British coast to attack merchantmen gathering for the Scandinavian run.

Off the Norwegian coast, a British-bound convoy fought its way through a stiff north-westerly wind, with rain squalls and heavy seas. At 1200hr, the German destroyers ravaged the six merchantmen, two destroyers and four armed trawlers. The destroyers, HMS *Partridge* and HMS *Pellew*, had no answer to superior German gunnery. Help to the west, in the form of two cruisers and four destroyers from the Grand Fleet, was too far away.

Lieutenant Commander Reginald Hugh Ransome and the crew of *Partridge* fought desperately to no avail. Their ship was swiftly reduced to a floating, powerless target. Three torpedoes ripped into her during the fight. She sank within thirty minutes after a display of remarkable courage. *Pellew*, captained by Lieutenant Commander James Robert Carnegie Cavendish, crawled away, one engine out of action, into a providential rain belt. She was the sole survivor among the convoy and its escorts.

All four German destroyers returned safely to base. The remainder of the flotilla had had only slim pickings around the Northumberland coast. They sank two lone merchant ships and a fishing trawler.

In December 1917, as Christmas Day approached, Geddes struck. He informed Jellicoe, in writing, that he 'had come to the conclusion that a change is desirable in the post of First Sea Lord'.

Jellicoe responded with dignity. 'You do not assign a reason for your action,' he wrote, 'but I assume that it is due to a want of confidence in me.' He would, he continued, 'be glad to be relieved as soon as possible'. Sir Rosslyn Wemyss took over as First Sea Lord.

Jellicoe's sacking caused controversy throughout the Royal Navy. Arguments raged. Some muttered of resignation but Jellicoe squashed such thoughts. He had borne major responsibility as Commander-in-Chief of the Grand Fleet or as First Sea Lord since the war began. He may have dragged his feet on the convoy issue, although, in truth, there was little evidence to show that they would work. He certainly preferred an offensive against the U-boats rather than defending merchant shipping from attack. Like many naval officers, he found it hard to grasp the idea that the number of U-boats sunk was totally immaterial to the battle. What really mattered was protection. The wolves may roam through the forest as much as they like; if they cannot reach the sheep, their presence means little.

With Jellicoe out of the way, Wemyss lost no time in removing the obdurate Sir Reginald Bacon from the Dover Patrol. Bacon was a Jellicoe man; there was no room for supporters of the admiral in positions where they could obstruct the new regime. In his place came Keyes.

The move pleased Lloyd George. Keyes was a thruster, the very man to carry through the long-proposed assault on the North Sea ports of Zeebrugge and Ostend. Jellicoe and Bacon, in Lloyd George's view, had dragged their feet on the issue. Like Prime Ministers before and after him, Lloyd George was a fire-eater from the safety of Downing Street.

The Admiralty and the War Cabinet were obsessed with the menace of Zeebrugge. Intelligence reports over-egged the pudding to confirm the importance of the Kapersnest, the Pirates' Lair, on the Belgian coast. In fact, the Flanders Flotilla, brave and dedicated as it was, accounted for only one-third of the ships sunk in the U-boat offensive. Most Zeebrugge boats were the smaller coastal vessels. The real troublemakers were the deep-water U-boats. They lived in even bigger pirate lairs but those targets presented formidable problems.

The introduction of convoys, allied with the almost universal adoption of torpedo attacks instead of 'stop, search, scuttle', effectively ended the role of the Q-ship. Flower Class sloops and PQ Class patrol boats gave up independent roaming to become convoy sloops, positioned at the head, tail or sides of a convoy in the hope that an unsuspecting U-boat would attack them. By January 1918, the Admiralty decreed that they were no longer decoy vessels but were to be treated as ordinary sloops or patrol boats.

By February 1918, Bayly's fleet of decoys at Queenstown had shrunk to three vessels. All were small ships, none over 750 tons. At Lowestoft, Granton and elsewhere, the same applied. Chances of trapping a lone U-boat tumbled. The only hope was to ply the coastal waters. And if Vice-Admiral Charles Dare, commanding at Milford Haven, had his way, even that would vanish. He decided that the solution was to disband the hunting patrols and escort everything from coastal steamers to ships sailing to join a convoy. He explained this 'method would have at least one great advantage, in that a submarine would be compelled to attack within reach of a vessel capable of active retaliation. With the present system of patrols this is not the case: the enemy can, with the greatest ease, evade them, and only attack a merchant ship when they are absent.'

The admiral put the case for convoys into a nutshell. It had taken more than three years of war but the light had dawned. Without waiting for approval, he put his precepts into action on 1 December 1917. During the month, his ships escorted twelve convoys, a total of seventy-four ships, without a single loss. It took another six months for the system to be adopted for coastal waters. Some admirals preferred hunting with hounds.

In January 1918, Allied tonnage losses were 303,608 tons. In February, it rose slightly to 305,509. March saw a total of 320,708 tons lost. In January, only 33 U-boats went to sea; the total strength was 132. In February, of 129 boats in commission, 50 boats went on patrol.

By April 1918, some could see that, for all practical purposes, the U-boat war was won. April shipping losses fell below 300,000 tons. Further, new construction of merchant ships exceeded the losses for the first time since February 1917. For the rest of the year, losses would never outpace the building programme. Indeed, they would only once again exceed 300,000 tons, in August 1918.

April 1918 also saw the assaults on Zeebrugge and Ostend. Although the raids failed in the simple sense that neither port was put out of action, they became a triumph for British propaganda. A war-weary public, rationed in essential foodstuffs, readily swallowed the revelation that Keyes and the Dover Patrol had put the Flanders bases permanently out of action. Probably only unrelieved, unmitigated disaster would have stopped the Zeebrugge and Ostend raids being presented as enormous victories. That the attacks did nothing to reduce the work of the Flanders boats was carefully ignored.

U-boat tactics changed. Not only did they seek prey in coastal waters. Night attacks became more frequent.

In May 1918, the U-boat Flottillenadmiral of the High Seas Fleet, Kapitän zur See Andreas Michelsen, tried a fresh ploy. The idea was not new. His predecessor, Hermann Bauer, had proposed it a year earlier. Bauer's scheme was that several U-boats should act in concert. One of the big U-boat cruisers could be converted to act as a command U-boat. On board, a flotilla commander would use wireless to coordinate attacks by several boats on a convoy.

Michelsen decided against a flotilla leader in a command U-boat. It is surprising that it had taken twelve months for the U-boat command to come up with any suggestion to attack the increasingly successful convoys effectively.

On 10 May 1918, the operation, which lasted until 25 May, began in spasmodic fashion. Room 40 at the Admiralty identified several boats in the area of the Western Approaches. When the 'concentration' started, no less than nine convoys were in the area. Four boats lay in their path. None attacked. The next day, *U 86* managed to sink the *San Andres*, a 2,500-gross-tonnage steamer of the Thoresen Line on passage to Bristol. Apart from this single effort, the U-boats let the convoys pass.

Five boats – *U 43*, *U 70*, *U 92*, *U 103* and *UB 72* – took advantage of the night to congregate near the entrance to St George's Channel. Shortly before 0400 on 12 May, the RMS *Olympic*, sister to *Titanic*, saw a U-boat on the surface. Crammed with American soldiers, on her twenty-second troop-carrying trip across the Atlantic, *Olympic*'s bridge reacted quickly. The lookout on *U 103* had no chance to react to the darkened shape hurtling towards him. The steel bow of the liner cut into the U-boat at full speed. Ten of Kapitänleutnant Claus Rücker's crew died. He survived along with thirty-four others.

Less than sixty minutes later, Oberleutnant zur See Friedrich Träger and *UB 72* in Lyme Bay were struck by a torpedo from the submarine *D4*. Thirty-four men died. The British surfaced to pick up three survivors, retching in oil-heavy sea.

UB 72's patrol had not been a happy one. On her way to the rendez-vous, she ran the gauntlet of three depth charges dropped from an air-ship, twenty-three from a destroyer, one of which caused an oil leak that gave away her position the next morning, when a further twenty depth charges exploded near her. Shaking off that pursuit, she then suffered a further attack from a patrol boat that dropped a further five charges.

The disappointments continued. By the end of the concentration, only five ships fell victim out of a total of 298 escorted ships. By the end of the month, fourteen boats had been destroyed. Ten replacements arrived but the effectiveness of the U-boat arm declined. Efficiency fell because too many inexperienced crews now went to sea. Despite Allied claims that morale was low, prisoner interrogations show little sign of it.

In one specific area, the U-boats had a new enemy to face. Air power had arrived in the shape of aeroplanes and airships. They were not U-boat killers. The de Havilland 6, rescued from oblivion as a disastrous training aircraft, enjoyed various nicknames. These included 'the Clutching Hand', 'the Clockwork Mouse', 'the Dung Hunter', 'the Sky Hook' and 'the Chummy Hearse'. Underpowered, slow, it carried a pathetic load of four 25lb bombs, provided the observer remained on the ground. Pilots who flew the version with the American Curtiss OX-5 engine became accustomed to a spluttering, followed by a silence broken only by the gentle sound of a windmilling propeller. The aeroplane invariably obeyed the laws of flight to descend, more or less gracefully, to the waves below. One compensation for this unfortunate habit was that the DH 6 made an excellent boat and floated for long periods.

Flying boats became more worrying opponents. By 1917, the 5-ton Felixstowe F2A, developed from the American Curtiss designs, could cover 2,000 square miles of ocean on its patrols from air stations at Felixstowe, Great Yarmouth and the Clyde. Armed with two 230lb bombs, and up to seven Lewis guns, the F2A was an ominous harbinger of future anti-submarine warfare. Before the conflict ended, flying boats claimed two airships, three U-boats and a clutch of German seaplane fighters as victims. The U-boats claims, at least, were wildly optimistic.

Airships had a much longer range with enormous value as convoy escorts. Slow and relatively peaceful, they maintained station for many hours.

Both airships and aircraft were sufficient to force a U-boat to dive, for both could bring destroyers with their hated Wasserbomben into the area.

And out on the sea, a handful of decoys still roamed.

SIXTEEN

BLUE SMOKE CAME OUT OF HER

Lieutenant Harold Auten, RNR, commander of HMS *Stock Force*, was below, drinking an afternoon cup of tea, when the torpedo hit his ship at almost exactly 1645hr on 30 July 1918.

Auten, the schoolboy who joined the dignified Peninsular & Oriental in 1908, spent the first year of the war at Devonport. Able to boast that he was on the staff of the Captain of the Dockyard, he served humdrum days as junior assistant to a commander. They spent hours on the unexciting task of arranging the fitting-out of armed trawlers.

This relatively placid existence abruptly ended in September 1915. Auten went as first lieutenant to *Zylpha* at Portsmouth. The 3,000-ton collier, one of Sir Lewis Bayly's original Q-ships, came under the command of Lieutenant Commander John Kelty McLeod, RN. He and Auten, along with Campbell and others, transferred to Queenstown. Like many another Q-ship, *Zylpha* then spent months trailing her coat across the waters of the Irish Sea and the Western Approaches.

Other decoys engaged U-boats. *Zylpha* endured days and nights of long, uneventful patrols. The nearest she came to action was three months in Caribbean waters. Reports, nothing more than wild rumours in truth, reached the Admiralty that confirmed Whitehall's worst fears: U-boats on station in the Mexican Gulf, ready to strike at tankers on the oil routes.

The Kaiserliche Marine had already shown that operations in American waters were possible. Only months earlier, Kapitänleutnant Hans Rose with *U 53* caused a sensation when he arrived at Newport, Rhode Island, in October 1916. The U-boat with some of her ballast tanks modified to carry extra fuel, made the journey on Scheer's personal orders. The blockade runner and cargo U-boat, *Bremen*'s maiden voyage had been planned to reach America on 15 September 1916. The Royal Navy had sent a gaggle of warships to intercept *Deutschland*, her sister ship, on an earlier voyage. They failed, but Scheer reasonably anticipated that they would try again with *Bremen*. Rose had the job of spreading a little panic. He was to enter Newport harbour to show that Germany's U-boats owned an exceedingly long and lethal reach.

As it happened, *Bremen* never reached America. She vanished. Nobody knows why or how. The Royal Navy also failed to arrive. Agitation in Washington persuaded them to stay clear.

U 53 found only merchant ships in her path. US Navy destroyers watched Rose sink five of them, three British, one Norwegian and one Dutch, outside US territorial waters. The Kapitänleutnant took great care to act absolutely in accordance with international law and the Prize Regulations. Nobody died.

Zylpha spent weeks looking for the mysterious rumoured U-boat. Auten himself claimed that the boat was an old one, purchased from an unnamed South American navy. Its new owner, allegedly pro-German, intended to produce apparently authentic film footage of sinking merchantmen.

After three months, the Q-ship returned home to the cold, green waters around Ireland. Finally, in April 1917, she met *U 50* under the command of Kapitänleutnant Gerhard Berger. A torpedo swept by a few feet away after McLeod took evasive action. In the fight that followed, *Zylpha* was the target of some fifty-three shells, according to the bridge signalman who kept count. She at last opened fire at long range after the fiftieth shot. The decoy's first two rounds fell short. The third and fourth shots produced smoke on the U-boat's deck between the forward gun and the conning tower.

Berger made off. The crew of the *Zylpha* convinced themselves they had badly damaged the enemy. At Queenstown, her return set off a spate of rumours. Marine Hayward recorded that *Q6* 'was very lucky in action of 17th, having two torpedoes and 37 shells fired at her, only one shell hit, one sub sunk and another damaged'. McLeod went on to command the only ship specifically built for decoy work, the 600-ton HMS *Hyderabad*.

On 22 April 1917 Lieutenant Harold Auten took over HMS *Heather*, also known as *Q16*. She was one of the first Flower sloops built to look like a merchant ship. Her previous captain was killed by a shell splinter when *Heather* fought Kapitänleutnant Waldemar Haumann and *U 52*, west of Ireland.

Auten was not enamoured of HMS *Heather* as a decoy. He thought the Germans would recognise her as a trapship because of her earlier encounter. He was probably right. The Imperial German Navy made sure that their U-boat commanders received every ounce of information available about enemy warships.

Sir Lewis Bayly realised that the unrestricted U-boat campaign had changed the ground rules. 'German submarines', he wrote in March 1917, 'are now very cautious as to approaching a merchant ship, even when stopped and abandoned. Torpedoing ships without warning has become much more common, and when a torpedo is not used, the ship is shelled at long range for a considerable period.'

Heather's new captain had a fertile imagination, full of bright ideas. Auten claimed to have personally invented the scheme to pack holds with timber for extra buoyancy. Several other officers made identical claims. Auten also considered that he originated the concept of smoke pots, tubs of dried seaweed, placed at careful intervals around the deck. These were set alight when under fire, the notion being to fool the enemy into thinking he had scored hits. Others also demanded credit for the concept. In the closed world of decoys, like that of U-boats, discussions went the rounds. One man's orphan thought became another's mature idea.

May. June. July. August. September. Auten and *Heather* patrolled the Irish Sea with no success. The distant ripple of a periscope rarely disturbed the monotonous cruising, back and forth, back and forth. Colliers sank to the north, to the south. Coastal steamers blew up to the east and to the west when torpedoes smashed into them. HMS *Heather* sailed on, undisturbed. Auten decided that his ship was a liability, not an asset.

In September 1917, Auten bearded Sir Lewis in person. Bayly was an extremely approachable admiral, always prepared to listen to the men who did the actual dirty business of fighting the war.

Auten suggested that a small collier, a favourite target among the U-boat fraternity, would serve the purpose better than his own all too familiar convoy sloop. Carefully converted so her lines remained unchanged, she would have a better chance of success. To Auten's surprise, Bayly promptly agreed. 'I will send you away to the Bristol Channel ports,' Sir Lewis decreed. 'See if you can find a ship that is suitable. In the meantime, I will inform the Admiralty.'

The lieutenant found his ship on his first day in Wales. She lay at anchor in Cardiff Docks: *Stock Force*, a 361-ton collier. For the look of the thing, Auten visited Penarth, Newport, and Swansea but nothing matched his original choice. With a 29ft beam, she was a good 6ft wider than many contemporaries, able to take a pair of 4in guns without altering her lines.

After three months of back-breaking work that saw extra bulkheads installed, timber 'cargo' properly stowed, two 4in guns, two 12-pounders, one 3-pounder and two 14in torpedo tubes stationed and disguised, *Stock Force* looked exactly as she had done twelve weeks earlier. She was ready for action.

Auten, though, was not. Not merely imaginative, he was also a perfectionist. He wanted extra detail. He decided to improve his panic party with a black sailor. Non-white ratings were non-existent in the Royal Navy although many merchant steamers had them. After several interviews, Auten found his man. He had been torpedoed three times and did not suppose that another would harm him. 'He was a sportsman,' Auten wrote later, 'and that was what I wanted.' An English middle class male could deliver no higher praise. To be a good sport was to be one of the best.

In a final act of legerdemain, Auten and two trusted workmen created a further deceit. Imitation wooden sides appeared. They filled in the forward deck. A dummy boat, upside down, occupied the main hatch area. It looked for all the world as if it concealed a gun. The trio altered the rigging. They removed the mizzen mast. Spectators nudged each other. It was clear where the gun was hidden and the altered outline made her an obvious decoy.

As a final touch, Auten asked for false sailing orders. He then slipped out of harbour two days early. As soon as the collier was safe from prying eyes, the dummy boat went overboard, the bogus bulwarks smashed to splinters and the mizzen mast and rigging restored. *Stock Force* became just another grubby workhorse.

Auten had barely worked up his gun crews when new and secret orders sent him up the west coast of Ireland. The Irish question had haunted British politics for centuries. The Republican Easter Rising in Dublin in 1916 might have been suppressed. The agitator and traitor, in English eyes, Sir Roger Casement might have been hanged at Pentonville in August of the same year. Despite these deterrents, Whitehall continued to fear Irish revolution. Germany, it was believed, might try to land men and weapons by U-boat on some remote shore on Ireland's west coast. *Stock Force*, an innocent collier, was the ideal vessel to trail up and down in a hunt for gunrunners.

After several weeks, without a sight of a U-boat or even a rowing boat laden down with Mauser rifles, Auten and his men returned to decoy duty in July 1918.

Many people had already decided that the U-boat was effectively beaten. They had become a nuisance, not a menace. Monthly sinkings remained serious but containable. U-boat losses rose. Worse, from the German viewpoint, success rates fell. The big boats of the High Seas Fleet, the backbone of the campaign against Britain, enjoyed a strike rate in March 1917 of roughly one ship destroyed every two days. By June 1918, it had fallen, to one ship every two weeks.

Nobody, however, told the men of the Unterseebootflottillen that they faced defeat. Among the Zeebrugge boats, where losses cut deep, a captured officer mentioned that it was a point of honour to volunteer for the Flanders Flotilla. Morale remained high.

The German Naval Command certainly believed that victory was possible despite the deteriorating situation on the Western Front and the imminent collapse of her allies. Scheer was personally convinced the U-boats could and would succeed. In June 1918, a new construction programme for forty U Class boats, forty-four improved UB III boats and forty UC III pattern went forward. To help it along, 50,000 workers moved from Army contracts to U-boat production. Not only the Imperial Navy believed that U-boats were the key: the German government agreed.

On 19 July 1918, the U-boats showed they had lost none of their resolve. Kapitänleutnant Otto von Schrader in *UB 64* attacked the America-bound Convoy OLX39. Its seven ships included the 32,000-ton liner-turned-troopship *Justicia*, in dazzle-painted camouflage. The convoy had seven destroyers as escorts. About 23 miles south of Skerryvore Rock, itself 11 miles south of Tiree in the Hebrides, von Schrader stopped the *Justicia* with a single torpedo. The destroyers depth-charged busily without causing damage. Two hours later, as the liner came under tow, *UB 64* tried again. Her torpedo frothed harmlessly past. The destroyers, angrier, dropped more depth charges. *UB 64* stayed in position although the tin plates and mugs in the galley rattled. After another three hours, a third torpedo again missed the listing target. This time, the depth charges forced von Schrader to break off the action and head home.

By dawn the next morning, twelve destroyers, two sloops, two armed yachts and eight trawlers surrounded *Justicia* as she was towed to safety. The Kaiserliche Marine tried again. At 0910, Oberleutnant zur See

Hans Oskar Wutsdorff, in command of *UB 124* on her first war patrol, put two torpedoes into her. That ended the career of *Statendam II*, of the Holland-Amerika Line, requisitioned, still unfinished, by Britain from the Harland and Wolff yard in 1915. She was renamed *Justicia*, intended as a replacement for the *Lusitania*, but Cunard had no crew for her on completion. Anxious to use her as a troopship, the government passed the liner to the White Star Line. Their flag flew as she sank.

Wutsdorff's men were gallant but inexperienced; the U-boat lost her trim. She surfaced, submerged again as the now infuriated destroyers plastered the sea with depth charges, and then plunged to the bottom, hurt although not beaten. *UB 124* stayed submerged all day. At 1750, she surfaced to find HMS *Marne* and HMS *Millbrook* waiting impatiently. Chlorine gas was seeping through the boat. Battery acid had leaked into the bilges. Despite this, Wutsdorff dived, followed by a clutch of depth charges. Thirty minutes later, the U-boat came to the surface once more. With the diesels giving the best they could, *UB 124* headed for home. *Marne* and *Millbrook* intercepted her. Unable to dive, Wutsdorff scuttled his command.

Back in the Irish Sea in July 1918, *Stock Force* soon brushed with a U-boat. On a wet, rain-filled midnight, with a fierce wind and high seas, the officer of the watch saw the streak of a torpedo heading straight for the collier. It arrived – and came out on the other side, passing directly under the engine room. Decoy and U-boat feinted for position. At 0230, the U-boat fired another torpedo, its track sparkling white in the dark water. It swished by, 3ft in front of the bow. The night's excitement slowly died away.

Auten's next clash with the enemy, when the torpedo interrupted his tea, was not so inconclusive. The day was marked by minor irritation. The sun rose that morning on a placid sea. Overnight mist burned away as *Stock Force* plodded along the coast of northern France. To the left, sunlight glinted off the acres of glass houses that were Guernsey's fruit and flower trade.

Morse code yammered into the wireless room. A U-boat sighting. The enemy was working roughly on the line between the Casquets, a group of rocks 8 miles north west of Alderney, to 20 miles south of Start Point in Devon. *Stock Force* turned her nose to pass 5 miles south of Lizard Point, just another small collier trudging between Le Havre and Cardiff.

The French joined in at about 1000hr. Two Curtiss flying boats buzzed overhead, dropping messages to warn of a U-boat in the area. They advised the collier to clear out of the area. Auten waved, smiled, held his course.

The aircraft dropped bombs on an oil slick. Dead fish floated to the surface. An annoyed Auten knew full well that no U-boat would surface as long as aeroplanes were around. Eventually, at about noon, one of the Curtiss boats smacked onto the water, only to take off again short minutes later. At last, the aviators left for lunch.

The collier carried on. The afternoon ticked by. The watch changed. Auten retired to the saloon with the off-duty officers for tea.

The bridge watch saw the track of a torpedo heading directly at them. The alarm rattled throughout *Stock Force*. Over went the helm. The engines were rung to full astern. Auten reached the bridge in time to see the torpedo 50yd away. Almost at the end of its range, it seemed to move slowly through the water, innocent, harmless.

Until it struck.

It detonated directly on the second watertight bulkhead, blowing it through to the other side of the ship. Derricks splashed overboard, the deck twisted, planks and debris, shells and shackles flew through the air. Part of the bridge disappeared. Every man on it, with the exception of Auten, was wounded. Auten recollected only that he went up in the air with the blast and came to earth underneath the chart table.

A moment later, sea water, thrown up by the explosion, drenched every man on the bridge. Spluttering, nauseous, anticipating disaster, they moved to their action stations. Auten, stumbling to his feet, felt astonished and relieved to discover that none of the crew had died. Men took the wounded below. One man could not be moved. An officers' steward, Reginald Starling, lay pinned beneath a heap of wreckage and a 12-pounder gun.

To free the steward would take an hour or more. Time was not on Auten's side. *Stock Force* was settling, bow down, in the water. Auten told the wounded man that he would have to leave him for the time being.

Auten ordered the panic party to abandon ship. Below deck, the doctor worked frantically with the wounded. If the ship foundered, neither he nor his patients had a chance of escape.

Auten moved aft to the gun house. Both 4in guns remained unscathed. The roof shielding the foremost one had almost collapsed when the water spout descended. Water poured over the telescopic sights and cordite. Lieutenant Edward Grey, the Number One, in charge of the guns, promptly organised some men to hold up the roof with oars. If the roof gave way completely, it would expose the gun in all its glory for observers on the U-boat to admire.

And watchers there were. Kapitänleutnant Max Viebeg, commander of *UB 80* of the First Flanders Flotilla, took no unnecessary risks. The Pour le Mérite holder observed. He waited.

Auten observed. Auten waited. He could see all round his ship except for dead ahead. There, his panic party rowed around. There, the U-boat surfaced, 800m distant.

The conning-tower hatch opened. Two men came out. They observed. They waited. For fifteen minutes, long minutes. *Stock Force* sank lower in the water. Finally, *UB 80* moved forward delicately, slowly. The panic party pulled down the port side of *Stock Force*. They hoped to lure the U-boat after them. Under the collier's guns. *UB 80* followed. She crept into Auten's vision, 400yd distant, within the sights of one gun.

Auten held his fire. If she continued to move forward, both guns would bear. Three hundred yards distant. Beam on. In range. In sight of both guns.

'Submarine bearing red 90, range 300 yards. Stand by.' Auten whispered the command down the voice pipe. A moment's pause. 'Let go!'

The gun shutters collapsed. The White Ensign fluttered out. Both 4in guns opened fire. The after gun's first shot, the gun captain, Assistant Paymaster Athol Davis recalled, 'seemed to skim the conning tower'. Auten reckoned it took away the periscope and wireless mast. The second shot burst in the centre of the conning tower. One man, 'evidently the commanding officer' in Auten's words, went into the water.

The foremost 4in gun joined in. One shot smacked into the hull below the conning tower. Grey remembered that a 'lot of blue smoke came out of her and her bow went up in the air a bit, making a better target than ever. . . . We continued to fire, putting shells in as hard as ever.'

UB 80 went below the waves. Auten reckoned his guns scored twenty direct hits. By his account, wreckage littered the water. Grey saw the top of a table and what he thought were dead bodies. Not a man on board *Stock Force* doubted that they sent the U-boat to its doom.

The Kriegstagebuch of *UB 80*, the war diary, tells the story briefly and with several differences. Among them is the disconcerting thought that Viebeg identified the 361-ton collier as a tanker five times the size:

Attack on 1,500 ton approx. steamer (tanker). Course Guernsey to Lizard.

Fired G6AV torpedo. Hit. Range 1,200 metres. Remained at periscope depth and observed steamer that seemed suspicious and only sank slowly.

After about 15 minutes, the steamer started to sink at the bow. Surfaced at about 400 metres distant.

The steamer opened fire with several concealed guns. Crash-dive. During the dive, the boat took two hits. Went to 11 metres depth, fired a second torpedo despite inability to raise either periscope.

Remained submerged until dusk. Surfaced. One shot had penetrated the bridge shield and the periscope support. Both periscopes had broken lenses, were filled with seawater and useless. . . .

Without periscopes, the boat had to return round the north of England because of the light nights and the necessary use of a periscope for the Channel route.

Viebeg reckoned his boat took two hits, not twenty. He reported no casualties. The table that Grey saw may have been a piece of the bridge shielding. Certainly, *Stock Force* hit the conning tower to put both periscopes out of action.

Max Viebeg was hardly chastened by the experience. On his way home, on the long haul north, he took on what he estimated was an 8,000-ton ship escorted by two destroyers. He did not sink it; his torpedo failed to explode. Clearly, however, *UB 80* was no badly wounded casualty.

Auten called back his panic party. *Stock Force* was in a bad way. After the action, she listed heavily to starboard, her trim upset. Not a single compass survived. The wireless did not work. Steering meant pointing the bow in the direction of land in the hope of reaching it before the ship sank.

Auten's first job, once *Stock Force* was under way, became the rescue of Reginald Starling. He lay unconscious beneath the 12-pounder. One of his last memories before he slipped into oblivion was seeing the ship's black cat. She had been buried under waterlogged wreckage. Starling watched her fastidiously climb onto a plank, shake herself so that water sprayed in all directions, before she picked her way to a dry spot.

Auten's men dragged Starling clear before the water that seeped steadily into the ship reached him. They moved the other wounded, also menaced by the creeping sea, up ladders to the deck. After that, every fit man, walking wounded or not, bailed for their lives with hand pumps, buckets, saucepans, any containers that held water. As bailing developed a rhythm, Auten detached a few men to make some rafts. The boats could not take everybody.

The water rose faster than the crew could clear it. The 40ft hole in the side, the slow collapse of the bulkhead between engine room and stoke hold, gave *Stock Force* mere hours to live. Only the timber, packed with such care into the hold, stopped the collier from slipping under.

Hearts lightened at about 1830hr. Smudges of smoke appeared on the port bow. Two trawlers, drawn by the sound of gunfire, bustled up. One immediately took the wounded and most of the survivors, including a damp cat. Auten, Grey and a small group of volunteers remained to try and save the ship.

Two torpedo boats arrived. In the engine room, the water reached the boilers. The chief engineer and his men came on deck. Now it was when she would sink, not if she would. With a lurch, *Stock Force* heeled further over to starboard. The lifeboat on that side was all but afloat. Auten ordered his remaining crew to abandon ship. He and Grey waited for the end. It was not long coming.

Stock Force started to settle. Auten and Grey walked to the dinghy. They paddled across to a torpedo boat. At 2125, the collier went down. Torpedoed at 1645, 27 miles from land, she was within 8 miles of the shore when she finally succumbed.

Despite the conviction of every man on board that they had sent their opponent to the bottom of the sea, the Admiralty was not completely convinced. Other apparently doomed U-boats had returned home. This did not, though, detract from the gallantry of Lieutenant Harold Auten and his men. Of forty-four men on board, twenty-three received medals or were Mentioned in Despatches. Auten himself received the highest honour. The *London Gazette*, in sparse words, notified the world that he was awarded the Victoria Cross for his action against 'an enemy submarine'.

On 28 July 1918, Admiral Reinhard von Scheer arrived at German Supreme Headquarters at Spa in Belgium. He came to discuss the proposal to extend the U-boat blockade to the United States of America. Only three boats from the U-cruiser flotilla were available for the job. Scheer protested. He wanted them in mid-Atlantic, finding convoys, calling up the smaller boats to attack them in concerted actions nearer land.

A compromise that left the big boats cruising up and down the US coastline did little to help the dying war effort. They sank a considerable number of ships, for it was just like the old days before convoys. They fatally mined the cruiser USS *San Diego*, although the battleship USS *Minnesota*, holed but afloat, made it to safety.

No matter how often the U-boats patrolled, they had failed one major test. The ships that brought American troops, American supplies across the Atlantic stayed largely unscathed. The great strategic concept of a blockade degenerated into a series of isolated attacks on stray steamers.

And it showed.

SEVENTEEN

A NICE CUP OF ENGLISH TEA

In August 1918, the German army on the Western Front reeled backwards at the Battle of Amiens. On 8 August, Haig's armies spawned, in Ludendorff's bitter phrase, the 'black day of the German Army in the history of the war'. The Fourth Army took 22,000 prisoners and more than 400 field guns. It was a devastating reverse. It shook the Kaiser. 'We have nearly reached the limit of our powers of resistance,' he glumly declared. 'The war must be ended.'

Worse followed. The British Third Army, in the Battle of Bapaume on 21 August, captured 34,000 prisoners and 270 guns. On 26 August 1918, the First Army entered the fray.

In September the fissures deepened. The Allies worked in concert to hit the enemy in successive attacks, not only in the west. Germany's weaker allies came under the cosh. Turkey, Bulgaria, Austria-Hungary reeled under deadly assaults.

What Keyes' raid failed to do in April came with the success of Douglas Haig's troops. The German army could not hold Flanders. The Kaiserliche Marine abandoned the harbours of Zeebrugge and Ostend, along with the repair shops and dockyard at Bruges. Ships and U-boats that could not be moved were scuttled. Among them was Captain Fryatt's *Brussels*. Moored alongside the Zeebrugge Mole, she had spent the two previous years as classrooms for the Flanders Flotilla.

The Hindenburg Line, that bastion of German defences, fell. At Schloss Wilhelmshöhe, the Kaiser broke down when he heard the news. 'Our army is at the end of its tether,' he wailed to a group of startled dinner guests. 'The senior officers have all gone. It means nothing more or less than that we have lost the war!'

The Kaiser felt unable to swallow more than a few morsels. Even more startling to his entourage, he spoke hardly a word before he went early to bed. He stayed there the next morning.

Hindenburg issued a manifesto. It appeared in the press and on posters throughout Germany:

'We are engaged in a relentless battle with our foes. If numerical superiority alone guaranteed victory, then Germany would long have lain crushed in the earth. The enemy knows, though, that Germany and her allies will not be defeated by arms alone. . . . He wants to poison our will and believes that the German sword will be blunted if Germany's spirit is corroded.'

On 12 September, Pershing launched the US offensive against the St Mihiel Salient, the blunted spearhead that pointed at Paris. By 14 September, the Americans had bagged 16,000 prisoners, 443 guns and vast quantities of supplies.

The next day, a combined British–French–Serbian–Greek force on the backwater of the Salonika Front smashed through the Bulgarian lines. Their German stiffening had already left for the Western Front. Aware that the Allies were going to win the war, the Bulgarians fled in huge numbers.

In Palestine, the same day, Allenby swept aside the Turkish army with his troops. The end was clearly near.

Scheer continued blithely to plan for 1919, when the planned production of U-boats would be twenty-three per month. On 24 September, the Kaiser, voluble once more, visited the U-boat school at Eckernförde. Mere words failed to turn the tide of war. On 5 October 1918, the Reichstag learned from the Chancellor, Prince Max of Baden, that the government had asked President Woodrow Wilson to arrange 'the immediate conclusion of an armistice on land, water and in the air'.

The U-boat arm did this request no favours. News reached the White House of a torpedo attack off Ireland on SS *Harano Maru*, a liner, in which 292 died. Less than a week later, another torpedo doomed the Irish mail boat *Leinster*. As she sank, a further torpedo slammed into her. With 527 dead in that attack, Woodrow Wilson turned the screw. In a formal reply, he declared that neither the United States nor its allies would

. . . consent to consider an armistice as long as the armed forces of Germany continue the illegal and inhumane practices which they still persist in. At the very time that the German Government approaches the Government of the United States with proposals of peace, its submarines are engaged in sinking passenger ships at sea – and not the ships alone but the very boats in which their passengers and crews seek to make their way to safety.

Berlin had no choice. On 20 October 1918, Germany replied in suitably humble terms. She denied strongly, for the honour of the Imperial Navy, that the U-boats destroyed either lifeboats or their occupants.

'The Cabinet', Ludendorff recorded, 'had thrown in the sponge.'

On 21 October, Scheer ordered all U-boats home. The offensive had failed. Germany had lost the war.

The bitter irony that accompanies conflict did not fail at the last. Fifty miles out to sea, on the murky autumn afternoon of 15 October 1918, HMS *Cymric* chased after the fleeing *U 6*. Rumours of the war nearing its end would not save this survivor from the Kaiserliche Marine.

She rapidly caught her. The submarine, stern down, was sinking. Her wireless chattered frantically sending out a series of calls for help. *Cymric* arrived to find the submarine's small boat out. Men struggled in the water. British submariners. From *J6*, based at Blyth. The decoy picked up thirty survivors. One died before *Cymric* reached port.

The Court of Inquiry convened the next day. At the conclusion of the hearing, the Court recorded its opinion that *Cymric*'s commanding officer 'was not justified in opening fire before he established her identity, *J6* being in full buoyancy, men on conning tower, mast up, ensign flying, gun unmanned and not acting in any way suspiciously'.

The papers went up the line. The Commodore (S), Sydney Hall, expressed his opinion coldly:

It does not appear reasonable that an officer whose particular business it was, should be capable of mistaking the silhouette of *J6* for *U 6*, even if he did not know that *U6* had sunk 3 years ago.

The CO of *Cymric* seems to have expected J6 to challenge and to be unaware that it is clearly laid down that the surface craft should challenge, and the submarine only reply.

To expect a German submarine in this position to have mast up and colours flying, gun not manned and men on deck in low visibility shows a further want of judgement – particularly as he was in an area where he must have known that British submarines are constantly on passage.

The Admiralty deliberated. Commodore Hall made a further submission:

The '*J6*' should not be confusable with '*U6*' at 1,200 to 1,800 yards. The silhouette is as unlike that of any U as one submarine can be unlike another and this should have been immediately evident to the CO of *Cymric* if he had known his business.

Taken in conjunction with the mast being up, flag flying, men on deck, gun not manned and his being off Blyth where J Class have always been based, also that he waited whilst her bearing changed from ahead to abaft the beam, and her range altered from 2½ to 3 miles, to 1,200, to 1,800 yards, the action of CO of *Cymric* showed a great want of judgement and knowledge of his duty.

The Admiralty decided.

On 19 January 1919, the Senior Naval Officer at Granton received the official letter. The commanding officer of HMS *Cymric* would face no further action. The letter stressed that the officer had 'done excellent service and the fact that officers and men of HM Service have lost their lives through his action is sufficient punishment'. Too many lives had been ruined during the war. To stain another was unnecessary.

In Germany, Scheer had attempted to use the High Seas Fleet in one last glorious assault on the Royal Navy. He planned to send his big ships to draw out the Grand Fleet to the south, towards the Firth of Forth. There the U-boats would wait. There the U-boats would strike the final blow. They had been forbidden to sink civilian liners but warships remained legitimate targets.

Scheer planned the operation for 30 October 1918. The chosen vessels of the High Seas Fleet duly assembled off Wilhelmshaven on 28 October. Unlike the men of the U-boat service, the surface sailors on the capital ships had spent more than two years in idleness. They had no stomach for a death-or-glory finale. When orders came to raise steam, late on the night of 29 October 1918, the officers of the Kaiserliche Marine learned, in no uncertain terms, where to put their epaulettes.

The destroyer and U-boat flotillas stayed loyal to the oath. And the last bitter pill came for Kapitänleutnant Johannes Spiess, the 'Heinrich' who stood with Otto Weddigen four years earlier, when *U 9* showed the world what U-boats could do. *Aboukir, Cressy, Hogue.*

Now a captain himself, commanding *U 135*, Spiess finished the war with his U-boat's torpedo tubes pointing directly at the battleship SMS *Helgoland*. In response, she trained her guns on the U-boat. The stand-off ended eventually when the most disciplined fleet in the world openly mutinied. The Red Flag replaced the Imperial Ensign.

Sunday 10 November 1918, at Witte Huis, Eijsden, a small Dutch village on the Belgian frontier near Maastricht, promised to be as uneventful as all the other Sundays before it. As in Jonchery, four years and fourteen weeks earlier, nothing ever happened on a Sunday. Everything changed at 0600hr. Hauptmann Sigurd von Ilsemann, an aide-de-camp to the Kaiser, recalled the arrival on the German-held side of the frontier:

In front of us was a great barrier of barbed-wire. The border! We had made it. Country bumpkin Bavarian militia rummaged around the cars. One of them looked in wonder at the travel-stained Imperial crest on our car and called over some others. My hand tightened on the butt of my carbine. If they did not let us through voluntarily, we would have to use violence. Those of us in the Kaiser's vehicle stayed seated and did nothing to draw attention to ourselves. Frankenberg and Zeyss got out and spoke in a friendly manner to a few sleepy soldiers who emerged from the border post.

'General von Frankenberg with some officers who have important business in Holland!' That was clear. The armistice was obviously imminent. The gateway to peace was opened, a soldier jumped on to the running-board and soon afterwards the German Kaiser was on neutral ground. The German Supreme Commander could no longer fall into the mutinous hands of his own soldiers.

Six men of the 48th Landweerbataljon, the local militia, looked after the crossing on the Dutch side of the frontier. They came under the command of 25-year-old Sergeant Pieter Wilhelmus Hubertus Pinckaers. He had his orders. No Germans, bristling with weapons or not, could enter the country without permission. He explained to the general that nothing could be done until the checkpoint officially opened in one hour's time. A collapsing Empire was no reason to open the office early. 'Dat kan niet,' Pinckaers declared and that was the end of the matter. As sergeants have done since the days of the Spartans, he then told higher authority. The border office had no telephone of its own, so he walked to a local factory. From there, he alerted Major van Dijl, garrison commander at Maastricht, to the arrival of the German Emperor.

Ilsemann described the scene:

Hardly anybody was about. . . . Presently, though, came signs of life. Soldiers and civilians appeared from the houses, curious about the

German vehicles seeking safety. Several poked their heads into our car.

The Kaiser took out a cigarette. 'Children, smoke if you wish. You have earned it.' These were the first words he had spoken in about an hour. When he finished his cigarette, he suggested we got out.

Slowly the sun rose above the hills of a countryside that had been spared this terrible war. Church clock bells welcomed the Sunday morning. I said softly to Hirschfeld: 'Hear that? Those are chimes of peace.'

The Kaiser, walking close by, put his hand on my shoulder. 'Ilsemann, where are your parents now, and what news do you have of them?'

'In Darmstadt, Your Majesty, but I don't believe they will stay there because the French want to occupy the town.'

Still talking, the Kaiser walked with us up and down the village street. It was cold, almost icy, but gradually warming in the sunshine. Towards eight o'clock in the morning, the local district commandant, the major of police with his adjutant and a Dutch diplomat, Verbrugge van's Gravendel, who had left Brussels at eleven o'clock the previous night to tell the commandant of the Kaiser's arrival. Because we showed-up earlier, we had taken the border guards by surprise.

These gentlemen were most proper in the presence of His Majesty and suggested that we went to Eijsden station to wait for the royal train . . . an hour later the special train was on neutral ground. Until then, the Kaiser walked to and fro on the platform with the Dutch major.

People came from all around. There were continual shouts of 'Ah, Kamerad Kaput!' or 'Vive La France!' We saw shaking fists and looks of hatred and revulsion. There were catcalls and shrill whistles. I felt great sadness for the unfortunate Emperor. He, however, walked quietly to and fro, up and down the platform as if he saw or heard nothing. Photographers took snapshots. It was a mercy when the train arrived to protect the Kaiser from further humiliation. We took a small breakfast in the restaurant car but the blinds had to be lowered because the factory workers (mostly Belgian) continued their abuse. For a while, we feared that they might start throwing stones.

Finally, in the middle of the morning, soldiers and police on bicycles arrived to seal off the station and restore order so that we were shielded from further annoyance.

Telephone calls and telegrams buzzed between Eijsden, Maastricht and The Hague. A strict Sunday observance law hindered swift communication. Telephone calls could only be made during certain hours to allow the operators to observe the Sabbath.

Queen Wilhelmina held an emergency cabinet meeting. She personally felt great sympathy for the Kaiser's plight. Some of her ministers worried what the Allies might do. The Belgians, the French and the British wanted revenge. Kaiser Wilhelm II, the All-Highest, the Supreme War Lord was a prime target for wrath. Wilhelmina won the day. By the late evening, Wilhelm knew that the Netherlands was prepared to grant him asylum.

Wilhelm took refuge with Count Godard van Aldenburg Bentinck, a man who had cousins on both sides of the conflict. Reluctant to become the Kaiser's host, he gave way when Wilhelm, being Wilhelm, tartly reminded the Count of his duty. Wilhelm was Master of the Order of Saint John of Jerusalem. Bentinck was a Knight of the Order. As such, they had taken an oath to succour any fellow knight in distress. Refusal was not an option.

Wilhelm arrived at Kasteel Amerongen on a cold, rainy day, a little over four hours after the guns fell silent across Europe. A sprightly Kaiser rubbed his hands together after he had greeted his host.

'What I would like now', he said cheerfully, 'is a nice cup of English tea.'

It all worked out rather well for the aristocratic Hauptmann Sigurd von Ilsemann, who stayed loyal to his emperor. He married one of the Count's daughters in 1920.

EPILOGUE

The wrecks of merchant ships, decoys, warships and U-boats from what was once known simply as the Great War litter the seabeds around the British Isles. The sunken hulks, in shallower water at least, sometimes receive visits from amateur divers. Most lie undisturbed, which is right and proper, for many are the tombs of the men who once sailed in them.

Nobody knows precisely how many decoys, the Q-ships, actually saw service. Most estimates suggest that more than 200 roamed the seas in a search for U-boats. Some put the total as high as 400. The truth probably lies somewhere in between. Some argue that Crisp's *Nelson*, for instance, was not a Q-boat at all but a simple armed smack.

Whatever the definition, only two vessels associated with Q-ships remain.

Along London's Victoria Embankment, the curious will find HMS *President* (1918). She is a 'riverside venue'. The promotional literature describes her as 'a boat'. Long ago, she bore the name HMS *Saxifrage*. Built to resemble a merchant ship, she served as a convoy sloop. In 1988 she was sold to a private company by a government perhaps a mite too contemptuous of tradition and history.

The remaining survivor is the schooner *Result*, otherwise known as *Q23*. She sits on dry land at Cultra, the home of the Ulster Folk and Transport Museum. Built at Carrickfergus, she now resides not far from where she was made.

Of their opponents, even less survives. The original *U 1* is preserved in Munich. She never went to war.

A section of *UB 46* is to be found in Turkey; rumour suggests that a section of *UC 13* may also appear there. Vienna has a portion of *U 20*.

Some forty-four Q-ships sank in the war against the U-boat. No accurate record exists of how many combats they fought. About seventy is the generally accepted number. A meticulous calculation from German records reveals that the decoys destroyed, at most, eleven U-boats, plus two more that fell to trawler/submarine combinations.

Despite the bravery, and the lavish awards of decorations that accompanied them, Q-ships did very little to defeat the U-boats. The real factors in containing the threat were, eventually, the convoy system and the late arrival of better mines.

Many hopeful and exaggerated claims dot the official records. The Admiralty's largesse in paying a bounty for successful encounters led to some bad faith. Embellishment of combat accounts was not unknown. It was even rumoured that some Auxiliary Patrol vessels were not above depth-charging recently sunk Scandinavian ships in the hope of persuading a body to float loose. Scandinavian uniforms looked very similar to those of the Germans. And £1,000 bought a lot of beer.

For the British public, the men who served on Q-ships deserved every decoration, every honour, every privilege that came their way. Each one was another Saint George or Beowulf. Every man was a hero who fought sea dragons.

For Germans, the U-boat men were champions of freedom. They, too, fought dragons, especially the British one that wanted to destroy their country. It is dispiriting to realise that xenophobic propaganda has changed little in a century.

Perhaps the final words should come from a member of Campbell's crew on the *Dunraven*:

As so many VCs were given to ships in the Q boat service I think the captain of the U boat that attacked the *Dunraven* deserved the VC or Iron Cross. He knew we were a Q boat or armed ship but he carried on fighting. I would like to have met the captain.

When we sunk a U boat you give a hurray when she was sinking but inside of you, you were sorry. It might have been the opposite way round. They were only serving their country.

From the other side of the wire come the words of von Spiegel, commander of *U 93*, the man who fought *Prize*. Captain Albert Spencer, a close friend of Sanders, recorded:

Von Spiegel and Sanders used to play cards in the evening. They were quite friendly. Von Spiegel asked Sanders, 'After the war, you must come to my place in Bavaria and spend a month's holiday with me.

We will go shooting in the forest.' And Sanders said, 'No fear. You get me over there, and you'll shoot me.' And von Spiegel looked at him in great surprise and said, 'Why? Why should I? You have treated me very well on board here, and after the war we can be friends. I am fighting for my country, and you are fighting for yours. That's right and proper for both of us.'

Duty. Honour. Sacrifice.
Still words with meaning.

BIBLIOGRAPHY AND SOURCES

The First Battle of the Atlantic has, in many ways, been overshadowed by the grimmer affair of the Second World War. No writer about the period, however, can ignore the work of Robert M. Grant, whose lifetime study of the U-boats of the Kaiserliche Marine is both an inspiration and a daunting example.

In these days of internet access, even a simple research yields tens of dozens of sites. Many of them repeat inaccurate information from another site. Others yield a remarkable amount of carefully checked information, including such delights as a complete list of the officers of the Kaiser's Navy. I have, however, only mentioned a few sites that do provide consistently accurate information; these are of great value to any author of the period.

BOOKS

Auten, Lieutenant Commander Harold, *'Q' Boat Adventures*, London, 1919 (reprinted Penzance, Periscope Publishing, 2003)

Beaverbrook, Lord, *Men and Power*, London, Hutchinson, 1956

Bridgland, Tony, *Sea Killers in Disguise*, Barnsley, Pen & Sword, 1999

——, *Outrage at Sea*, Barnsley, Pen & Sword, 2002

Brown, Malcolm and Meehan, Patricia, *Scapa Flow*, Allen Lane, London, 1968

Campbell, Rear Admiral Gordon, *My Mystery Ships*, Hodder & Stoughton, London, 1928 (reprinted Penzance, Periscope Publishing, 2002)

——, *Number Thirteen*, London, Hodder & Stoughton, 1932

Chatterton, E. Keble, *Q-ships and Their Story*, London, Sidgwick & Jackson, 1922

——, *Gallant Gentlemen*, London, Hurst & Blackett, 1931

——, *Fighting the U-boats*, London, Hurst & Blackett, 1942

Coles, Alan, *Slaughter At Sea*, London, Robert Hale, 1986

Corbett, Sir Julian (vols 1–3)/Newbolt, Sir Henry (vols 4–5), *Official History of the War – Naval Operations*, London, Longmans, 1922–8

Crompton, Kapitänleutnant Iwan, *Der Baralong Fall*, Berlin, Ullstein, 1917

——, *Englands Verbrechen an U 41*, Gütersloh, Bertelsmann, 1941

Crutwell, C.R.M.F, *A History of the Great War 1914–1918*, Oxford, Oxford University Press, 1934

Dixon, Professor Norman, *On the Psychology of Military Incompetence*, London, Jonathan Cape, 1976

Dönitz, Grossadmiral Karl, *Zehn Jahre und zwanzige Tage: Erinerungen 1935–1945*, Frankfurt-am-Main, Athenäum-Verlag, 1958

Forstner, Freiherr Georg-Gunter von, *Als U-boots Kommandant Gegen England*, Berlin, Ullstein, 1916

Fürbringer, Kapitänleutnant Werner, *Alarm! Tauchen!*, Berlin, Ullstein, 1933

Gibbs, Philip, *The Struggle In Flanders*, London, Heinemann, 1919

Gibson, R.H. and Prendergast, Maurice, *The German Submarine War 1914–1918*, London, Constable, 1931

Gordon, Andrew, *The Rules of the Game*, London, John Murray, 1996

Grant, Robert M., *U-Boats Destroyed*, London, Putnam, 1964

——, *The U-Boat Hunters*, Penzance, Periscope Publishing, 2003

Gray, Edwyn, *British Submarines in the Great War*, Barnsley, Leo Cooper Reprint, 2001 of A *Damned Un-English Weapon*, London, Seeley Service, 1971

——, *The Killing Time*, London, Seeley Service, 1972

'Griff' (A.S. Griffith), *Surrendered. Some Naval War Secrets*, Cross Deep, privately published, 1927

Hoogendijk, J.H. (collator) and de Balbian Verster, J.F.L. (ed.), *De Nederlandische Koopvaardij in den oorlogstijd (1914–1918)*, Amsterdam, NV Holkema & Warendorf, 1930

Horton, Edward, *Illustrated History of the Submarine*, London, Sidgwick & Jackson, 1974

Ilsemann, Sigurd von, *Der Kaiser in Holland*, Munich, Biederstein Verlag, 1967

Jameson, Rear Admiral Sir William, *The Most Formidable Thing*, London, Hart-Davis, 1965

Jane, Fred T., *Jane's Fighting Ships, 1914*, London, Sampson Low Marston, 1914 (reprinted by Newton Abbot, David & Charles, 1968)

Kemp, Paul, *U-Boats Destroyed*, London, Arms & Armour Press, 1997

Lake, Deborah, *The Zeebrugge and Ostend Raids, 1918*, Barnsley, Pen & Sword, 2003

Lambert, Nicholas (ed.), *The Submarine Service, 1900–1918*, Aldershot, Navy Records Society, 2001

Langsdorff, Werner von, *U-Boote am Feind*, Gütersloh, Bertelsmann, 1937

Lipscomb, Commander Frank, *Historic Submarines*, London, Hugh Evelyn Limited, 1970

Lomas, David, *Mons, 1914*, Oxford, Osprey Publishing, 1997

Massie, Robert K., *Castles of Steel*, London, Jonathan Cape, 2004

Muhlhauser, G.H.P., *Small Craft*, London, Bodley Head, 1920

Niemöller, Oberleutnant zur See Martin, *Vom U-Boot zur Kanzel*, Berlin, Martin Warneck-Verlag, 1934 (published also in English as *From U-Boat to Pulpit*, London, William Hodge, 1936)

Ritchie, Carson, *Q-ships*, Lavenham, Terence Dalton, 1985

Roskill, Stephen, *Hankey: Man of Secrets*, London, Collins, 1970

Rössler, Eberhard, *The U-Boat*, London, Cassell, 2002

Salter, J.A., *Allied Shipping Control*, London, Clarendon Press, 1921

Satterthwaite, Susan, *Bonner VC, The Biography of Gus Bonner: VC And Master Mariner* SR Print Management, Aldridge, 2008

Scheffer, H.J., *November 1918*, Utrecht, De Bataaafsche Leeuw, 1918

Snelling, Stephen, *VCs of the First World War – The Naval VCs*, Stroud, Sutton Publishing, 2002

Terraine, John, *Business in Great Waters*, London, Leo Cooper, 1989

Thomas, Lowell, *Raiders of the Deep*, London, Heinemann, 1929 (reprinted Penzance, Periscope Publishing, 2002)

Toland, John, *No Man's Land*, London, Eyre Methuen, 1980

Valentiner, Kapitänleutnant Max, *300,000 Tonnen Versenkt!*, Berlin, Ullstein, 1917

———, *U-38: Wikingerfahrten eines deutschen U-bootes*, Berlin, Ullstein, 1934

Wiebicke, Karl, *Die Männer von U 96 Errinerungen an Fahrten unseres U-Bootes*, Leipzig, Kohler, 1934

Wiest, Andrew, *Passchendaele and the Royal Navy*, Connecticut, Greenwood Press, 1995

Williamson, Gordon, *German U-Boat Crews 1914–45*, Oxford, Osprey Publishing, 1995

JOURNALS, MAGAZINES, ARTICLES, ETC.

Boersma, M.Th.L.W., *Uit Eijsdens verleden*, Maastricht, 1979

Coder, Lieutenant Commander Barbara J, USN, 'Q-ships of the Great War' (a research report submitted to the Air University Faculty, US Air Command and Staff College, 2002)

Wills, Richard, H.L. 'The *Hunley* In Historical Context' (a paper of the Department of the Navy, Naval Historical Center, Washington Navy Yard, Washington, DC)

INTERNET SITES

www.battleships-cruisers.co.uk
www.britsub.net
www.history.rochester.edu
home.foni.net/~adelsforschung1/rall10.htm
www.kaiserliche-marine.de
uboat.net
www.u-boot-net.de
www.uk-muenchen.de

GENERAL INDEX

Abbreviations: KL = Kapitänleutnant, OL = Oberleutnant.
People, places and vessels with a single mention are not listed except if judged of
particular importance.

INDEX OF VESSELS